Ethical AI and Education

Ethical AI and Education: Reality, Opportunities, Governance, and Consequences of AI in the Classroom examines how artificial intelligence (AI) is entering schools and what responsible use requires from educators, leaders, and policymakers. It moves beyond claims of inevitable transformation to ask how decisions about AI are made, who holds responsibility, and what is at stake when educational judgment is shaped by automated systems.

The book develops a governance-based approach to AI in education, grounded in ethics, law, and institutional practice. It addresses core issues including bias, datafication, academic integrity, teacher agency, and global inequality, while placing recent developments such as generative AI within a longer trajectory of educational technology. Drawing on international frameworks, including the European Union Artificial Intelligence Act, it provides practical guidance for schools seeking to implement AI in ways that are lawful, accountable, and educationally meaningful. The central argument is that ethical AI in education depends not on tools alone, but on structures of oversight, professional judgment, and institutional responsibility.

For researchers, educators, and policymakers seeking to understand not only how AI is entering education, but how it should be governed, this book provides both analysis and direction.

AAAI/CRC Press Advances in AI Ethics Series

As artificial intelligence technology continues to evolve at a fast pace, the need for a nuanced understanding of the ethical concerns surrounding this technology, and how to address them, has become more crucial than ever.

This CRC Press series, in collaboration with the Association for the Advancement of Artificial Intelligence (AAAI), leverages AAAI's expertise and leadership in AI to address the ethical implications of this emerging technology. As the premier scientific society in AI, AAAI's deep engagement with the field ensures this series offers cutting-edge insights and a roadmap for navigating the future of AI ethics.

AAAI/CRC Press Advances in AI Ethics Series serves as a vital resource for researchers, students, policymakers, technologists, and anyone invested in ensuring that AI advancements contribute to a fair, just, and equitable society.

Ethical AI and Education: Reality, Opportunities, Governance, and Consequences of AI in the Classroom
Clara Hawking & Darren Coxon

Ethical AI and Education

Reality, Opportunities, Governance, and Consequences of AI in the Classroom

Clara Hawking and Darren Coxon

CRC Press
Taylor & Francis Group
Boca Raton London New York

CRC Press is an imprint of the
Taylor & Francis Group, an **informa** business

Designed cover image: Florian Fastina

First edition published 2027
by CRC Press
2385 NW Executive Center Drive, Suite 320, Boca Raton FL 33431

and by CRC Press
4 Park Square, Milton Park, Abingdon, Oxon, OX14 4RN

CRC Press is an imprint of Taylor & Francis Group, LLC

ISBN: 9781041120919 (hbk)
ISBN: 9781041120902 (pbk)
ISBN: 9781003662945 (ebk)

DOI: 10.1201/9781003662945

Typeset in Times
by Newgen Publishing UK

For my children.
As in all things.

—Clara Hawking

For my family,
Who govern everything I do.

—Darren Coxon

For the generations who will inherit the world we are building.
And for the future that belongs to them.

—Clara Hawking and Darren Coxon

Contents

Preface

This book was written at a moment when artificial intelligence (AI) moved rapidly from the margins of educational technology into the centre of public and professional debate. The release of generative AI systems brought questions that had been developing for years into immediate focus. Schools, universities, and governments were asked to respond quickly, often without the structures, evidence, or shared language required to do so with confidence.

Much of the early discussion framed AI in education in terms of opportunity or threat. Less attention was given to the conditions under which these systems should be used, and the responsibilities they create for institutions. This book begins from the position that AI is neither neutral nor self-justifying. Its use in education must be examined through the same standards that apply to any system that shapes learning, assessment, and decision-making.

The chapters that follow do not attempt to provide a single answer to the question of AI in education. Instead, they develop a framework for thinking and action grounded in governance, ethics, and institutional responsibility. This includes attention to issues of bias, data use, professional judgment, global inequality, and regulatory accountability, as well as the practical realities schools face when adopting new technologies.

The intention is not to reject innovation, but to place it within a structure that preserves educational purpose. If AI is to play a role in schools, it must do so in ways that support, rather than displace, the human relationships and professional expertise on which education depends.

This book is written for those responsible for making decisions in this space: educators, school leaders, policymakers, and researchers. It assumes that the central challenge is not whether AI will be used in education, but how it will be governed, and in whose interests.

Acknowledgements

This book draws on work developed across multiple educational and institutional contexts, and we are grateful to the educators, school leaders, and organisations who continue to engage seriously with the challenges of AI in education. Their questions, concerns, and professional judgment have shaped the direction of this work far more than any single framework or policy.

We also acknowledge the wider research and policy communities whose contributions have informed the arguments presented here. The field of AI in education is developing rapidly, and this book builds on a growing body of scholarship and international dialogue that continues to refine how these systems are understood and governed.

Finally, we recognise the practitioners working daily within classrooms and schools, often under conditions of uncertainty and pressure. It is their responsibility, and their restraint, that will ultimately determine how AI is integrated into education.

About the Authors

Clara Hawking is an AI governance leader and ethicist. With a background in computer science and a specialisation in AI ethics, she works with schools, governments, and international organisations to support the responsible and effective integration of AI into learning environments. Clara has led large-scale AI governance initiatives across international school groups and has trained thousands of educators and leaders on ethical and lawful AI use. She is a contributing advisor on AI in education to global institutions and a frequent speaker on AI policy, governance, and the future of education. Her work focuses on aligning technological innovation with educational purpose, safeguarding, and institutional responsibility.

Darren Coxon is an education leader, researcher, and writer with extensive experience in digital strategy, educational technology, and institutional development. His work focuses on the intersection of pedagogy, technology, and system-level change in schools. Darren has held senior leadership roles in international education and has contributed to research and practice in areas including digital transformation, curriculum innovation, and the impact of emerging technologies on teaching and learning. His writing explores the practical and philosophical implications of technology in education, with a particular focus on how schools can respond thoughtfully to rapid technological change.

Introduction 1

Setting the Stage for Ethical AI in Education

Generative artificial intelligence did not enter education quietly. It arrived with headlines, panic, excitement, and a remarkable amount of projection.

Within months of the public release of large language model AI tools, such as ChatGPT, in late 2022 and early 2023, schools, universities, ministries, and families found themselves pulled into a global argument about what education was becoming. Teachers worried about plagiarism, assessment integrity, deskilling, and whether students would stop thinking for themselves. Students experimented, improvised, and in many cases moved faster than the adults responsible for governing their learning environments. Policymakers oscillated between encouragement and alarm. Technology companies promised transformation at scale. Across the world, one message was repeated with unusual force: education had changed, and there was no going back (Dwivedi et al., 2023; Kasneci et al., 2023).

That message was only partly true.

What changed suddenly was not the existence of artificial intelligence in education, but its visibility. By the time generative AI became public spectacle, schools had already spent decades absorbing digital systems that captured data, shaped decisions, mediated communication, and normalised new forms of institutional dependence. Recommendation systems, predictive analytics, plagiarism detection, adaptive platforms, automated writing support, behaviour tracking, and platform ecosystems had already altered educational life long before many schools began calling these systems "AI" (Selwyn, 2016; Holmes, Bialik and Fadel, 2019). The current moment, then, should not be read as a clean technological beginning. It is better understood as an acceleration and exposure of patterns that were already well underway.

This distinction matters because it changes the ethical question.

If artificial intelligence in education is treated as a sudden disruption, the temptation is to respond tactically: update the academic honesty policy, run a short training session, assign the issue to the Head of IT, purchase a detection tool, or simply wait for the market to settle. But if AI is understood as part of a longer transformation in how educational institutions see, classify, support, govern, and sometimes misrecognise students, then a different response is required. The issue is no longer whether a school adopts one

DOI: 10.1201/9781003662945-1

tool or another. The issue is whether educational institutions have the governance, ethical language, legal literacy, and human clarity to decide what role intelligent systems should play in the lives of children.

That is the real subject of this book.
This is not a book about whether artificial intelligence is "good" or "bad" for education. It is not a guide to prompt writing. It is not a celebration of innovation for its own sake, nor a nostalgic rejection of technological change. It is an argument for keeping hold of reality in a field unusually vulnerable to hype.

That reality begins with a simple observation. Education is not like most other sectors. It does not merely deliver services or optimise transactions. It forms persons. It distributes opportunity. It shapes civic habits, epistemic trust, and social futures. Decisions made in educational environments can widen or narrow the life chances of children long before those children understand the systems acting upon them. For that reason, AI in education raises questions that are not only technical or economic, but ethical, legal, political, and deeply human.

Those questions are now urgent.
Across jurisdictions, schools are being encouraged to adopt systems that promise personalised learning, improved efficiency, earlier intervention, better data, reduced workload, and future readiness. Some of these promises hold genuine potential. Many do not. Most are difficult to evaluate in conditions of institutional strain, uneven evidence, and aggressive commercial marketing. As earlier waves of educational technology have shown, schools do not fail because they refuse innovation. They fail because they are too often asked to absorb it without the structures needed to govern it well (Selwyn, 2016; UNESCO, 2023).

This book therefore begins from a different premise: the most important AI question for education is not what technology can do. It is what schools are prepared to permit, protect, resist, explain, and remain accountable for.

From that premise, the argument unfolds in three movements.
The first movement is historical and diagnostic. Chapters 2 to 4 show that the current AI moment did not emerge from nowhere. It sits within a longer history of digitising education, marked by recurring cycles of promise, shallow adoption, weak oversight, and institutional forgetting. The story runs from early classroom computing to one device per child policies, from MOOCs and virtual learning environments to pandemic platform dependence and the contemporary AI EdTech market. These chapters show that many of the structural vulnerabilities now associated with AI were seeded long before generative systems became headline news. Schools were already becoming datafied environments. Automated judgment was already entering educational decision making. Commercial platforms were already becoming infrastructure.

The second movement is normative and practical. Chapters 5 to 8 ask what must be built if artificial intelligence is to be governed responsibly. These chapters shift the debate away from hype and toward the conditions of legitimate use: ethics in practice, school level governance frameworks, regulatory literacy, and the human rights foundations needed to evaluate systems that increasingly shape children's educational lives. The argument here is that AI governance cannot be reduced to an IT issue, a procurement decision, or a compliance exercise. It is a whole institution's responsibility. It must reach safeguarding, leadership, pedagogy, contracting, family communication, student participation, and mechanisms of redress. It must also move beyond abstract principles. Schools need operational language, structures of accountability, and a framework for deciding not only what is lawful, but what is educationally justified (OECD, 2019; UNESCO, 2021).

The third movement is forward looking. Chapters 9 and 10 turn to the horizon already emerging: agentic systems, advanced analytics, spatial computing, robotics, simulation environments, and the wider convergence of infrastructures likely to shape classrooms in the years ahead. These chapters argue that the future of educational AI will not be determined by a single tool, but by the interaction of multiple systems and the institutional cultures into which they are absorbed. This makes ethical preparation more, not less, important. If schools fail to build strong governance and professional capacity now, the result will not simply be technical confusion. It will be a widening ethical deficit, in which innovation moves faster than the institutions responsible for children can think.

Across all three movements, a common thread runs through the book.
Artificial intelligence in education is ultimately a question of power. Who designs the systems? Who profits from them? Who is made visible to them? Who is misread by them? Who can challenge them? Who remains responsible when they fail? And above all, whether children remain subjects of education or become objects of optimisation inside infrastructures they did not choose and cannot meaningfully contest.

The book does not claim that these questions have easy answers. Nor does it pretend that the evidence base is complete. One of the difficulties facing researchers, school leaders, and policymakers alike is that educational AI is moving faster than long term scholarship can stabilise. Not every jurisdiction is equally represented in the literature. Not every technology discussed here will mature as predicted. Some of the most consequential decisions are being made in conditions familiar to the history of technology: partial evidence, uneven governance, and considerable commercial pressure. This makes conceptual clarity and ethical seriousness all the more necessary.

It also makes collaboration necessary. No single group can resolve these challenges alone. Educators understand pedagogy and institutional reality. Students understand the lived experience of digital systems from within. Families understand local context and trust. Policymakers shape legal and funding conditions. Developers build the infrastructures that increasingly structure educational possibilities. The future of AI in education will be shaped not by any one of these actors, but by whether they can develop forms of shared responsibility strong enough to resist both panic and complacency.

That is why this book takes the approach it does. It treats AI in education not as a narrow technical matter, but as a field in which the core problems of AI ethics become unusually visible. Questions of fairness, accountability, transparency, dignity, human oversight, democratic legitimacy, and child protection do not arrive later, after the technology is in place. They are present from the start. In that sense, education is not a secondary application domain for AI ethics. It is one of the places where the ethical stakes are clearest.

To keep it real, in this context, is not to reject ambition. It is to resist fantasy. It is to refuse the seductive language that turns every platform into transformation, every dashboard into insight, every automated output into neutrality, and every efficiency gain into educational progress. It is to insist that education remains a moral and public project even as its tools become more computational, more predictive, and more opaque.

That insistence matters because the current policy environment often encourages the opposite. In too many settings, AI enters schools through procurement rather than public deliberation, through market urgency rather than pedagogical clarity, and through institutional fatigue rather than informed collective choice. The result is a dangerous mismatch. Systems with significant implications for children's rights and developmental environments are being adopted by institutions that often lack sufficient governance structures, training, legal literacy, or evaluative capacity to absorb them responsibly. This problem is not confined to one country or one sector. It appears in public systems and private systems, in highly resourced schools and low resource settings, and in both highly regulated and weakly regulated jurisdictions. The forms vary. The pattern does not.

The governance imperative therefore extends beyond individual schools. It raises broader questions about public responsibility in an era in which educational technology is increasingly shaped by multinational platform companies, uneven national regulation, and the geopolitical distribution of digital power. Recent years have shown the cost of leaving educational infrastructure to evolve without sufficient public oversight. During the pandemic, schools across the world became dependent on digital platforms with little time to assess the implications for privacy, surveillance, or long-term institutional autonomy. Human Rights Watch documented the extent to which government endorsed online learning tools exposed children to intrusive data practices unrelated to education itself (Human Rights Watch, 2022). That episode was not an anomaly. It was a warning about what happens when crisis, convenience, and weak governance combine.

This is why the second half of the book moves steadily from ethics to governance, from governance to law, and from law to human rights. Regulation matters. Institutional policy matters. Professional development matters. But beneath them all lies a deeper question: *what is a child owed in an educational environment increasingly mediated by intelligent systems*? The answer cannot come from the market alone. It cannot come from technical capability alone. It must come from a moral and political account of what education is for, and of what schools owe the children whose futures they help shape.

This is also why the book gives serious attention to teachers. No discussion of AI in education can proceed honestly without confronting the anxieties technologies generate within the profession. Workload, deskilling, automation, professional authority, and the fear of becoming peripheral to systems that claim to personalise and optimise learning more efficiently than human beings are not trivial concerns. They are central. Yet the argument developed here is that the answer is not to pit teachers against technology. It is to insist that educational technology remain accountable to professional judgment rather than displacing it. If AI is introduced into schools without strengthening teacher agency, then the institution has misunderstood both the technology and the profession.

Finally, this book proceeds with a degree of humility. Artificial intelligence in education is changing rapidly. Some of the tools discussed here will mature. Others will fail. Some concerns will intensify. Others will mutate. The book does not offer a final settlement. It offers a framework: historical, ethical, legal, and practical. Its purpose is not to predict every development. It is to help readers think clearly enough to meet them.

What follows begins with history because institutions that do not understand how they arrived at a crisis rarely govern their way out of one. Before schools can decide what to do about artificial intelligence, they need to understand the longer pattern of technological promise, weak oversight, and educational compromise that made this moment possible.

That is where the book begins.

REFERENCES

Dwivedi, Y.K., Kshetri, N., Hughes, L., Slade, E.L., Jeyaraj, A., Kar, A.K., Baabdullah, A.M., Koohang, A., Raghavan, V., Ahuja, M., Albanna, H., Albashrawi, M.A., Al-Busaidi, A.V., Balakrishnan, J., Barlette, Y., Basu, S., Bose, I., Brooks, L., Buhalis, D., Carter, L., Chowdhury, S., Crick, T., Cunningham, S.W., Davies, G.H., Davison, R.M., Dé, R., Dennehy, D., Duan, Y., Dubey, R., Dwivedi, R., Edwards, J.S., Flavián, C., Gauld, R., Grover, V., Hu, M-C., Janssen, M., Jones, P., Junglas, I., Khorana, S., Kraus, S., Larsen, K.R., Latreille, P., Laumer, S., Malik, F.T., Mardani, A., Mariani, M., Mithas, S., Mogaji, E., Nord, J.H., O'Connor, S., Okumus, F., Pagani, M., Pandey, N., Papagiannidis, S., Pappas, I.O., Pathak, N., Pries-Heje, J., Raman, R., Rana, N.P., Rehm, S-V., Ribeiro-Navarrete, S., Richter, A., Rowe, F., Sarker, S., Stahl, B.C., Tiwari, M.K., van der Aalst, W., Venkatesh, V., Viglia, G., Wade, M., Walton, P., Wirtz, J. and Wright, R. (2023) 'Opinion Paper: So what if ChatGPT wrote it? Multidisciplinary perspectives on opportunities, challenges and implications of generative conversational AI'. *International Journal of Information Management*, 71, 102642. Available at: https://doi.org/10.1016/j.ijinfomgt.2023.102642

Holmes, W., Bialik, M. and Fadel, C. (2019) *Artificial Intelligence in Education: Promises and Implications for Teaching and Learning*. Boston: Center for Curriculum Redesign. Available at: www.consorciosthem.com/wp-content/uploads/2025/02/sthem-ia-07-holmes-fadel-bialik-artificial-intelligence-in-education-promise-and-implications-for-teaching-and-learning-2019.pdf

Human Rights Watch (2022) *"How Dare They Peep into My Private Life?" Children's Rights Violations by Governments that Endorsed Online Learning during the Covid-19 Pandemic*. New York: Human Rights Watch. Available at: www.hrw.org/report/2022/05/25/how-dare-they-peep-my-private-life/childrens-rights-violations-governments

Kasneci, E. et al. (2023) 'ChatGPT for good? On opportunities and challenges of large language models for education', *Learning and Individual Differences*, 103, 102274. Available at: https://doi.org/10.1016/j.lindif.2023.102274

OECD (2019) *Recommendation of the Council on Artificial Intelligence.* Paris: OECD Publishing. Available at: https://legalinstruments.oecd.org/en/instruments/OECD-LEGAL-0449

Selwyn, N. (2016) *Education and Technology: Key Issues and Debates.* 2nd edn. London: Bloomsbury. Available at: www.bloomsbury.com/ca/education-and-technology-9781350145566/

UNESCO (2021) *Recommendation on the Ethics of Artificial Intelligence.* Paris: UNESCO. Available at: https://unesdoc.unesco.org/ark:/48223/pf0000380455

UNESCO (2023) *Global Education Monitoring Report 2023: Technology in Education: A Tool on Whose Terms?* Paris: UNESCO. Available at: https://unesdoc.unesco.org/ark:/48223/pf0000385723

A Brief History of Digitising Education

2

Promises and Pitfalls

THE STATE OF EDUCATION TECHNOLOGY

Before artificial intelligence arrived in our classrooms, education systems had already passed through multiple technological transformations. Each arrived accompanied by ambitious claims about its potential to reshape learning, teaching, and the structure of schooling itself. Each was introduced with confidence that new tools would personalise learning, increase engagement, reduce teacher workload, close attainment gaps, and prepare students for a rapidly changing world.

The historical records suggest a more complicated outcome.
Across the past four decades, global educational systems have repeatedly adopted new digital technologies at scale. Calculators, desktop computers, interactive whiteboards, virtual learning environments, tablets, and large-scale online learning platforms have each been presented as catalysts for transformation. Governments have invested substantial resources in infrastructure, software, and devices. Schools have adapted curricula, retrained teachers, and reorganised classroom practice in response to these technological shifts.

Nonetheless, the evidence base has rarely supported the scale of the original claims.
Meta-analyses of educational technology research consistently show small to modest average effects on student learning outcomes, with significant variation depending on implementation and context (Hattie, 2009; Tamim et al., 2011). Even widely adopted

DOI: 10.1201/9781003662945-2

technologies often produce measurable gains that fall below expectations set by policy rhetoric and commercial marketing. The gap between promise and evidence has become one of the defining features of educational technology adoption.

This pattern has been observed across multiple decades of innovation. New technologies generate initial enthusiasm, rapid policy adoption, and large public investments. Early evaluations report mixed results. Over time, the technology becomes absorbed into everyday practice, often serving more limited purposes than originally envisioned. The revolutionary narrative fades, only to re-emerge when the next technology arrives. Then the cycle begins again.

Understanding this history is not simply an academic exercise. The ethics and governance challenges now associated with artificial intelligence represent an amplification of issues that emerged during earlier waves of educational technology adoption. Questions about evidence, equity, procurement, and teacher training and pedagogical integration were frequently left unresolved during previous technological transitions. These issues now reappear with greater urgency as AI systems enter classrooms.

Educational institutions have often demonstrated what might be described as a limited institutional memory regarding technology adoption. Lessons learned during one wave of innovation are rarely systematically applied to the next. As a result, education systems repeatedly encounter similar implementation challenges despite decades of experience with digital technologies.

The historical cases examined in this chapter illustrate this pattern clearly. From the calculator debates of the 1980s to the rapid expansion of interactive whiteboards, from large-scale infrastructure initiatives such a *Building Schools for The Future* in the UK, to the global enthusiasm surrounding *Massive Open Online Courses* (MOOCs) and one-to-one device programmes, each technological wave reveals recurring tensions between aspiration and evidence.

These patterns are directly relevant to the present moment. Artificial Intelligence arrives in education accompanied by claims that exceed those associated with previous technologies. AI systems are expected not only to support teaching but to fundamentally redesign how learning occurs, enabling highly personalised instruction at scale while automating many tasks traditionally performed by teachers. History suggests caution.

The purpose of this chapter is therefore not to dismiss educational technology. Digital tools have undeniably shaped modern education and continue to offer meaningful opportunities for improving teaching and learning. Rather, the aim is to examine why technological revolutions in education so often fall short of their transformative promises. The lessons are both humbling and instructive. They suggest that technology alone transforms nothing; that implementation matters more than innovation; that context shapes outcomes more than capabilities; and that the hardest problems in education are human problems that technology can support but cannot solve. By understanding the structural reasons behind these outcomes, educators and policymakers may be better positioned to approach artificial intelligence with the critical perspective necessary for responsible governance. The historical record that follows offers both a warning and a guide.

PART I: CYCLES OF TECHNOLOGICAL PROMISE IN EDUCATION

The calculator wars and the Cockcroft legacy

One of the earliest global technology debates in modern education concerned the introduction of electronic calculators into mathematics classrooms. Although it now appears almost quaint, the arrival of affordable handheld calculators during the late 1970s and early 1980s represented a genuine paradigm shift in mathematics education. Educators, policymakers and parents raised fundamental questions. Should students be allowed to use calculators? Would reliance on electronic calculation undermine mental arithmetic? Was education risking the development of a generation unable to perform basic numerical reasoning?

These concerns reflected a deeper anxiety about the relationship between technology and cognitive development. Mathematics education had long emphasised mental and written calculation as core intellectual skills. The introduction of devices capable of performing arithmetic instantly therefore appeared to challenge longstanding pedagogical assumptions about how mathematical understanding should develop. Looking back and comparing with now, it seems remarkably simple. Schools today face far greater challenges.

The calculator debate reached its most influential moment in the United Kingdom in 1982, with the publication of the Cockcroft Report, *Mathematics Counts* (Cockcroft, 1982), commissioned by the Department of Education and Science. The report remains one of the most comprehensive examinations of maths education ever undertaken in Britain. Over three years, the Cockcroft Committee investigated how mathematics was taught and learned across the education system. The inquiry gathered evidence from teachers, employers, mathematicians and researchers, reviewed existing studies, and conducted extensive consultations across schools, universities and workplaces.

The report's conclusions on calculators were notably balanced. Rather than presenting calculators as either a threat or a solution, the committee argued that they should be understood as tools that could support mathematical understanding when used appropriately. The report recommended that calculators be made available to pupils at all stages of the primary curriculum, while simultaneously emphasising that students must continue to develop strong mental and written calculation skills (Cockcroft, 1982). Calculators were therefore framed not as replacements for mathematical thinking but as instruments that could support particular forms of problem solving and exploration. The key phrase was to think of calculators "as an aid to teaching and learning"; to ensure that the calculator supplemented rather than replaced fundamental skills (Cockcroft, 1982).

What's remarkable about the Cockcroft Report, when viewed from the perspective of contemporary global educational technology debates, is the seriousness with which the committee approached questions of evidence and implementation. The report carefully distinguished between different pedagogical uses of calculators. For example, calculators could be used for checking work, exploring numerical patterns, or managing complex computations during problem solving. These uses were not pedagogically equivalent. Some supported deeper mathematical understanding, while others risked bypassing conceptual development. The committee therefore emphasised that the educational value of calculators depended heavily on *how* teachers integrated them into instruction.

This approach reflected a broader recognition that the impact of technology in education is shaped less by the tool itself than by the surrounding pedagogical context. Research conducted in subsequent decades broadly supports this conclusion. Studies have found that calculators can support mathematical problem solving and conceptual understanding when used strategically, particularly in tasks that emphasise reasoning rather than routine computation (Ellington, 2003; Hembree and Dessart, 1986; Stacy and Groves, 1994). At the same time, other studies have raised concerns that excessive reliance on calculators may weaken aspects of number sense and estimation, particularly when foundational numerical skills are insufficiently developed (Reys et al., 1999; Stacey and Groves, 1994).

The evidence therefore remains nuanced rather than definitive. Calculators appear to benefit students in some contexts while offering fewer advantages in others. As with many educational technologies, outcomes depend heavily on instructional design, teacher expertise, and the stage of students' mathematical development.

Still, the calculator debate established a pattern that would recur with later technologies. Initial resistance from traditionalists was followed by strong advocacy from technological innovators. Over time, calculators became normalised within mathematics education, and the original controversy largely disappeared. What is more striking, however, is how rarely education systems returned to examine systematically whether the technology ultimately delivered the learning gains that early policy debates had anticipated.

Calculators became ubiquitous in mathematics classrooms across the world. In many cases they are now so embedded in everyday practice that they are no longer even considered a form of educational technology. However, the long-term evidence regarding their educational impact remains mixed. Some research suggests that calculator use enables students to engage earlier with complex mathematical tasks and supports higher-level problem solving (Ellington, 2003). Other research indicates that heavy reliance on calculators may weaken students' intuitive understanding of numbers if introduced prematurely or used without appropriate pedagogical scaffolding (Reys et al., 1999; Sowder, 1992).

What the calculator episode ultimately reveals is not the success or failure of a particular technology, but a recurring institutional weakness within education systems. Technologies are introduced, debated, and eventually absorbed into practice, yet the infrastructure required for sustained evaluation and learning is rarely developed. Once the initial controversy fades, systematic assessment often disappears with it.

This pattern would become characteristic of subsequent waves of educational technology adoption. The experience of calculators therefore provides an early example of a recurring dynamic in educational innovation: rapid adoption followed by limited long-term evaluation of how technology actually reshapes learning.

Understanding this pattern is essential when considering contemporary developments such as artificial intelligence. Without systematic reflection on earlier technological transitions, education risks repeating the same cycle of enthusiasm, adoption and partial understanding each time a new technology enters the classroom.

Interactive whiteboards: A UK cautionary tale

If any technology illustrates the gap between promise and evidence in education, it is the interactive whiteboard. During the early 2000s the United Kingdom became one of the most enthusiastic adopters of the technology anywhere in the world, investing heavily in large scale classroom deployment. By the mid-2000s interactive whiteboards had become a common feature of British classrooms, with adoption rates far exceeding those of most other countries. In effect, the UK education system became a national test bed for the large-scale integration of this technology.

Government investment was substantial. Through initiatives such as the *Primary National Strategy* and the *Schools Whiteboard Expansion* programmes, thousands of classrooms were equipped with interactive whiteboards in a relatively short period of time. The scale of the rollout was such that it attracted international attention from both researchers and commercial providers. As Higgins, Beauchamp and Miller note, the United Kingdom rapidly became one of the most prominent contexts in which the educational impact of interactive whiteboards could be studied (Higgins, Beauchamp and Miller, 2007).

The enthusiasm surrounding the technology was driven by a powerful narrative. Interactive whiteboards promised to transform pedagogy by making lessons more visual, interactive and collaborative. They appeared to offer a bridge between traditional classroom instruction and the increasingly multimedia digital culture in which young people were growing up. Teachers could annotate digital content in real time, incorporate video and simulations into lessons, and invite students to manipulate objects directly on screen. In policy discourse and commercial marketing alike, the technology was presented as a catalyst for a more engaging and modern form of teaching.

These claims were not entirely without foundation. Early classroom observations did identify examples of teachers using interactive whiteboards in ways that supported collaborative problem solving, shared annotation of student work, and the visual explanation of abstract concepts (Higgins, Beauchamp and Miller, 2007). In some classrooms teachers did adapt aspects of their instructional practice to take advantage of these possibilities.

However, the emerging research literature quickly revealed a more complicated reality. In many classrooms interactive whiteboards were used primarily as projection devices rather than as genuinely interactive tools. Rather than transforming pedagogy, the boards frequently functioned as digital replacements for traditional blackboards or overhead projectors. Reviewing the early research, Higgins, Beauchamp and Miller concluded that although teachers and students often reported positive attitudes towards the technology, the pedagogical uses observed in practice were frequently limited and did not necessarily represent substantial changes in teaching methods (Higgins, Beauchamp and Miller, 2007).

The policy narrative nevertheless remained compelling. Interactive whiteboards were widely promoted as technologies that would make lessons more interactive, improve classroom organisation, and enable teachers to share digital lesson materials with students. The technology appeared to embody many of the characteristics associated with modern education: visual presentation, multimedia integration, and increased opportunities for participation.

This vision was also linked to broader assumptions about how contemporary learners engage with information. Advocates argued that students raised in environments saturated with digital media might respond more positively to visually rich and interactive forms of teaching than to more traditional instructional approaches. Interactive whiteboards, it was suggested, could meet students within this digital culture by incorporating multimedia content, interactive tasks, and dynamic visual explanation into everyday classroom practice.

Yet something important was often missing from these discussions. The policy debate focused heavily on the technological capabilities of the tools themselves, while paying less attention to the conditions required for those capabilities to translate into meaningful learning outcomes. The question of how such technologies would be integrated pedagogically, supported through professional development, and evaluated over time was often secondary to the enthusiasm surrounding the devices themselves.

The UK government's response to this uncertainty was notable. Rather than relying solely on assumptions about impact, it commissioned large scale evaluation studies designed to measure the educational effects of interactive whiteboard adoption. The Primary Schools Whiteboard Expansion Project, conducted between 2004 and 2006, examined the impact of the technology across a substantial sample of primary schools and pupils aged 9 to 11 (Somekh et al., 2007).

The research design was unusually rigorous for an educational technology initiative of this scale. Using multilevel statistical modelling, the study analysed attainment outcomes in literacy, mathematics, and science while controlling for prior attainment, school characteristics, and teacher effects. In principle, this methodology allowed researchers to examine whether the presence of interactive whiteboards was associated with measurable improvements in pupil progress.

The results were encouraging but complex. The evaluation found evidence of positive gains for pupils aged seven and eleven, and these gains appeared to be related to the length of time pupils had been taught in classrooms equipped with interactive whiteboards. In several subjects, pupils who had experienced longer exposure to the technology showed somewhat greater progress than those who had not. These gains were particularly noticeable among pupils of average and above-average prior attainment. The researchers therefore identified what appeared to be a form of dose-response relationship: greater exposure to interactive whiteboard-supported teaching was associated with improved outcomes in certain contexts (Somekh et al., 2007).

At the time, these findings were widely interpreted as evidence that the substantial investment in interactive whiteboards had been justified. The technology appeared capable, at least in some contexts, of supporting measurable improvements in pupil attainment.

But then came the secondary school research.

The *Secondary Whiteboard Expansion* (SWE) scheme substantially increased interactive whiteboard provision in London secondary schools, providing another opportunity for rigorous evaluation (Moss et al., 2007). This time the findings were different. Statistical analysis showed no measurable impact on pupil performance in English, mathematics, or science during the first year in which departments became fully conversant with the technology. The same technology that appeared to support some gains in primary classrooms showed no observable effect on secondary students.

The evaluators attempted to make sense of this discrepancy. One possibility was that secondary teaching differs fundamentally from primary teaching. Secondary lessons are often more content-dense and examination-driven, leaving less room for the kinds of interactive activities that appeared to support learning among younger pupils. Another explanation was that secondary teachers may simply have needed more time to adapt their pedagogical practices to the technology. It was also possible that the technology itself required longer exposure before any measurable effects would appear. Finally, researchers considered whether the initial novelty reported by both teachers and pupils might have faded before any lasting benefits could emerge.

This final explanation proved particularly prescient. Higgins, Beauchamp and Miller observed that while pupils often welcomed interactive whiteboards when they were first introduced, the motivational increase frequently appeared short-lived (Higgins, Beauchamp and Miller, 2007). What initially appeared innovative could quickly become routine once the technology was integrated into everyday classroom practice. The tool that promised to transform engagement often became simply another classroom fixture.

Higgins, reviewing the broader research evidence, later characterised the impact of interactive whiteboards on attainment as generally modest and often short-lived. Teachers and pupils frequently perceived the technology as beneficial, yet these perceptions did not consistently translate into measurable improvements in learning outcomes. In many cases the subjective experience of engagement did not correspond with observable gains in attainment.

This finding raises an uncomfortable question. The United Kingdom invested heavily in interactive whiteboard technology, yet the research evidence suggests that the effects on learning outcomes were limited. In several studies the observed effect sizes were small, and in some contexts they disappeared entirely. Nevertheless the investment continued, and the technology became firmly embedded in everyday classroom practice.

Part of the explanation lies in how educational technologies are evaluated. Many teachers reported that interactive whiteboards made lessons easier to organise and that students appeared more engaged. These benefits are not trivial. Teacher satisfaction and classroom engagement matter. However, they differ from the substantial improvements in attainment that had often been promised in policy rhetoric and commercial marketing. If interactive whiteboards had been presented primarily as tools that might make lessons somewhat easier to manage and occasionally more engaging, the technology might reasonably have been considered a modest success. Instead they were promoted as mechanisms for raising achievement, and the evidence for that claim remained limited.

The interactive whiteboard experience also reveals something about the psychology of educational technology adoption. Once a technology becomes established, schools have already invested financial resources and teachers have invested time learning how to use it. Under these circumstances questioning the effectiveness of the technology becomes difficult. Economists describe this dynamic as the sunk cost effect, in which previous investment influences future decisions even when evidence of effectiveness is uncertain.

Another issue concerns the problem of comparison. Teachers using interactive whiteboards often reported higher levels of engagement than they had experienced with traditional boards. Still, this comparison assumes that the relevant alternative was simply the absence of the technology. In reality the same financial investment could potentially have been directed towards other educational interventions such as reducing class sizes, employing additional teaching assistants, or improving curriculum materials. Few evaluations compared interactive whiteboards with these alternative uses of the same resources.

The experience therefore reveals several broader lessons about educational technology adoption. Engagement and achievement are not the same outcome. *Initial enthusiasm does not reliably predict long-term impact.* Large-scale investments are often made before the evidence base is fully established. And once technologies are widely embedded, honest evaluation becomes institutionally and politically difficult.

In this respect the interactive whiteboard episode should have provided an important warning. Education systems might have learned that enthusiasm for new tools must be accompanied by careful evaluation, and that technological adoption should be guided by evidence rather than expectation. Notwithstanding, the historical record suggests that these lessons were only partially absorbed. Subsequent waves of educational technology have reproduced many of the same patterns.

Building schools for the future: Technology as architecture

While the examples discussed in this section draw primarily from the United Kingdom, the dynamics they illustrate are far from uniquely British. Over the past four decades, education systems around the world have undertaken large scale investments in digital infrastructure, often accompanied by ambitious claims about how new technologies and learning environments would transform teaching and learning. The UK case is therefore best understood not as an isolated experience but as a particularly well documented example of a broader global pattern: technological optimism, substantial public investment, and mixed evidence regarding educational impact.

The interactive whiteboard investment was substantial, but it paled in comparison to what came next. In 2004, Prime Minister Tony Blair announced *Building Schools for the Future* (BSF), the most ambitious school building programme in British history. The programme aimed to rebuild or refurbish every secondary school in England over a fifteen year period, with a projected lifetime cost of roughly £52 billion to £55 billion (National Audit Office, 2009). Technology was integral to the vision. These would be schools designed for the digital age, with architecture intended to enable rather than constrain new forms of teaching and learning.

The vision, as presented by the government, was undeniably compelling. Rather than reproducing the Victorian school model with its fixed rows of desks and teacher dominated layouts, the new buildings would feature flexible learning spaces that could be reconfigured for different activities, ICT suites with up-to-date equipment, wireless networks enabling anytime, anywhere learning, and classrooms designed around collaboration rather than instruction. The buildings themselves would also model sustainability, with visible environmental technologies and design features intended to cultivate resource awareness. In policy terms, BSF was framed not simply as a construction programme but as an attempt to align the physical environment of schooling with the social and technological conditions of the twenty-first century.

Fourteen local authorities entered the first wave in 2005 and 2006. New schools were planned with network infrastructure designed for technologies that had not yet fully emerged, with flexible spaces intended for technology enhanced learning, and with environments expected to enable the pedagogical transformation that earlier technology investments had failed to deliver. The underlying argument was that education had been trying to pour new wine into old wineskins: that it was difficult to realise twenty first century learning in buildings designed for nineteenth and twentieth century forms of instruction.

The premise was not unreasonable. Physical space does shape pedagogical possibilities. Collaborative learning, project-based work, and the embedded use of digital tools are all harder to sustain in classrooms designed primarily for lecture-based instruction. ICT suites that require advance booking limit spontaneity. Buildings with weak electrical or network infrastructure constrain the everyday use of computing. In this sense, the argument that physical infrastructure can enable or restrict educational innovation had genuine force. Research on school architecture and spatial layout supports this broader point: built environments can influence patterns of movement, interaction, visibility, and the kinds of teaching that become easier or harder to enact (Sailer, 2018).

However, the programme also became a case study in the challenges of large-scale educational investment. The procurement process proved extraordinarily complex, involving local authorities, private finance initiative partners, architects, and contractors in negotiations that often took years. Local Education Partnerships were established to manage these arrangements, adding further layers of governance and administration. The National Audit Office later concluded that the programme had underestimated the time required for delivery and raised concerns about complexity, cost, and the burdens placed on participating authorities (National Audit Office, 2009).

Another key challenge centred on how these new spaces would actually be used for learning. Considerable thought had gone into architectural design, but far less had been devoted to preparing teachers or adapting curriculum models to suit the pedagogies such spaces seemed to assume. Some of the design thinking drew inspiration from Scandinavian examples such as *Hellerup School* and *Ørestad Gymnasium* in Denmark, both of which became well known for open and flexible learning environments (Danish Ministry of Foreign Affairs, 2009). Those schools, however, are closely tied to wider pedagogical models and organisational cultures that support more project-based and collaborative approaches to learning. Importing the architecture without the corresponding educational philosophy risked producing a mismatch between space and practice (Marcarini et al., 2020).

That mismatch is not merely theoretical. In some BSF schools, teachers left traditional buildings in July and returned in September to radically different environments with limited preparation. Open plan layouts, hub and spoke models, and large shared spaces were expected to support new forms of collaboration, yet many teachers were still working within timetables and subject structures organised around conventional one-hour lessons. In such contexts, acoustic spillover, competing teaching styles, and the difficulty of sustaining focused instruction in adjacent open spaces became serious practical problems. In some cases, movable partitions proved insufficient and walls had to be retrofitted to make the spaces workable.

The irony of this was noted at the time. In a House of Commons debate in July 2008, Dr John Pugh referred back to the earlier fashion for open plan schools in the 1970s and observed that many such buildings had later required walls to be added when educational fashions changed. The point was less architectural nostalgia than institutional memory: school design has repeatedly been shaped by ambitious ideas about pedagogy, only for everyday practice to reassert itself later in more conventional forms (House of Commons, 2008).

What became increasingly clear was that the problem did not lie in openness itself, but in the failure to align architecture, curriculum, teacher preparation, and organisational practice. A siloed curriculum, with mathematics followed by English followed by geography, often still required a degree of spatial separation if each subject was to be taught effectively. The Danish examples that inspired some of the designs worked because the building matched a broader educational philosophy. New wineskins, on their own, were never going to improve the wine.

The final blow to BSF came after the 2010 general election. On 5 July 2010, Education Secretary Michael Gove announced the cancellation of the programme, describing it as bureaucratic and wasteful. More than seven hundred projects already underway did not proceed. In the end, just over five hundred secondary schools were rebuilt or substantially renovated, far fewer than originally envisioned (National Audit Office, 2009). The cancellation remains politically contested, with critics pointing to the loss of long promised renewal and defenders pointing to delays, cost, and excessive bureaucracy.

What received less attention in these political arguments was the central educational question: whether the technology-rich environments promised by BSF would actually have transformed education. The research that exists is cautious at best. Studies of school design and organisational change suggest that where educational transformation did occur, it was associated less with the physical fabric of buildings than with leadership, culture, and pedagogical practice (Burman, Mumovic and Kimpian, 2018). In other words, architecture could enable possibility, but it could not by itself generate new forms of teaching.

This is where the ethical dimension becomes impossible to ignore. Large public investments in technology and infrastructure are usually justified in terms of expected benefits for students. Yet if those benefits depend not only on the tools or buildings themselves, but on teacher preparation, institutional culture, organisational design, and ongoing support, then there is an ethical responsibility to plan for those conditions rather than assume they will arise on their own. To promise transformation without building the human and institutional capacity required to realise it is not merely a technical failure. It is a failure of stewardship.

That lesson matters directly for AI governance. Technology enables, but it does not determine. New capabilities create possibilities, but realising those possibilities requires changes in practice that are fundamentally human. Buildings designed for collaboration do not make teachers collaborative. AI tools designed for personalisation will not, by themselves, make learning personalised. In both cases, the ethical question is not simply whether the technology works, but under what conditions it can be deployed responsibly, fairly, and in ways that genuinely serve educational purposes.

Even the environmental performance of BSF buildings offers a cautionary parallel. A later study of five BSF schools found that all fell short of their design intentions in operational terms, with carbon emissions higher than expected (Burman, Mumovic and Kimpian, 2018). The gap between what the buildings were designed to do and what they actually did in practice mirrors a wider problem in educational technology: systems are too often judged by design aspiration rather than by lived use.

Gove later stated that cancelling BSF was his "biggest mistake in office" (Marrs, 2016). Whether that judgement is accepted or not, the available evidence suggests that even had the programme continued, the educational transformation promised by its architects would not automatically have followed. Transformation requires more than bricks, bandwidth, and devices. It requires attention to professional practice, institutional memory, and ethical responsibility. That is precisely why the story of BSF belongs in a history of AI governance.

As the chapter now moves beyond the UK case, the pattern becomes more clearly global. The next wave of educational technology would no longer be embedded primarily in walls, wiring, and school estates, but in platforms, networks, and online systems that promised to extend learning beyond the classroom itself.

The Virtual Learning Environment Promise

While some technologies arrived with fanfare, others emerged gradually before pandemic circumstances (2020–2023) thrust them into prominence. *Virtual Learning Environments (VLEs)*—online platforms for sharing resources, submitting work, and managing learning—evolved steadily through the 2000s and 2010s, adopted by schools at varying rates and with differing levels of enthusiasm.

The concept appeared straightforward: an online space where teachers could post resources, students could submit work, and learning could extend beyond the physical classroom. In principle, VLEs promised anytime-anywhere learning, improved visibility for parents into students' work, and reduced reliance on paper-based administration. By the early 2010s, many schools and universities across Europe and North America had adopted some form of digital learning platform (Selwyn, 2016).

In the United Kingdom the VLE market developed its own ecosystem, somewhat distinct from what was happening internationally. Moodle, the open-source platform that dominated universities globally, never achieved the same penetration in schools. Its university-oriented structure often proved difficult to translate into the pedagogical and administrative realities of primary and secondary education. Moodle assumed users capable of navigating complex folder structures and managing their own learning independently, while younger students required greater scaffolding and guidance. What worked effectively for university students studying independently could feel overwhelming to younger learners and their teachers (Selwyn, 2016).

The market consequently fragmented. Some schools adopted platforms such as *Frog*, others used *It's Learning* or *Edmodo*, while others built custom systems on *SharePoint* or *Google Sites*. The lack of standardisation created significant challenges. Teachers moving between schools often had to learn entirely new systems, and interoperability between platforms remained limited. A resource created within one VLE could rarely be transferred easily to another. For many teachers this contributed to a growing sense of "innovation fatigue" as successive digital initiatives appeared and disappeared without long term stability.

One British success story was *Firefly*, founded in 2000 by two students at St Paul's School in London (Firefly Learning, 2023). Simon Hay and Joe Mathewson developed the platform to solve a problem they themselves experienced: the fragmentation of digital resources and the difficulty of managing coursework online. The origins of the platform illustrate an important pattern in educational technology: systems designed in response to authentic user needs are often more likely to gain traction. By 2014 *Firefly* was reportedly used by more than 250 schools in the United Kingdom, and by 2016 adoption had expanded internationally to hundreds of schools across multiple countries.

The *Firefly* story is interesting because it emerged from an authentic pain point—students who wanted to solve a problem they actually had. Nevertheless, even successful platforms faced a familiar challenge. Adoption did not guarantee pedagogical transformation. In many schools VLEs functioned primarily as digital filing cabinets, repositories where teachers uploaded worksheets and students occasionally retrieved them. Interactive features remained unused, discussion forums stayed empty, and digital submission systems often duplicated rather than replaced paper processes. The technology existed, but the deeper transformation that early advocates imagined rarely materialised.

As with many educational technologies, the schools that used VLEs most effectively relied on champions: enthusiastic teachers or leaders who invested time in training colleagues and developing model resources. Without such leadership adoption remained shallow. Platforms could remain present for years without becoming fully integrated into everyday teaching practice.

Then came 2020.

As the COVID-19 pandemic spread globally, schools closed at unprecedented scale, and digital platforms shifted almost overnight from supplementary tools to essential infrastructure. The moment revealed both the value and the limits of prior digital investment. Schools with established platforms, routines, and teacher familiarity were generally better placed to maintain continuity, while others struggled to do so.

The experience also exposed deep inequalities. Access to devices, connectivity, and digitally confident teaching became decisive, and for many students digital learning meant exclusion rather than opportunity (Engzell, Frey and Verhagen, 2021; ITU, 2021). At the same time, the rapid deployment of educational technologies raised urgent questions about privacy, surveillance, and children's rights that were often secondary under emergency conditions (Human Rights Watch, 2022).

The pandemic did not settle the question of digital transformation in education. It clarified it. Technology could sustain elements of continuity, but it could not by itself resolve the social, pedagogical, and ethical conditions on which education depends. Because these lessons are central to the argument of the next chapter, they are explored there in greater depth.

The MOOC mirage

As virtual learning environments began to take hold in schools and universities, a parallel revolution was said to be unfolding in higher education. Massive Open Online Courses, or MOOCs, emerged in the early 2010s amid impressive claims about democratisation, scale, and disruption. Elite institutions partnered with platforms like Coursera, edX, and later FutureLearn, presenting free online courses as a route to world class learning for anyone with an internet connection. In 2012, the moment was so heavily mythologised that *The New York Times* declared it "The Year of the MOOC" (Pappano, 2012). FutureLearn's own launch materials framed the project in similarly expansive terms, promising wider access to higher education in the United Kingdom and beyond (FutureLearn, 2012).

The rhetoric was not merely optimistic. It was transformational. MOOCs were presented as a mechanism through which elite teaching could be detached from elite campuses, costs could be radically reduced, and longstanding exclusions might finally be overcome. In the broader discourse around online disruption, some commentators went further and predicted institutional collapse in conventional higher education. What mattered here, however, was not simply the boldness of the forecast. It was the moral claim beneath it: that scale, openness, and technical delivery could produce educational justice almost by themselves. This assumption would become one of the defining ideas of digital education, and one of its most persistent illusions.

Early evidence did show genuine strengths. Many MOOCs offered high production values, strong academic content, flexible access, and opportunities for transnational participation. For adult learners seeking professional development, intellectual exploration, or subject specific upskilling, these features were significant. Yet the gap between enrolment and meaningful educational participation quickly became impossible to ignore. Jordan's analysis of 221 MOOCs found completion rates ranging from 0.7 per cent to 52.1 per cent, with a median of 12.6 per cent (Jordan, 2015). Reich and Ruipérez Valiente later argued that the central problems of the MOOC model had not substantially improved over time, noting persistently low completion rates and highly unequal global participation (Reich and Ruipérez Valiente, 2019). A more recent comparative study by Celik and Cagiltay found that conventional completion measures still remain low, even if alternative ways of calculating participation can produce more generous figures (Celik and Cagiltay, 2024).

The numbers from the earliest flagship courses were especially revealing. Research on MITx and HarvardX reported that the first wave of high-profile MOOCs attracted enormous initial registration, but only a small fraction of those registrants completed the courses. In the widely discussed MITx course *Circuits and Electronics*, nearly 155,000 learners enrolled and just over 7,100 earned a certificate, a completion rate of under 5 per cent (Breslow et al., 2013; Ho et al., 2014). Scale, in other words, was real. Educational transformation was less evident. This distinction matters. Access to a platform is not the same thing as sustained learning, and registration statistics can easily function as a marketing proxy for impact rather than evidence of it.

The ethical problem runs deeper when participation is examined demographically. Empirical work repeatedly found that MOOCs were used disproportionately by learners who were already relatively advantaged: adults with prior education, stronger study skills, and better digital access. Rohs and Ganz concluded that MOOCs, despite their egalitarian rhetoric, were mostly used by people with higher levels of education and risked reinforcing rather than reducing inequality (Rohs and Ganz, 2015). Reich and Ruipérez Valiente similarly observed that growth in participation was concentrated in the world's most affluent countries (Reich and Ruipérez Valiente, 2019). This is not a minor implementation problem. It raises a central ethical question for digital education: who is actually positioned to benefit when "open" learning is built on assumptions of connectivity, time, confidence, and self-direction that many learners do not possess.

Seen in this light, the limitations of MOOCs are both pedagogical and ethical. They expose the weakness of a recurring idea in educational technology: that widening formal access is enough to widen genuine opportunity. But, meaningful participation in online learning depends on far more than course availability. It depends on infrastructure, digital literacy, language, time, family circumstance, institutional recognition, and the presence of support structures that help learners persist. UNESCO has since made the same point in broader terms, warning that the digital divide excludes millions from education and that connectivity has become integral to the right to education itself (UNESCO, 2023a). The ethical lesson is clear. A system cannot plausibly claim democratisation while leaving the conditions of participation untouched.

For this reason, the MOOC story is best understood not as a failure of online learning in general, but as a caution against technological solutionism. MOOCs proved more durable when they supplemented existing educational pathways than when they claimed to replace them. They found clearer value in lifelong learning, professional development, and exploratory study than in any wholesale substitution for universities. This pattern is likely to recur in contemporary debates about AI in education. Systems that promise frictionless personalisation at global scale may once again confuse reach with impact, exposure with learning, and access with justice. The history of MOOCs suggests that educational ethics begins precisely where such confusions are challenged.

Curiosity, access, and the limits of self-directed learning

The limitations of MOOCs reveal a deeper assumption that has long shaped educational technology discourse: the belief that access to digital tools, at sufficient scale, will naturally produce meaningful learning. This assumption has appeared repeatedly in different forms across the history of digital education. One of the most influential examples emerged more than a decade before the rise of MOOCs in Sugata Mitra's widely discussed "Hole in the Wall" experiment.

Beginning in 1999, Mitra and colleagues placed publicly accessible computers in low income communities in India and observed how children interacted with them without formal instruction (Mitra and Rana, 2001). The results quickly attracted international attention. Children with no prior exposure to computers appeared to learn basic operational skills through experimentation and peer collaboration. Within hours they could manipulate the mouse and navigate the interface, and within days, they were opening programmes, exploring software and accessing digital media. These observations quickly circulated through academic and policy discussions about digital learning. The narrative that emerged was extraordinarily powerful. Here, apparently, was evidence that curiosity combined with access to technology could overcome educational disadvantage and allow children to teach themselves complex skills without formal instruction.

The experiment later inspired the development of Self Organised Learning Environments and Mitra's widely viewed TED project, *School in the Cloud* (TED, 2013). The appeal was obvious. It seemed to show that children could teach themselves if adults simply stepped back and technology stepped in.

Once again, the evidence base proved more fragile than the story. The original Hole in the Wall studies were observational and exploratory, not controlled trials. They suggested that children could acquire certain forms of operational computer literacy, but they did not establish that unguided digital access reliably produced deeper learning across domains such as literacy, mathematics, or sustained conceptual understanding. Arora's later fieldwork in the Central Himalayas found that two Hole in the Wall sites had failed to take root and raised serious questions about sustainability, local context, and the assumptions built into the project's theory of change (Arora, 2010). The issue was not whether children are capable of peer learning or experimentation. They plainly are. It was more whether those capacities justified the far larger claim that formal instruction could be displaced by minimally supervised access to technology.

Related evidence from other one to one technology initiatives pointed in the same direction. In a large-scale randomised evaluation of Peru's One Laptop per Child programme, increased access to computers led to greater use at school and at home, but no measurable improvement was found in mathematics or language test scores (Cristia et al., 2017). This finding closely reflected Warschauer's earlier argument that technology alone does not resolve educational disadvantage because meaningful inclusion depends on social context, institutional support, and the capacities required to use tools well (Warschauer, 2003). The ethical significance of this literature is substantial. It shows that children can be given devices, platforms, and even apparent freedom, while still being denied the conditions necessary for meaningful educational benefit.

Taken together, MOOCs and the Hole in the Wall experiments reveal a recurring pattern in the history of educational technology. New tools are frequently accompanied by compelling narratives about access, empowerment, and transformation. Yet when those narratives are examined through systematic research, the educational outcomes often appear more modest and far more dependent on context than early claims suggest. The promise of scale does not automatically translate into meaningful learning, and access to powerful tools does not, by itself, overcome the social, institutional, and pedagogical conditions that shape educational success.

This pattern carries an important warning. Technologies that appear to democratise learning can, without careful design and support, reinforce existing inequalities by favouring those who already possess the time, resources, and prior knowledge needed to benefit from them. The history of digital education therefore challenges a persistent assumption: that technological access alone is sufficient to produce educational opportunity.

For a book concerned with AI ethics, this matters. The central question is not whether intelligent systems can expand educational reach. They almost certainly can. The harder and more important question is whether they do so in ways that are equitable, evidence based, and consistent with education's obligations to human flourishing rather than technological spectacle.

Answering that question requires moving beyond the narratives that so often accompany new technologies and toward the research literature on learning itself. Over the past two decades, education researchers have attempted precisely this task, synthesising thousands of studies in an effort to identify which interventions actually improve learning outcomes. Among the most influential of these efforts is the work of John Hattie, whose large-scale synthesis of educational research sought to measure the relative impact of different teaching practices and innovations.

The Hattie effect: What does the evidence actually show?

The historical pattern identified in the previous sections raises an obvious question. If technological enthusiasm repeatedly produces ambitious claims about educational transformation, what does the research evidence actually show about the impact of different interventions on learning outcomes?

One of the most influential attempts to answer this question appears in the work of John Hattie. Hattie's synthesis of educational research has become one of the most widely cited attempts to measure the relative effectiveness of different teaching practices, policies, and innovations.

Hattie's 2008 book Visible Learning synthesised more than 800 meta-analyses relating to educational achievement, a body of work that in later updates expanded to over 1,200 meta-analyses encompassing tens of thousands of individual studies (Hattie, 2009; Hattie, 2015). His approach was to calculate effect sizes for different educational interventions in order to estimate their relative impact on student achievement.

Within this framework, Hattie proposed a benchmark effect size of 0.40, which he described as a "hinge point" representing approximately one year of learning growth during one year of schooling (Hattie, 2009). Interventions with effect sizes above this threshold could therefore be interpreted as having a greater than average impact, while those below the hinge point might warrant more cautious investment.

The appeal of this approach was immediate. Education systems are saturated with competing claims about what works. Teachers, school leaders, and policymakers are routinely encouraged to adopt new initiatives, technologies, and reforms, often without clear evidence of their effectiveness. Hattie's synthesis appeared to offer something rare in education policy debates: a systematic framework for comparing interventions and identifying which practices were most strongly associated with improved learning outcomes.

Where did technology appear within this evidence base?

In Hattie's synthesis, the category "computer assisted instruction" produced an average effect size of approximately 0.31 (Hattie, 2009). This value indicates a modest positive effect on student achievement, but one that falls below the hinge point of 0.40. In other words, computer-based learning interventions appeared to produce measurable gains, yet those gains were not, on average, as large as those associated with many other educational practices.

By comparison, several instructional strategies demonstrated substantially larger effect sizes. Feedback to students, for example, showed an average effect size of 0.73, while teacher clarity, formative evaluation, and classroom discussion also produced consistently higher impacts across the research base (Hattie, 2009; Hattie, 2015).

Importantly, some of the most powerful effects emerged not from technology itself but from the quality of interaction between teachers and students, particularly where feedback enabled teachers to adapt instruction to student needs.

Taken at face value, these findings offered a sobering perspective on the transformative claims frequently attached to educational technology. Despite significant investment in information and communication technologies across many education systems, the overall research synthesis suggested that digital tools alone rarely produced the largest improvements in learning outcomes.

However, Hattie's methodology has also attracted significant criticism, and the findings must therefore be interpreted with care. Scholars such as Schulmeister and Loviscach argued that the statistical procedures used in the synthesis may have produced misleading interpretations, particularly when effect sizes from very different contexts and interventions were aggregated into single averages (Schulmeister and Loviscach, 2014).

Other critics have raised concerns about the comparability of the underlying studies. Meta-analyses conducted across different decades, educational systems, and technological contexts were combined within the same synthesis. As a result, studies examining early drill-and-practice software from the 1980s could appear alongside research on interactive simulations or collaborative learning platforms developed decades later. While such aggregation allows broad comparison, it may also obscure important contextual differences in how technologies are implemented and used.

A further point of controversy concerned the interpretation of certain variables within the synthesis. The variable "self-reported grades," which appeared with one of the highest effect sizes in the dataset, derived from research examining the accuracy with which students report their own academic performance rather than an instructional intervention designed to improve learning (Kuncel, Credé and Thomas, 2005). Critics argued that treating this variable as if it represented a strategy for improving achievement risked confusing correlation with causation.

Despite these methodological debates, several conclusions from the broader research literature remain widely accepted. First, educational technologies tend to produce modest positive effects on learning outcomes on average, but rarely dramatic improvements on their own (Tamim et al., 2011). Second, the impact of technology varies widely depending on how it is implemented.

Some interventions show meaningful benefits, while others produce little measurable effect.

Perhaps most importantly, the evidence consistently suggests that pedagogy matters more than the technology itself. Digital tools can support learning when they are embedded within effective instructional design, but they are rarely sufficient on their own. Interactive whiteboards used for active instruction, collaborative problem solving, or formative assessment may produce different outcomes than the same devices used primarily as projection screens. Similarly, access to computer laboratories or online platforms can support learning in some contexts while producing little measurable benefit in others.

The implication is not that technology is irrelevant to education. Rather, it is that its effects are mediated through the practices of teaching and learning that surround it. The same technology can support powerful learning in one environment and remain largely inert in another.

From an ethical perspective, this finding is significant. It suggests that the value of educational technologies cannot be assessed solely in terms of technical capability or scale of adoption. Their impact depends on the institutional, pedagogical, and social conditions within which they are deployed.

For debates about artificial intelligence in education, this history offers a useful point of caution. AI systems may well support new forms of feedback, assessment, and personalised learning. Yet the broader research record suggests that technological innovation alone rarely transforms education. Gains tend to be incremental, uneven, and deeply dependent on the surrounding educational environment. The ethical responsibility therefore lies not only in developing new tools, but in understanding how those tools interact with existing educational practices, inequalities, and institutional structures.

CONCLUSION TO PART I: LESSONS FROM THE FIRST WAVE OF DIGITAL EDUCATION

Taken together, the developments examined in this chapter reveal a consistent pattern in the history of educational technology. From early virtual learning environments to the rise of MOOCs and experiments such as Hole in the Wall, new technologies have repeatedly been accompanied by narratives of educational transformation.

Yet the empirical record is more restrained. Digital technologies can support learning, but their effects are rarely automatic and seldom revolutionary. Access does not guarantee participation, participation does not guarantee learning, and learning outcomes remain shaped by the broader educational environment.

These historical lessons matter for contemporary debates about artificial intelligence. They suggest that the ethical challenge of educational technology lies not simply in the capabilities of new systems, but in the conditions under which they are introduced into schools and universities.

The next phase of the story illustrates this point in an unexpected way. The most significant technological transformation in education during the past two decades did not arrive through carefully planned institutional reforms or educational platforms. It arrived in the pockets of students.

PART II: SMARTPHONES: THE TECHNOLOGY WE DIDN'T PLAN FOR

While educators debated the merits and drawbacks of interactive whiteboards and virtual learning environments, a different technology arrived that would prove both more transformational and disruptive: the smartphone. Unlike previous educational technologies, smartphones were not introduced to schools through procurement processes or pedagogical planning. They arrived in students' pockets, and schools were forced to decide how to respond.

The adoption curve was breathtakingly fast. The iPhone launched in 2007; by 2010 smartphones were already common among teenagers, and by the middle of the following decade they had become widespread among young people across many developed countries. Unlike computers, which require dedicated spaces and scheduled access, smartphones are always present, always connected, and capable of delivering a continuous stream of notifications, messages, and media. They therefore present an unprecedented challenge to the controlled information environments schools have traditionally attempted to maintain.

The scale of smartphone penetration among young people is striking. In the United Kingdom, Ofcom reported in 2024 that 98 per cent of 16–17-year-olds owned a smartphone, while 96 per cent of children aged 12–15 owned one. Even among younger children, ownership has increased rapidly: 61 per cent of children aged 8–11 now have their own smartphone (Ofcom, 2024). As a result, even primary schools increasingly face questions of device management that were once associated primarily with secondary education.

Smartphones have also become the primary point of internet access for many young people. Ofcom data indicates that 71 per cent of children aged 5–15 use a smartphone to go online, making it the most common means of internet access. Among 16–17-year-olds, 97 per cent use mobile phones to access the internet (Ofcom, 2024). The desktop computer that education systems invested in so heavily during the early waves of digital learning has therefore been eclipsed by devices that schools themselves did not purchase.

From a classroom perspective, smartphones pose a significant challenge to behaviour management and sustained attention. Many schools have responded with strict policies: phones prohibited on school grounds, confiscation for violations, and escalating disciplinary measures for repeated breaches. The reasoning behind these policies is straightforward. Smartphones can distract from learning, enable cyberbullying, and provide access to inappropriate content. Schools are educational environments, and many educators argue that smartphones undermine the conditions necessary for focused learning.

However, enforcement has proven difficult. Students conceal devices in creative ways or carry multiple phones. Confiscation policies can lead to confrontations with parents and increase administrative burdens for school staff. Time spent policing device use is time not spent teaching or supporting students. At the same time, some educators recognise that smartphones can support learning activities, including quick research, collaborative communication, translation, and access to educational applications.

Survey data illustrates how schools are attempting to navigate these tensions. Research conducted by the Children's Commissioner for England in 2024 found that nearly all schools had policies restricting smartphone use during the school day. Primary schools tended to enforce stricter policies: 72 per cent required phones to be handed in or stored securely. Secondary schools reported similar but slightly lower rates at 66 per cent (Children's Commissioner for England, 2024). In most cases, phones were prohibited during lessons, though policies differed on whether limited use was permitted during breaks.

Governments have also begun to intervene. In England, the Department for Education issued guidance in 2024 (updated February 2026) encouraging schools to prohibit phone use during the school day, including during breaks and lunchtime. The guidance stopped short of imposing a statutory ban but signalled clear policy support for restriction, suggesting that "All schools should be mobile phone-free environments by default; anything other than this should be by exception only." (Department for Education, 2026).

Similar debates have emerged internationally. France introduced a national ban on mobile phones in primary and lower secondary schools in 2018, reflecting growing concern about distraction, cyberbullying, and student wellbeing. Other education systems have adopted comparable measures. In Sweden, the Education Act was amended in 2022 to clarify schools' authority to confiscate mobile phones and other disruptive digital devices during lessons. In Australia, several states have introduced system wide restrictions. Victoria implemented a statewide ban on student mobile phones during the school day in government schools in 2020, while New South Wales introduced a similar ban across public high schools in 2023.

More centralised approaches have also emerged. In China, the Ministry of Education issued national regulations in 2021 limiting students from bringing mobile phones into schools without parental consent and requiring that devices, if present, be managed by school authorities. In the United Arab Emirates, where digital governance has increasingly intersected with broader child protection frameworks, education authorities have also introduced stricter guidance around student device use and online safety as part of wider digital wellbeing and cyber safety initiatives.

Taken together, these measures illustrate how smartphone governance has moved from a matter of individual school discipline to a policy issue addressed at regional and national levels. UNESCO's global monitoring of education systems indicates that a growing number of countries now restrict or prohibit smartphone use in schools, reflecting a shared recognition that the device has become a central factor shaping attention, behaviour, and student wellbeing within contemporary learning environments (UNESCOb, 2023).

The use of social media applications on smartphones further complicates the issue. Platforms such as TikTok, Instagram, and Snapchat set minimum user ages of 13. Yet Ofcom data shows that three quarters of social media users aged 8–17 have their own account despite these restrictions, and around 60 per cent of children aged 8–12 have created profiles while under the official age threshold (Ofcom, 2024). Age verification mechanisms are easily circumvented, leaving schools to address the behavioural and pastoral consequences of platforms they neither control nor regulate.

The educational implications are significant. Social media platforms are designed to maximise engagement through constant notifications, algorithmic recommendation systems, and short form content streams that reward rapid switching of attention. When accessed through smartphones that students carry throughout the school day, these systems introduce persistent opportunities for distraction both inside and outside the classroom. OECD analysis of student digital behaviour has found that frequent use of digital devices for leisure activities during lessons is associated with increased distraction and lower academic performance in many education systems (OECD, 2024).

The effects extend beyond school hours. Because smartphones accompany students' homes, the same platforms can compete directly with homework, reading, and sleep. A growing research literature links heavy or problematic social media use among adolescents with reduced concentration, disrupted sleep patterns, and increased psychological distress, although causal relationships remain complex and contested (Odgers and Jensen, 2020). For schools, this creates a paradox. Institutions are increasingly expected to support student wellbeing and academic focus, yet many of the digital environments shaping those outcomes exist beyond the school's authority.

In this sense, the challenge posed by smartphones is both technological *and* structural. Schools can regulate devices within their own walls, but they cannot regulate the design incentives of global social media platforms. The behavioural effects of those platforms therefore enter classrooms indirectly, mediated through devices that students carry with them throughout the day.

The concerns raised by educators and policymakers are meaningful. A growing body of research links heavy social media use with increased anxiety, depression, and reduced wellbeing among adolescents, particularly girls (Odgers and Jensen, 2020). Constant connectivity can fragment attention and disrupt sleep, while cyberbullying extends peer conflicts beyond school hours and into students' private lives. These are social and psychological harms that schools are increasingly expected to manage despite having limited authority over the platforms that generate them. Australia more recently responded to this by banning social media outright for under-16s, citing that "the risks of social media, such as cyberbullying, harmful content, and online predators, outweigh the positives" (UNICEF, 2026).

At the same time, the smartphone challenge illustrates a broader lesson about educational technology. *The most consequential technologies affecting learning are not always those designed specifically for education.* Smartphones were developed as consumer communication devices rather than pedagogical tools. Their influence on learning environments emerged indirectly as a consequence of widespread adoption among young people (Ofcom, 2024).

This dynamic reveals important governance implications. Educational policy and institutional oversight traditionally focus on technologies that schools intentionally procure, such as learning platforms, assessment systems, and, more recently, artificial intelligence tutoring systems. These technologies pass through formal procurement processes and are therefore subject to institutional review, regulatory compliance, and policy oversight. Consumer technologies operate differently. Their adoption is driven primarily by markets rather than educational strategy, yet their influence on students' learning, behaviour, and wellbeing may be far greater (OECD, 2024).

The boundaries that once separated school and home, education and entertainment, have therefore become increasingly porous. Smartphones allow social media platforms, messaging systems, and entertainment applications to accompany students throughout the school day and into their home environments. Research has shown that frequent use of digital devices for leisure activities during lessons is associated with increased distraction and lower academic performance in many education systems (OECD, 2024). Beyond school hours, heavy or problematic social media use has also been associated with disrupted sleep patterns and increased psychological distress among adolescents, although causal relationships remain complex and contested (Odgers and Jensen, 2020; Kelly et al., 2018; Carter et al., 2016).

Technologies that initially appear unrelated to schooling can therefore shape how students learn, communicate, and experience the world. The governance frameworks developed for institutionally adopted technologies may be poorly suited to technologies that enter classrooms through students themselves.

In this sense, the arrival of smartphones marked a turning point. Schools were no longer responding only to technologies they had chosen to adopt; they were responding to technologies already embedded in students' everyday lives. As later chapters will explore, the rapid emergence of generative AI tools followed a remarkably similar pattern. Students encountered these tools independently, often through personal devices and accounts, before schools had time to develop policies or pedagogical frameworks.

Part I of this chapter has shown that the history of educational technology is characterised by cycles of promise, adoption, and reassessment. The smartphone represents a particularly vivid example of this pattern. It was not introduced with a clear pedagogical rationale, yet it quickly became one of the most influential technologies shaping the modern classroom. The next section examines one of the first attempts by education systems to respond to this new mobile computing environment through deliberate adoption: the introduction of tablet devices, particularly the iPad, and the pedagogical framework commonly associated with their use, the SAMR model.

PART III: IPADS AND THE SAMR MODEL

Of all the technologies introduced into schools over the past four decades, the iPad was among those that generated the greatest optimism. For the first time, many educators believed that a device had arrived that might genuinely reshape classroom practice, shifting the teacher's role from the traditional "sage on the stage" to a "guide on the side".

Ruben Puentedura first articulated the SAMR model in 2006 as part of his work with the Maine Learning Technology Initiative. The model was designed to provide educators with a common language for discussing how digital technologies could be integrated into teaching and learning. Wider recognition followed when Puentedura presented the model publicly in 2010, establishing SAMR as one of the most widely referenced frameworks for thinking about educational technology integration (Puentedura, 2010).

The timing was fortuitous. Apple released the first iPad in 2010 and the iPad 2 in 2011, and schools around the world quickly embraced the device. Tablets promised mobility, intuitive interfaces, and a vast ecosystem of applications. Many policymakers and school leaders believed they had found the long-awaited tool capable of transforming the classroom.

The adoption of the SAMR model remains important for understanding later debates about artificial intelligence in education. The framework illustrates both the promise and the limitations of attempting to structure technological innovation within relatively narrow conceptual categories.

The first level of the SAMR model is *substitution*.

At this stage, technology simply replaces an existing tool without altering the underlying task. Students might read a PDF textbook on an iPad rather than a printed copy, or write an essay in a word processor rather than by hand. The activity remains fundamentally unchanged. Substitution rarely enhances the learning process directly, yet it often represents the first stage of technological integration in schools. It can improve efficiency. Digital textbooks reduce the weight of schoolbags, and teachers can store lesson materials electronically rather than maintaining extensive paper archives. Even today, much technology use in education remains at this level. Artificial intelligence systems frequently operate in a similar way, replacing existing processes rather than transforming them.

The second level is *augmentation*.

Here technology still supports the same learning activity but introduces functional improvements. Collaborative writing tools such as Google Docs allow students to edit shared documents simultaneously, while digital texts can include search functions, hyperlinks, and embedded dictionaries. The task itself remains recognisable, but the technology offers advantages that traditional tools cannot easily provide. Students may receive immediate feedback while writing or access supporting information instantly. The learning activity becomes more efficient, but it is not fundamentally restructured.

The third level is *modification*.

At this stage technology begins to reshape the design of learning tasks. Students might create multimedia presentations, produce short films, or explore geographical landscapes through interactive mapping tools such as Google Earth. These activities allow students to demonstrate understanding in ways that were previously difficult to achieve in traditional classroom settings. Technology is no longer simply improving efficiency; it is enabling new forms of expression and exploration. Apple's marketing of the iPad emphasised precisely this possibility, presenting the device as a tool capable of liberating students from conventional formats such as the five-paragraph essay and encouraging richer forms of knowledge creation.

The final level is *redefinition*.

Here technology enables tasks that would previously have been inconceivable. Students might collaborate on projects with peers in other countries, participate in virtual field trips, or develop digital artefacts such as websites and applications addressing real-world problems. In theory, Redefinition represents the highest aspiration of technology-enhanced learning: students acting as creators, collaborators, and participants in global knowledge networks rather than passive recipients of teacher-generated content.

The promise of the iPad was that it might accelerate movement toward these higher levels of transformation. Yet, as with earlier waves of educational technology, the reality proved more complicated.

In practice, the SAMR model proved far easier to describe than to implement. Technical limitations quickly became apparent. Tablet screen sizes were often small for extended academic work, typing on touchscreens was cumbersome, and stylus input did not always provide a reliable substitute for handwriting. Battery life degraded over time, and students frequently arrived at school with partially charged devices. Schools found themselves investing in charging stations or adapting classroom layouts to accommodate limited power outlets.

Device management presented further challenges. The application ecosystem surrounding tablets was largely designed for entertainment rather than education, requiring schools to rely on mobile device management systems to control access during lessons. Even with such systems in place, maintaining focus proved difficult. Tablets could easily conceal distractions behind screens angled away from teachers. The situation sometimes resembled placing students in a digital environment rich with entertainment options and asking them to ignore most of them.

Durability also proved problematic. Although tablets are constructed from strengthened materials, breakages occur regularly and repairs can be costly. For many schools, the financial burden of maintenance and replacement quickly became apparent.

These practical challenges were accompanied by pedagogical pressures. The SAMR model encouraged teachers to pursue increasingly sophisticated uses of technology, sometimes emphasising novelty rather than educational effectiveness. Teachers already managing heavy workloads were asked to redesign lessons in ways that demanded new technical skills and unfamiliar pedagogical approaches. In some cases, technology integration became associated with performative innovation rather than demonstrable improvements in learning.

Large-scale implementation projects illustrated these risks clearly. The Los Angeles Unified School District initiative is among the most widely cited examples. In 2013 the district launched a programme to distribute iPads to more than 600,000 students as part of a digital curriculum initiative. The project encountered serious difficulties. Students quickly bypassed device restrictions, the digital curriculum was incomplete, and the procurement process became the subject of a federal investigation. The superintendent eventually resigned, and the programme was widely regarded as a cautionary example of poorly governed educational technology adoption (Herold, 2014).

Cases such as this highlight an important lesson. Technologies originally designed for consumer markets rarely translate seamlessly into educational contexts. Without careful planning, training, and governance, even well-intentioned initiatives can generate significant disruption while delivering limited pedagogical benefit.

The experience of iPad implementation therefore reinforces a recurring theme in the history of educational technology: transformation rarely occurs simply because a new device enters the classroom. Meaningful change requires thoughtful integration, sustained professional development, and governance structures capable of aligning technological capability with educational purpose.

These lessons are directly relevant to the contemporary debate around artificial intelligence. As with earlier technologies, enthusiasm for AI has been accompanied by ambitious claims about transformation. Yet the history of previous digital innovations suggests that successful integration will depend less on the technology itself than on how institutions implement, evaluate, and govern it.

CHAPTER CONCLUSION: WHAT HISTORY TEACHES US

Looking across four decades of educational technology, several patterns become visible. These patterns are not merely historical observations. They provide a framework for understanding how new technologies, including artificial intelligence, are likely to shape education.

The first pattern concerns the persistent gap between promise and evidence. New technologies frequently arrive accompanied by claims of transformation. Calculators were expected to revolutionise mathematical reasoning, interactive whiteboards promised unprecedented engagement, virtual learning environments promised learning anytime and anywhere, and massive open online courses were heralded as a democratisation of education. In practice, rigorous research reveals more modest effects. Technology can support learning, but rarely in the dramatic ways early advocates predict.

This does not mean such technologies lack value. Calculators did influence mathematics teaching, interactive whiteboards sometimes improved classroom interaction, and online learning platforms proved essential during periods of school closure. Yet the historical record suggests that the rhetoric of transformation consistently outpaces empirical evidence. For AI, the implication is clear: extraordinary claims require careful evaluation.

A second pattern concerns implementation. Technologies do not operate independently of context. The same tool may produce very different outcomes depending on how it is used, who is using it, and what support structures exist. Technology should therefore be understood not as a programme to be implemented but as a capability that institutions must learn to employ effectively.

This insight has important implications for governance. Asking whether "AI works" is too simplistic. A more meaningful question concerns which forms of implementation produce beneficial outcomes, in which contexts, and for which students.

A third pattern concerns equity. Educational technologies often amplify existing inequalities rather than reducing them. Students and schools with greater resources and expertise are frequently better positioned to benefit from new tools, while disadvantaged communities may struggle to access or implement them effectively. Early evidence from previous technological waves suggests that new tools often reinforce existing educational advantages.

Artificial intelligence may follow a similar trajectory. Schools with stronger digital infrastructure and more extensive professional development resources may be able to integrate AI effectively, while others may lag behind. Addressing this imbalance requires governance frameworks that explicitly prioritise equitable access and support.

A fourth pattern concerns sustainability. Technological adoption rarely ends with the initial purchase. Devices require maintenance, software must be updated, and teachers require ongoing training as platforms evolve. Many educational technology initiatives fail not because the technology itself is ineffective, but because the long-term costs and organisational demands of sustaining its use were underestimated.

Artificial intelligence systems are likely to intensify this challenge. They depend on continuous software updates, evolving datasets, licensing arrangements, and ongoing staff development. Effective governance must therefore consider the entire lifecycle of technological adoption rather than focusing solely on initial deployment.

A fifth pattern concerns the enduring importance of teachers. Repeated predictions have suggested that digital technologies would eventually replace educators. Yet throughout successive technological waves, teaching has proven remarkably resilient. Technologies change, but the core role of educators in guiding, motivating, and supporting learners remains central.

AI systems may assist teachers by automating certain tasks or providing new forms of feedback. However, they remain fundamentally reactive systems. They respond to prompts and inputs but do not initiate learning in the way skilled educators do. Motivation, encouragement, and pastoral care remain difficult to replicate technologically.

A sixth pattern concerns path dependency. Decisions about technology platforms can shape future possibilities in ways that are difficult to reverse. Schools that adopted particular digital platforms during earlier waves of technological adoption now find themselves embedded within specific technological ecosystems. These choices influence the AI tools that can be integrated into existing infrastructure.

This raises important governance questions about long-term flexibility and institutional autonomy. Decisions made under time pressure may have consequences that extend far beyond their original context.

Finally, there is the persistent governance gap. Educational technologies often enter classrooms before regulatory or institutional frameworks have fully developed. Schools experiment, adapt, and respond in real time while policymakers attempt to understand the implications.

Artificial intelligence is currently following this familiar trajectory. Students and teachers are already experimenting with AI systems while broader governance debates continue.

History suggests that the success of AI in education will depend less on technological capability than on the quality of the governance frameworks developed around it. The challenge is not simply to adopt new tools but to integrate them thoughtfully, evaluate their impact rigorously, and ensure that their benefits are distributed fairly across education systems.

The remainder of this book explores how such governance frameworks might be designed.

REFERENCES

Arora, P. (2010) 'Hope in the wall? A digital promise for free learning', *British Journal of Educational Technology*, 41(5), 689–702. Available at: https://bera-journals.onlinelibrary.wiley.com/doi/10.1111/j.1467-8535.2010.01078.x

Breslow, L., Pritchard, D.E., DeBoer, J., Stump, G.S., Ho, A.D. and Seaton, D.T. (2013) 'Studying learning in the worldwide classroom: Research into edX's first MOOC', *Research and Practice in Assessment,* 8, 13–25. Available at: www.researchgate.net/publication/237091973_Studying_Learning_in_the_Worldwide_Classroom_Research_into_edX's_First_MOOC

Burman, E., Mumovic, D. and Kimpian, J. (2018) 'Building schools for the future: Lessons learned from performance evaluations of five secondary schools and academies in England', *Frontiers in Built Environment*, 4, Article 22. Available at: www.frontiersin.org/journals/built-environment/articles/10.3389/fbuil.2018.00022/full

Carter, B., Rees, P., Hale, L., Bhattacharjee, D. and Paradkar, M.S. (2016) 'Association between portable screen-based media device access or use and sleep outcomes: A systematic review and meta-analysis', *JAMA Pediatrics*, 170(12), 1202–1208. Available at: https://pubmed.ncbi.nlm.nih.gov/27802500/

Celik, B. and Cagiltay, K. (2024) 'Uncovering MOOC completion: A comparative study of completion rates from different perspectives', *Open Praxis,* 16(3), 446–457. doi: 10.55982/openpraxis.16.3.606 Available at: https://openpraxis.org/articles/10.55982/openpraxis.16.3.606

Children's Commissioner for England (2024) *The Big Ask: Children's Views on Phones and Social Media.* London: Children's Commissioner. Available at: www.childrenscommissioner.gov.uk

Cockcroft, W.H. (1982) *Mathematics Counts: Report of the Committee of Inquiry into the Teaching of Mathematics in Schools.* London: HMSO. Available at: https://education-uk.org/documents/cockcroft/cockcroft1982.html

Cristia, J., Ibarrarán, P., Cueto, S., Santiago, A. and Severín, E. (2017) 'Technology and child development: Evidence from the one laptop per child program', *American Economic Journal: Applied Economics,* 9(3), 295–320. Available at: www.aeaweb.org/articles?id=10.1257/app.20150385

Danish Ministry of Foreign Affairs (2009) *Learning from Denmark.* Available at: https://storbritannien.um.dk/en/the-trade-council/projects/learning-from-denmark

Department for Education (2026) *Mobile Phones in Schools: Guidance for Schools.* London: Department for Education U.K. Available at: www.gov.uk/government/publications/mobile-phones-in-schools

Ellington, A.J. (2003) 'A meta-analysis of the effects of calculators on students' achievement and attitude levels in precollege mathematics classes', *Journal for Research in Mathematics Education*, 34(5), 433–463. Available at: www.jstor.org/stable/30034795?origin=crossref

Engzell, P., Frey, A. and Verhagen, M. (2021) 'Learning loss due to school closures during the COVID-19 pandemic', *Proceedings of the National Academy of Sciences*, 118(17), 4–5. Available at: www.pnas.org/doi/10.1073/pnas.2022376118

Firefly Learning (2023) *Firefly: A Veracross Solution – The Firefly Journey (About: Who We Are).* Available at: www.fireflylearning.com/about/who-we-are (Accessed: 15 March 2026).

FutureLearn. (2012, December 14) *FutureLearn Launches.* Available at: www.futurelearn.com/info/feature/futurelearn-launches

Hattie, J. (2009) *Visible Learning: A Synthesis of Over 800 Meta-Analyses Relating to Achievement.* London: Routledge. Available at: https://inspirasifoundation.org/wp-content/uploads/2020/05/John-Hattie-Visible-Learning_-A-synthesis-of-over-800-meta-analyses-relating-to-achievement-2008.pdf

Hattie, J. (2015) *Visible Learning Updated.* London: Routledge.

Hembree, R. and Dessart, D.J. (1986) 'Effects of hand-held calculators in precollege mathematics education: A meta-analysis', *Journal for Research in Mathematics Education*, 17(2), 83–99. Available at: www.jstor.org/stable/749255?origin=crossref

Herold, B. (2014) 'FBI Investigation Leaves L.A. iPad Initiative in Further Disarray', *EducationWeek*, 3 December. Available at: www.edweek.org/teaching-learning/fbi-investigation-leaves-l-a-ipad-initiative-in-further-disarray/2014/12

Higgins, S., Beauchamp, G. and Miller, D. (2007) 'Reviewing the literature on interactive whiteboards', *Learning, Media and Technology*, 32(3), 213–225. Available at: www.tandfonline.com/doi/full/10.1080/17439880701511040?utm_source=researchgate.net&utm_medium=article

Ho, A.D., Reich, J., Nesterko, S.O., Seaton, D.T., Mullaney, T., Waldo, J. and Chuang, I. (2014) *HarvardX and MITx: The First Year of Open Online Courses* (HarvardX and MITx Working Paper No. 1). Available at: https://papers.ssrn.com/sol3/papers.cfm?abstract_id=2381263

House of Commons (2008) *Building Schools for the Future*, House of Commons Debate (Hansard), 8 July 2008. London: UK Parliament. Available at: https://hansard.parliament.uk/commons/2008-07-08/debates/0807091000002/BuildingSchoolsForTheFuture

Human Rights Watch (2022) *How Dare They Peep into My Private Life? Children's Rights Violations by Governments that Endorsed Online Learning during the Covid-19 Pandemic.* Available at: www.hrw.org/report/2022/05/25/how-dare-they-peep-my-private-life/childrens-rights-violations-governments

ITU (2021) *Measuring Digital Development: Facts and Figures.* Available at: www.itu.int/en/ITU-D/Statistics/Documents/facts/FactsFigures2021.pdf

Jordan, K. (2015) 'Massive open online course completion rates revisited: Assessment, length and attrition', *The International Review of Research in Open and Distributed Learning,* 16(3), 341–358. Available at: www.irrodl.org/index.php/irrodl/article/view/2112

Kelly, Y., Zilanawala, A., Booker, C. and Sacker, A. (2018) 'Social media use and adolescent mental health: Findings from the UK Millennium Cohort Study', *EClinicalMedicine*, 6, 59–68. Available at: www.thelancet.com/journals/eclinm/article/PIIS2589-5370(18)30060-9/fulltext

Kuncel, N., Credé, M. and Thomas, L. (2005) 'The validity of self-reported grade point averages', *Review of Educational Research*, 75(1), 63–82. Available at: https://journals.sagepub.com/doi/10.3102/00346543075001063

Marcarini, M.F., Galvani, G., Imbesi, S. and Pinheiro, C. (2020) 'Pedarchitecture: Which learning environments for the personalisation of teaching and learning?', In Peters, M. and Heraud, R. (eds.) *Knowledge, Education and Cultural Change*. Singapore: Springer. Available at: https://link.springer.com/chapter/10.1007/978-981-15-7497-9_8

Marrs, C. (2016) 'Gove: 'I regret scrapping Building Schools for the Future'', *Architect's Journal.* Available at: www.architectsjournal.co.uk/news/gove-i-regret-scrapping-building-schools-for-the-future

Mitra, S. and Rana, V. (2001) 'Children and the internet: Experiments with minimally invasive education in India', *The British Journal of Educational Technology,* 32(2), 221–232. Available at: https://bera-journals.onlinelibrary.wiley.com/doi/10.1111/1467-8535.00192

Moss, G., Jewitt, C., Levačić, R., Armstrong, V., Cardini, A. and Castle, F. (2007) *The Interactive Whiteboards, Pedagogy and Pupil Performance Evaluation: An Evaluation of the Schools Whiteboard Expansion (SWE) Project: London Challenge.* London: Institute of Education, University of London / Department for Education and Skills. Available at: https://discovery.ucl.ac.uk/id/eprint/10000905/1/Moss2007whiteboardsRR816.pdf

National Audit Office (2009) *The Building Schools for the Future Programme: Renewing the Secondary School Estate.* London: The Stationery Office. Available at: www.nao.org.uk/reports/the-building-schools-for-the-future-programme-renewing-the-secondary-school-estate/

Odgers, C.L. and Jensen, M.R. (2020) 'Annual research review: Adolescent mental health in the digital age: Facts, fears, and future directions', *Journal of Child Psychology and Psychiatry*, 61(3), 336–348. Available at: https://pubmed.ncbi.nlm.nih.gov/31951670/

OECD (2024) *Students, Digital Devices and Learning: Evidence from PISA*. Paris: OECD Publishing. Available at: www.oecd.org/education

Ofcom (2024) *Children and Parents: Media Use and Attitudes Report 2024*. London: Ofcom. Available at: www.ofcom.org.uk

Pappano, L. (2012, November 2) The year of the MOOC. *The New York Times*. Available at: www.nytimes.com/2012/11/04/education/edlife/massive-open-online-courses-are-multiplying-at-a-rapid-pace.html

Puentedura, R.R. (2010) *SAMR and TPCK: Intro to Advanced Practice*. Available at: http://hippasus.com/resources/sweden2010/SAMR_TPCK_IntroToAdvancedPractice.pdf

Reich, J. and Ruipérez Valiente, J.A. (2019) 'The MOOC pivot', *Science,* 363(6423), 130–131.

Reys, R., Reys, B., Emanuelsson, G., Johansson, B., McIntosh, A. and Yang, D.C. (1999) 'Assessing number sense of students in Australia, Sweden, Taiwan, and the United States', *School Science and Mathematics*, 99, 61–70. Available at: https://doi.org/10.1111/j.1949-8594.1999.tb17449.x

Rohs, M. and Ganz, M. (2015) 'MOOCs and the claim of education for all: A disillusion by empirical data', *The International Review of Research in Open and Distributed Learning*, 16(6), 14–15. Available at: https://doi.org/10.19173/irrodl.v16i6.2033

Sailer, K. (2018) 'Corridors, classrooms, classification: The impact of school layout on pedagogy and social behaviour', *UCL Bartlett School of Architecture Working Paper*. Available at: https://discovery.ucl.ac.uk/id/eprint/10048838/1/Sailer2018_PedagogyBehavLayout_final.pdf

Schulmeister, R. and Loviscach, J. (2014) 'Kritische Anmerkungen zur Studie "Lernen sichtbar machen" (visible learning) von John Hattie', *SEMINAR*, 2, 121–130. Available at: https://j3l7h.de/publications/MetaSchulmeisterLoviscach.pdf

Selwyn, N. (2016) *Education and Technology: Key Issues and Debates*. London: Bloomsbury.

Somekh, B., Haldane, M., Jones, K., Lewin, C., Steadman, S., Scrimshaw, P., Sing, S., Bird, K., Cummings, J., Downing, B., Harber S.T., Jarvis, J., Mavers, D., and Woodrow, D. (2007) *Evaluation of the Primary Schools Whiteboard Expansion Project*. Becta. Available at: https://downloads.smarttech.com/media/research/international_research/uk/becta_executive_expansion_summary.pdf

Sowder, J. (1992) Estimation and number sense. In: Grouws, D. (ed.) *Handbook of Research on Mathematics Teaching and Learning*. New York: Macmillan. Available at: www.emerald.com/books/edited-volume/20147/chapter-abstract/105408762/Estimation-and-Number-Sense?redirectedFrom=fulltext

Stacey, K. and Groves, S. (1994) *Calculators in Primary Mathematics*. University of Melbourne / Deakin University research project. Paper presented at the Annual Meeting of the National Council of Teachers of Mathematics (72nd, Indianapolis, IN, April 1994). Emerald Publishing Limited, USA. Available at: https://api.semanticscholar.org/CorpusID:54506646

Tamim, R.M., Bernard, R.M., Borokhovski, E., Abrami, P.C. and Schmid, R.F. (2011) 'What forty years of research says about the impact of technology on learning: A second-order meta-analysis', *Review of Educational Research*, 81(1), 4–28. Available at: https://journals.sagepub.com/doi/10.3102/0034654310393361

TED. (2013) *Sugata Mitra: Build a School in the Cloud*. Available at: www.ted.com/talks/sugata_mitra_build_a_school_in_the_cloud

UNESCO. (2023a) *Scaling up Digital Learning and Skills in the World's Most Populous Countries to Drive Education Recovery*. Available at: www.unesco.org/en/articles/scaling-digital-learning-and-skills-worlds-most-populous-countries-drive-education-recovery

UNESCO (2023b) *Global Education Monitoring Report 2023: Technology in Education – A Tool on Whose Terms?* Paris: UNESCO. Available at: https://unesdoc.unesco.org/ark:/48223/pf0000385723

UNICEF Australia (2026) *Social Media Ban.* Available at: www.unicef.org.au/unicef-youth/staying-safe-online/social-media-ban-explainer?srsltid=AfmBOoqYmYHbFoLLZlObOnq72Wy-i6EG7VDIY1loju3VFvAthvYTQ4wI

Warschauer, M. (2003) *Technology and Social Inclusion: Rethinking the Digital Divide.* Cambridge, MA: MIT Press.

3 The COVID-19 Effect

Opportunities and Unintended Consequences

In early 2020, stories emerged of a mysterious virus circulating in Asia. Like many viruses before it, the world took little notice. It was only when cases began to exponentially increase across the globe, and deaths were recorded well beyond the norm for other coronaviruses, that governments began to act. The virus was named *severe acute respiratory syndrome coronavirus* 2, abbreviated as *SARS-CoV-2*. The disease became known as *COVID-19*. The World Health Organisation (WHO) declared this novel coronavirus outbreak a global pandemic on March 11, 2020 (Cucinotta and Vanelli, 2020). Some countries took a hyper cautious approach from day one, and others were initially more lenient about safety precautions, but soon increased restrictions, bringing in lockdown, social distancing, mandatory face masks, and treatment centres.

COVID-19's impact on schools was profound and unprecedented in its global reach. According to UNESCO, 1.6 billion students were adversely impacted, with 188 countries closing schools in 2020 (UNESCO, 2021). As UNESCO states in their report *The State of the Global Education Crisis: a Pathway to Recovery*, "Globally, from late February 2020 until early August 2021, education systems were on average fully closed for 121 instructional days and partially closed for 103 days, with the world's poorest children disproportionately affected." (UNESCO, 2021). In the UK, when Education Secretary Gavin Williamson announced on 18th March that schools would close, the Department for Education had no pre-existing plan for mass disruption. The National Audit Office later criticised the DfE's approach as "largely reactive." (National Audit Office, 2021). Within days, schools scrambled to deliver remote learning with unequal results: Sutton Trust research found 54 per cent of private schools enabled their students

DOI: 10.1201/9781003662945-3

to have devices for online learning, compared to only 5 per cent of state schools (Sutton Trust, 2021). Numbers of students with internet access were similar: 50 per cent in private schools and 5 per cent in state schools. This immediately exacerbated an already wide digital divide, something that further widened as the pandemic progressed. The truth is that no one was ready, but some were less ready than others.

The government's response came through several initiatives. Oak National Academy launched in late April—remarkably, it was up and running only a few days after the first lines of code were committed (Nolan, 2021). Built rapidly by 40+ teachers from leading schools, it delivered 2 million lessons in its first week and reached 100 million lessons by February 2021 (Whitaker, 2020a). The DfE also announced a laptop scheme for disadvantaged pupils but most equipment arrived in June 2020—just weeks before summer term ended, severely limiting its immediate impact (Dickens, 2020). A case of too little, too late.

The second lockdown in January 2021 saw schools provide significantly improved remote learning. School provision for online learning changed radically between the two lockdowns. The Sutton Trust found that 54 per cent of teachers were using live online lessons by January 2021, up from just 4 per cent in March 2020—though 86 per cent of private schools were providing live lessons compared to just 50 per cent in the state sector (Sutton Trust, 2021). By the time schools fully reopened on 8 March 2021, the DfE was on course to deliver 1.3 million devices, though the NAO noted the department had initially considered providing 602,000 devices for all vulnerable children and priority year groups but scaled back to just 220,000 due to practical supply constraints—while Ofcom estimated between 1.14 million and 1.78 million children lacked home access to a laptop, desktop or tablet (Children's Commissioner, 2020).

THE GLOBAL DIGITAL DIVIDE: HIGH-INCOME VS. LOW-RESOURCE SCHOOL SYSTEMS

The pandemic exposed a profound digital chasm between wealthy and developing nations that had existed for decades but had rarely been so consequential for children's education. While around nine-in-ten people in developed economies reported using the internet in 2019, in low income countries it was less than one-in-five (Liu, 2021). At the domestic level, only 19 per cent of homes in low-income countries had online access, and less than 10 per cent had access to a computer at home (ibid). When schools closed globally, half of all learners did not have access to a household computer, and 43 per cent had no internet available at home—with these figures significantly higher in low-income nations (UNESCO, 2020). This made it almost impossible to maintain any semblance of continuity in these countries, putting the developed world at a profound advantage.

A joint report by UNESCO, UNICEF and the World Bank found that schoolchildren in low-and lower-middle-income countries lost nearly 4 months of schooling over the pandemic, compared to 6 weeks of loss in high-income countries (UNICEF, 2020). The simulations were stark: school closures of just 7 months could lead to a 10 per cent increase in the share of students in Learning Poverty and cost this generation of students $10 trillion in lifetime earnings, with an estimated 24 million students from pre-primary to tertiary deemed at risk of permanently dropping out of school (World Bank, UNESCO and UNICEF, 2021). These were genuine and potentially long-term risks and there was little that could be done about it, other than hope that governments the world over got on top of the virus sooner rather than later.

The disparity was not only about access to devices; it reflected fundamental differences in educational infrastructure, teacher preparedness, and governmental capacity to respond. In many ways, COVID brought more sharply into focus how unequal the world is when it comes to access to technology in school. Countries such as Estonia, Netherlands, and Finland had already excelled in digital education and learning prior to 2019, which made their transition to virtual teaching considerably easier compared with the rest of the world (Babbar and Gupta, 2022). Estonia, for example, successfully made the move to remote teaching in "basically a week" when COVID struck. As Estonian education officials noted, "We started really ahead of everybody else in the mid-90s, trying to equip schools with computers and improve the internet connection... we have also always paid a lot of attention to skills development so that teachers would be able to use technology." (Watson, 2021).

South Korea's response was similarly effective. Before the pandemic, 99.7 per cent of South Korean homes had full access to the internet, and 99.9 per cent of teenagers used high-speed internet in their daily lives (Inter-American Development Bank, 2020). Phased online-learning was implemented systematically, beginning with students in their final year of middle and high school on April 9, and was fully expanded to all remaining year groups by April 20. To avoid widening the digital divide, the South Korean government provided free digital device rental services, giving priority to students from low-income families, and through adopting a zero-rating policy, students received free mobile data access to education websites with support from the three major telecom companies.

These successes stood in stark contrast to countries with less developed digital infrastructure. Research published in *Globalisation, Societies and Education* showed how digital divides manifested between high- and low-income countries, rural and urban areas, and skilled and unskilled populations—inequalities that were particularly acute between developed and developing nations, with large sections of the population in countries like India, Pakistan, Bangladesh, Nepal and Afghanistan having limited access to basic digital infrastructure during lockdown (Mathrani, Sarvesh and Umer, 2021) In low-income households, particularly those in rural or semi-urban regions, digital inequality severely undermined the choices these families could make. In Nigeria, significant differences were seen in students' access to remote learning between government and private schools, with socioeconomic status a key factor in whether children could learn remotely at all (Azubuike et al., 2021). These divides were compounded by gender inequalities: research by Nigeria's Centre for Information Technology and Development found that 61 per cent of fathers in Northern Nigeria discouraged their daughters from using the internet, while 55 per cent of men did not want their wives to go online—barriers that took on new significance when education moved entirely online (Equal Access International). What COVID offered the world was a snapshot of how divided access to technology is—one that may have slightly improved in some parts of the world, but it still notably absent in others. This takes on added significance when we consider the potential that AI has as an always-ready tutor. As we saw in the last chapter, it is often those who least need it that have most access to it and therefore stand to benefit most greatly. Our largest concern continues to be this divide widening still further, with gendered attitudes such as those seen in Nigeria only making the problem more acute.

The financial response to funding recovery was equally unequal. The UK government committed £3.1bn for education recovery between 2020–21 and 2024–25—around £310 per pupil in total. In stark contrast, education catch-up plans for the Netherlands (£2,100 per pupil) and the US (£1,800 per pupil) were far larger and more ambitious (Education Policy Institute, 2021). Between April and October 2020, the Global Partnership for Education approved $467 million in COVID-19 accelerated grants to 66 countries—while significant, this represented a fraction of what would be needed to address the learning losses in the developing world (Global Partnership for Education, 2021). We still speak of the 'COVID effect' on learning loss, and this has as much to do with how countries responded once students went back to school as they did during the pandemic.

THE MICROSOFT / GOOGLE DIVIDE

The pandemic forced many schools to choose rapidly between Microsoft Teams and Google Classroom—a decision that five years later still shapes their AI governance options. Prior to the pandemic not every school had made that choice: however, the requirement for low-cost video conferencing necessitated choosing one over the other, as Zoom (an immensely popular business tool at the start of the first lockdown) was not economically feasible for large scale teaching, as well as not offering the kind of security required in education. The experience of one school in Singapore, whose students were exposed to 'lewd, obscene images' on a Zoom call owing to the call being hacked, demonstrated to the world that more secure options were needed (BBC News, 2020) .

The DfE partnered with Google and Microsoft to offer schools funded support to get set up on G Suite for Education or Office 365 Education, but England's decentralised system meant individual schools and Multi-Academy Trusts were left to make independent platform choices without national coordination. James Leonard, head of education at Google UK, told the Westminster Education Forum that many English schools had been "caught out in the rain"—partly due to the decentralised nature of the system, and partly because the focus on standards had made the use of edtech feel risky (Roberts, 2020). This was exemplified by the National Education Union, who warned teachers that online learning should not be undertaken, citing reasons such as teacher safeguarding, workload, and pupils without equipment missing out on live classes (Lough, 2020).

While the intentions were laudable, these were abnormal times so concessions did need to be made.

Wales had already invested in its national Hwb platform, Scotland had Glow, and Northern Ireland had C2k, meaning growth on those platforms was "exponential" once lockdown hit because there were virtually no technical or legal barriers to overcome. In England, by contrast, an existing network of managed service providers whose business models depended on keeping schools on-premise meant many institutions were starting from scratch (Roberts, 2020). There was, quite simply, no way to garner multiple, competing entities into a coordinated approach to ensure pupils had fast access to the platforms needed to deliver online learning.

The scale of worldwide tech adoption was staggering. As Akshat Sharma, lead product manager for Google Classroom, noted: "As the pandemic set in, our user base quadrupled from 40 million to 150 million in a few weeks" (Okoruwa, 2024). Schools chose platforms based on existing infrastructure: those with Microsoft environments gravitated to Teams for seamless integration with their single sign-on credentials, while primary schools favoured Google Classroom's simpler interface and Chromebook compatibility. Microsoft reported global education users growing from 7 million in September 2019 to 100+ million by January 2021 (Stuart, 2021). Cost played less role than expected—both platforms offered free education tiers—but Multi-Academy Trusts increasingly standardised on single platforms, with IT services providers emphasising unified cloud platforms.

Looking to today, this platform lock-in directly constrains current AI adoption. While prices of both Microsoft and Google AI-powered software licenses have decreased in recent years, costs do soon add up: a typical UK MAT of around 3,000 pupils and 200 teachers will see an annual bill close to £100,000—with the largest MAT seeing an eye-watering £1.8 million needing to be spent on Microsoft licenses for their pupils alone (Public Sector Executive, 2024). These are not insignificant sums, and in the schools we support they feel the strain of providing AI licenses for their teachers and students in order that they don't fall behind.

Critically, both AI assistants integrate deeply with their respective ecosystems: Copilot only works within Teams for meeting summaries, Gemini only within Google Meet. What is also notable is that Google has made their tools available to all age groups as part of Workspace for Education, whereas Copilot is still available only for 13+. Combine that with a more varied AI offer in Google (with NotebookLM and Google's Gems proving particularly popular with teachers), and the lower annual cost, and you can see how Google schools are currently at an advantage over their Microsoft counterparts.

The 5Rights Foundation warns that the largest platforms, such as Google and Microsoft, have subverted interoperability requirements by engaging with different education platforms as an identity provider, gaining a nodal position (5Rights Foundation). Schools theoretically remain free to choose alternative AI tools—Oak National Academy's publicly-funded Aila assistant, or third-party options such as TeachmateAI and Magic School—but data protection requirements, procurement efficiencies, and infrastructure dependencies practically constrain them to their platform vendor's AI offerings. This leads to different opportunities for AI exposure for both teachers and students and further widens the gap between those who can benefit from AI, and those who cannot. It is doubtful whether this will change any time soon.

HOW 'FREE' PLATFORMS INTRODUCED DEEPER DATA EXTRACTION

The rush to adopt EdTech during COVID created data governance problems that persist into 2026. Both Microsoft and Google collect extensive data from education users: identification data, behavioural metrics, learning analytics and device information. The Austrian Data Protection Authority ruled in 2024 that Microsoft 365 Education illegally tracked students using cookies without consent (noyb, 2025). It is the single most concerning area in all of edtech, and the rapid increase in technology use in schools through COVID meant that many of these governance areas were overlooked.

The scale of data extraction in the EdTech sector is alarming. Research by Internet Safety Labs found that 96 per cent of apps used or recommended by K-12 schools share students' personal information with third parties (Arundel, 2023). Researchers examined 1,357 apps recommended or required by schools across 663 schools in every US state, representing nearly half a million students. Of the 96 per cent of apps that shared data with third parties, 78 per cent of the time it was with advertising and data analytics entities, and often without user consent. Additionally, 79 per cent of the apps reviewed could access student location information, and 52 per cent could access calendar and contact information. Google was the most common third-party that received data from the apps used in schools, with nearly 70 per cent of all apps observed sending data to Google (Riley, 2022).

Human Rights Watch's investigation painted an even more disturbing picture. Their report, "How Dare They Peep into My Private Life?" examined 164 education technology products endorsed by 49 countries and found that of the 163 products reviewed, 145 (89 per cent) surveilled or had the capacity to surveil children, outside school hours, and deep into their private lives (Human Rights Watch, 2022). Many products harvested information about children such as who they are, where they are, what they do in the classroom, who their family and friends are, and what kind of device their families could afford for them to use for online learning. The data surveillance took place in virtual classrooms and educational settings where children could not reasonably object to such surveillance. Most EdTech companies did not allow students to decline to be tracked; most of this monitoring happened secretly, without the child's knowledge or consent.

The regulatory response has been fragmented and inadequate. The ICO's compulsory audit of the Department for Education (published October 2020) delivered damning findings: 139 recommendations for improvement, with over 60 per cent classified as urgent or high priority. Auditors found "data protection was not being prioritised," no Record of Processing Activity (a direct GDPR breach), and "cultural barriers and attitudes" limiting compliance (Whitaker, 2020b). The National Pupil Database contains over 21 million individuals' named records collected since 1996, never deleted. Between March 2012 and June 2021, nearly 2,500 data releases occurred—with over a third of approved requests for identifying data going to commercial companies (defenddigitalme, 2021).

Perhaps most alarming was the ICO's November 2022 reprimand regarding the Learner Records Service breach, involving "prolonged misuse of the personal information of up to 28 million children." (Whitaker, 2022). Gambling companies accessed student data. Information Commissioner John Edwards noted this "would have warranted £10 million fine"—but no fine was imposed because the company involved had dissolved.

Turning to today, the lack of transparency around AI algorithms compounds these concerns. EdTech's rapid adoption has become a growing concern for educators, students, and parents, often because the functionality of these tools and the data collected by them lacks transparency, and general-use technologies often lack the safeguards of those developed specifically for education use. More than half of education technology companies did not fully disclose how learner data was being collected and shared. Many Generative AI tools rely on large amounts of data to continuously train the underlying model that generates responses, raising questions about whether vendors use student personally identifiable information to train models, and whether any products created with those models are educational or commercial. The majority of better known EdTech platforms make a point of highlighting that they do not use school data for model training, but many use third party AI providers who may not be as transparent. When it comes to AI, data governance is an increasing minefield.

STUDENT OUTCOMES DURING EMERGENCY REMOTE LEARNING

The research evidence on student outcomes during emergency remote learning through COVID is now substantial and sobering. A comprehensive meta-analysis published in *Learning and Instruction* found that the pandemic had an overall negative effect on learning outcomes, with students losing more ground in mathematics and science than in other subjects (Di Pietro, 2023). Critically, the research showed that one year or more after COVID-19, students had not recovered from the initial learning loss. Systematic reviews and meta-analyses suggest an average learning loss attributable to COVID-19 school closures of 0.17 of a standard deviation, "equivalent to roughly a one-half year's worth of learning" (Patrinos et al., 2022).

The 2022 PISA results provided the most comprehensive international comparison. The assessment saw an unprecedented drop in performance across the OECD: compared to 2018, mean performance fell by 10 score points in reading and by almost 15 score points in maths—equivalent to three-quarters of a year's worth of learning (OECD, 2023). The decline in maths performance was three times greater than any previous consecutive change. For countries with more prolonged school closures, the declines were more significant among the lowest-achieving students: "students in countries with the shortest closures (10th percentile of all participating countries) lost around 8–10 points… . Students in countries with average closures lost around 12 points …, while students in countries with the longest closures (90th percentile) lost 15 points or more" (Jakubowski et al., 2025).

In England specifically, research consistently shows 2-3 months of learning loss from the first lockdown, with approximately 1 additional month from the second lockdown (less severe due to improved remote learning). The disadvantage gap—already significant pre-pandemic—widened substantially. Education Endowment Foundation research found the gap between disadvantaged and non-disadvantaged pupils equivalent to 7 months' progress by autumn 2020 (Education Endowment Foundation, 2021).

Subject and age patterns emerged clearly. Primary maths showed faster recovery than reading: Year 2 maths had recovered to above expected standards by summer 2021, while Year 1 reading deficits of 3 months persisted (EEF, 2021). The youngest pupils—those whose early years education was disrupted—face the longest-lasting effects. The 2023 KS1 cohort (disrupted Nursery/Reception) showed only 71 per cent achieving literacy score 5+ versus 77 per cent in 2019—a 6 per cent point drop (Thomson, 2024).

The data on student outcomes tells a story that should inform every decision we make about AI integration in education. The sheer scale of learning loss is staggering enough, but the patterns within the data are what demand our closest attention. The finding that the lowest-achieving students in countries with the most prolonged closures suffered losses nearly double those in countries with shorter closures tells us something fundamental: the duration and depth of disruption matters enormously, and it matters most for those who are already struggling. In England, the widening of the disadvantage gap from five months to seven months by autumn 2020 represented tens of thousands of children falling further behind their peers at a pace that, as the 2024 data confirms, we have still not fully reversed. This should give us serious pause as we contemplate the next major technological shift in our schools. If AI is deployed inequitably—if access, support, and quality vary along the same socioeconomic fault lines that determined who thrived and who floundered during the pandemic—we risk engineering a new version of precisely this pattern. The COVID data tells us that innovation without equity at its centre will widen the gaps we claim to be trying to close, and that once those gaps widen, they prove extraordinarily resistant to narrowing again.

TEACHER PERSPECTIVES: SUCCESSES IN RESOURCEFUL TECH USAGE VS. FRUSTRATIONS AT LACK OF TRAINING

Teachers demonstrated remarkable adaptability during the pandemic, but the experience also exposed fundamental gaps in professional development and support structures. A national survey of 3,404 UK teachers (published in Education Sciences by researchers using data collected during lockdown) found that 64 per cent reported having very little or no previous experience in online teaching, and only 26 per cent felt confident using Ed Tech to deliver lessons online. The same study found that 46 per cent of teachers felt happy and cheerful often during lockdown, with only 17 per cent saying they did not. 'Crucially, teachers felt that what they were doing was important and worthwhile,' the paper mentions, even if they were frequently exhausted, with just over a quarter saying they felt energetic often (See, 2024). The DfE's own review of pandemic research noted that there was no prior requirement for schools and colleges across England to engage in remote teaching before the pandemic, and investment in remote education solutions was lacking at the time of initial school closures. (Howard, Khan and Lockyer, 2021).

The problem was that the outbreak of COVID-19 was so sudden that there was little or no time for many schools to design and implement learning programmes specifically designed to support children's learning at home. Qualitative research revealed several themes related to challenges, including time constraints, locating and selecting appropriate digital resources, keeping students engaged, collaborating with families, plagiarism, a lack of support, navigating technological challenges, effective assessment, and lack of leadership direction (DeCoito and Estaiteyeh, 2022).

There was rightly much focus on what was best for pupils at home, but teachers were often overlooked, expected to 'step up' into an entirely new mode of teaching delivery without ever having been shown how. This, coupled with their own challenges (devices, internet access, and their own families to deal with) meant that the strain on teachers through the pandemic was vast.

Working online meant teachers had to adapt to new ways of teaching for which they had not been trained (Winter et al., 2021). Some teachers saw digital literacy training as laborious and time-consuming and detracted from their core business of delivering quality learning. There were also competing demands among teaching, administration, and research that led to work overload, with criticisms emerging regarding the quality of learning and the validity of assessments.

That said, there were some genuine successes. By the second lockdown, 54 per cent of teachers used online live lessons compared with just 4 per cent in March 2020 (Weale, 2021). NEU surveys of 10,000+ members found 69 per cent favoured new technology working methods; 57 per cent wanted schools to retain online parents' evenings (Whitaker, 2021).

Contrary to some research, many teachers agreed that the transition to online instruction provided opportunities to be innovative and to learn to teach with new technologies. The general perception of online teaching due to the COVID-19 pandemic was mostly positive among teaching staff who also reported being provided with relevant equipment and technology as well as training for online teaching. Goudarzi et al discovered that the perceived benefits of online for teachers included "the feasibility of teaching regardless of time and place, cost-effectiveness, non-necessity of physical attendance, the existence of a variety of choices, saving time, studying simultaneously with working, and the development of participatory and independent types of learning" (Goudarzi et al., 2023). The need to innovate meant that teachers did rise to the challenge, and many were surprised at their newfound technical skills.

Pre-pandemic teaching development also proved vital for facing the challenges resulting from the pandemic. Teachers with enhanced professional development felt better prepared to face pedagogical and technological challenges. The PISA 2022 results confirmed this: teacher support proved particularly important in times of disruption (OECD, 2023). The availability of teachers to help students in need had the strongest relationship to maths performance across the OECD, compared to other experiences linked to COVID-19 school closure. Maths scores were 15 points higher on average in places where students agreed they had good access to teacher help (ibid.).

But there were many challenges to this preparation. Pre-pandemic, 79 per cent of primary teachers in England said they had received some ICT training, yet only 41 per cent felt prepared when they finished their studies (OECD, 2019). There was no prior requirement for schools and colleges across England to engage in remote teaching and learning before the pandemic, and investment in remote education solutions was lacking at the time of the initial school closures in March 2020 (DfE, 2022). The consequences were immediate and personal. A May 2020 NASUWT survey found that 36 per cent of members reported they did not have adequate IT equipment to provide online learning (Bond and Bolan, 2021). Workload increased substantially: research into UK teachers' experiences during the first lockdown found that on average, teachers spent 15 hours a week on marking alone, with 41 per cent spending over 20 hours per week on planning, management, and admin (See, 2024). The cumulative toll on the profession was profound. The NASUWT Wellbeing at Work Survey 2024, drawing on responses from nearly 12,000 teachers and using the Warwick-Edinburgh Mental Wellbeing Scale, recorded an overall score of 38.4—a figure significantly below the typical mean of around 50–52 reported for the general population (NASUWT, 2024).

The pandemic experience offers a direct and uncomfortable lesson for those now tasked with implementing AI in schools. It is a familiar pattern: technology arrives promising transformation, schools cannot prepare quickly enough, professional development lags behind deployment, and the burden of adaptation falls unfairly on already overworked teachers. A 2025 DfE survey found that 43 per cent of teachers rated their AI confidence at just 3 out of 10, with over 60 per cent requesting help applying AI to planning and support tasks—and nearly all wanting safety guidance and additional training (DfE, 2025). These figures are strikingly similar to what TALIS 2018 revealed about ICT readiness on the eve of the pandemic. History, it seems, is already repeating itself. What the pandemic made abundantly clear is that technology does not implement itself, and that the quality of any Ed Tech impact cannot be split from the professional conditions in which teachers work. Deploying AI into schools whose teachers are exhausted, under-trained, and already carrying a wellbeing score two standard deviations below the population norm is not a governance strategy—it is a repetition of the same mistake. Combine that with government ministers who have never been teachers shouting from the rooftops that AI will transform workloads and you have a recipe for disaster. Effective AI implementation requires what emergency remote teaching never had: sustained, structured professional development; equity of access to infrastructure; and governance frameworks designed around teacher capacity rather than market enthusiasm. We need to learn our lesson.

APPLYING LESSONS LEARNED

So what are these lessons, and how can we apply them in our governance of AI in education? We experienced a lot. We saw learning loss, that much is obvious. Yet it is challenging to attribute this solely to the move from face-to-face to online: some students preferred online learning. This was particularly the case with those who found conventional classroom arrangements challenging for concentration. There were so many other factors—families whose breadwinners were suddenly without income causing massive strain on family life, lockdowns forcing families to spend considerable amounts of time with one another without the ability to 'escape', and the abovementioned technical challenges to name but three. Online learning per se cannot and should not be seen as the only reason why pupils of all ages experienced such profound and longlasting learning loss. It is more a case of being away from a learning environment, with families trying their best to share devices and limited internet connectivity while dealing with myriad other challenges, that led to so many pupils falling so far behind.

As we continue to adopt AI technologies into our schools, we need to be aware of the multiple reasons why pupils either gain or lose progress in relation to their peers. If we simply say 'face-to-face is good, online-with-AI is bad' then we are missing a broader point. AI can be a tremendous force multiplier, but only if it is coupled with an understanding that what it multiplies must include the school *and* home environment, access to technology, and the broader wellbeing of the pupil *and* their family. COVID taught us that the medium of instruction mattered far less than the ecosystem surrounding it. A child with a quiet room, a dedicated device, supportive parents, and a stable internet connection could thrive in online learning—as many pupils demonstrated. A child sharing a phone with three siblings in a household reeling from sudden unemployment could not. The variable was never simply 'online versus offline'; it was the totality of circumstances in which learning was attempted.

This is a lesson we must carry forward with considerable care as AI enters our classrooms. The temptation will be to evaluate AI tools in isolation—does this adaptive learning platform improve maths scores? Does this AI tutor help pupils write better essays? These are important questions, but they are insufficient ones. We must also ask: who has access to these tools at home, and who does not? Are we creating a new digital divide where pupils whose families can afford AI-enhanced learning platforms pull further ahead of those who cannot? Are we accounting for the fact that a tool which works brilliantly for a pupil with strong self-regulation may be counterproductive for one who needs the structure and accountability of human interaction? During COVID, many schools made quick decisions about which platforms to adopt based on what was available rather than what was optimal. The consequences of these decisions are with these schools to the present day.

The parallels with the current rush to integrate AI are striking and should give us pause. Schools that adopted Microsoft Teams during the pandemic, for instance, now find themselves steered towards Microsoft's AI ecosystem; those that chose Google Classroom face a similar gravitational pull towards Google's offerings. These are not neutral choices. They are governance decisions with long tails, and they deserve to be treated as such. What COVID revealed, perhaps more starkly than any previous disruption to education, is that learning is not a transaction that can be reduced to the delivery of content through a particular channel. It is a deeply human process, shaped by relationships, environment, emotional state, and a hundred other variables that no technology—however sophisticated—can fully account for.

The pupils who reported learning better at home were not making a case for online learning in the abstract. They were telling us something important about the conditions under which they personally thrived: fewer social distractions, greater autonomy over their pace of work, the comfort of familiar surroundings. Had their home circumstances been different—had they been dealing with food insecurity, domestic tension, or the anxiety of a parent's illness—their experience would almost certainly have been different.

AI governance in education must therefore resist the false binary of technology-good or technology-bad and instead embrace the messier but more honest reality that outcomes depend on context. A school with robust pastoral support, a clear understanding of its community's socioeconomic profile, and a governance framework that asks hard questions about equity and access will be far better placed to integrate AI beneficially than one that simply purchases the latest platform and hopes for the best. The learning loss of the pandemic was not a failure of technology. It was a failure of preparedness, of equity, and in many cases of governance. We would do well to ensure we do not repeat those failures simply because the technology on offer is seemingly more impressive this time around.

REFERENCES

Arundel, K. (2023) 'School apps share student personal information', *K-12 Dive*, 14 February. Available at: www.k12dive.com/news/school-apps-share-student-personal-information/639913/

Azubuike, O.B., Adegboye, O. and Quadri, H. (2021) 'Who gets to learn in a pandemic? Exploring the digital divide in remote learning during the COVID-19 pandemic in Nigeria', *International Journal of Educational Research Open*, 2, 100022. Available at: https://doi.org/10.1016/j.ijedro.2020.100022

Babbar, M. and Gupta, T. (2022) 'Response of educational institutions to COVID-19 pandemic: An inter-country comparison', *Policy Futures in Education*, 20(4), 469–491. Available at: https://doi.org/10.1177/14782103211021937

BBC News (2020) 'Singapore home-based learning: Zoom utilised by hackers to show obscene images to students', *BBC News*, 10 April. Available at: www.bbc.co.uk/news/world-asia-52240251

Bond, M. and Bolan, F. (2021) *What Have We Learned about Online Learning? UK and Global Evidence on the Emergency Remote Education of Schoolchildren during COVID-19*. The International Public Policy Observatory. Available at: https://theippo.co.uk/what-have-we-learned-about-online-learning-summary-evidence-emergency-remote-education-schoolchildren-during-covid-19/

Children's Commissioner (2020) 'Children without internet access during lockdown'. *Children's Commissioner*. Available at: www.childrenscommissioner.gov.uk/blog/children-without-internet-access-during-lockdown

Cucinotta, D. and Vanelli, M. (2020) 'WHO declares COVID-19 a pandemic', *Acta Bio-Medica: Atenei Parmensis*, 91(1), 157–160. Available at: https://doi.org/10.23750/abm.v91i1.9397

DeCoito, I. and Estaiteyeh, M. (2022) 'Transitioning to online teaching during the COVID-19 pandemic: An exploration of STEM teachers' views, successes, and challenges', *Journal of Science Education and Technology*, 31, 340–356. Available at: https://doi.org/10.1007/s10956-022-09958-z

defenddigitalme (2021) 'The ICO audit of the Department for Education — One year on', *defenddigitalme*, 7 October. Available at: https://defenddigitalme.org/2021/10/07/the-ico-audit-of-the-department-for-education-one-year-on/

Department for Education (2022) *Learning during the Pandemic: Review of Research from England*. London: DfE. Available at: www.gov.uk/government/publications/learning-during-the-pandemic/learning-during-the-pandemic-review-of-research-from-england

Department for Education (2025) *AI Revolution to Give Teachers More Time with Pupils*. GOV.UK, 6 January. Available at: www.gov.uk/government/news/ai-revolution-to-give-teachers-more-time-with-pupils

Di Pietro, G. (2023) 'The impact of Covid-19 on student achievement: Evidence from a recent meta-analysis', *Educational Research Review*, 39, 100530. Available at: https://doi.org/10.1016/j.edurev.2023.100530

Dickens, J. (2020) 'DfE fails to meet target of delivering 230k laptops by end of June', *Schools Week*, 3 July. Available at: https://schoolsweek.co.uk/dfe-fails-to-meet-target-of-delivering-230k-laptops-by-end-of-june/

Education Endowment Foundation (2021) 'New study finds "significantly lower achievement", with a "large and concerning gap" for disadvantaged pupils', *EEF News*. Available at: https://educationendowmentfoundation.org.uk/news/eef-publishes-new-research-on-the-impact-of-covid-19-partial-school-closures

Education Policy Institute (2021) *Education Recovery and Resilience in England: Phase Two Report*. London: EPI. Available at: https://epi.org.uk/publications-and-research/education-recovery-and-resilience-in-england-phase-two-report-october-2021/

Equal Access International (n.d.) *Closing the Gender Digital Divide: Tech4Families*. Equal Access International. Available at: www.equalaccess.org/our-work/projects/closing-the-gender-digital-divide-tech4families/

5Rights Foundation (n.d.) 'Competing interests in education data: Schools must resist big EdTech', *Education Data Futures*. Available at: https://educationdatafutures.5rightsfoundation.com/essays/competing-interests-in-education-data/schools-must-resist-big-edtech/

Global Partnership for Education (2021) 'COVID-19 (Coronavirus): What you need to know'. *Global Partnership for Education*. Available at: www.globalpartnership.org/covid19

Goudarzi, E., Hasanvand, S., Raoufi, S. and Amini, M. (2023) 'The sudden transition to online learning: Teachers' experiences of teaching during the COVID-19 pandemic', *BMC Medical Education,* 23, 895. Available at: https://doi.org/10.1371/journal.pone.0287520

Howard, E., Khan, A. and Lockyer, C. (2021) *Learning during the Pandemic: Review of Research from England. Coventry: Ofqual*. Available at: www.gov.uk/government/publications/learning-during-the-pandemic/learning-during-the-pandemic-review-of-research-from-england

Human Rights Watch (2022) *'How Dare They Peep into My Private Life?': Children's Rights Violations by Governments that Endorsed Online Learning During the Covid-19 Pandemic'*. 25 May. Human Rights Watch. Available at: www.hrw.org/report/2022/05/25/how-dare-they-peep-my-private-life/childrens-rights-violations-governments

Inter-American Development Bank (2020) 'Responding to COVID-19 in South Korea: Discovering online education as a key for future education', *IDB Blog*. Available at: www.iadb.org/en/blog/education/responding-covid-19-south-korea-discovering-online-education-key-future-education

Jakubowski, M., Gajderowicz, T. and Patrinos, H. (2025) 'COVID-19, school closures, and student learning outcomes: New global evidence from PISA', *npj Sci. Learn.*, 10(5). Available at: https://doi.org/10.1177/2158244021106081

Liu, J. (2021) 'Bridging digital divide amidst educational change for socially inclusive learning during the COVID-19 pandemic', *SAGE Open*, 11(4), 2. Available at: https://doi.org/10.1177/21582440211060810

Lough, C. (2020) 'Coronavirus: Teachers should not live stream lessons', *TES*. Available at: www.tes.com/magazine/archive/coronavirus-teachers-should-not-live-stream-lessons

Mathrani, A., Sarvesh, T. and Umer, R. (2021) 'Digital divide framework: Online learning in developing countries during the COVID-19 lockdown', *Globalisation, Societies and Education*, 20(5), 625–640. Available at: https://doi.org/10.1080/14767724.2021.1981253

NASUWT (2024) *Teacher Wellbeing Survey*. Available at: www.nasuwt.org.uk/advice/health-safety/teacher-wellbeing-survey.html

National Audit Office (2021) *Support for Children's Education during the Early Stages of the Covid-19 Pandemic*. London: NAO. Available at: www.nao.org.uk/reports/support-for-childrens-education-during-the-covid-19-pandemic/

Nolan, L. (2021) 'How Oak National Academy went from vision to virtual education in 6 days [part 1]', *Mux Blog*, 8 April. Available at: www.mux.com/blog/how-oak-national-academy-went-from-vision-to-virtual-education-in-6-days-part-1

noyb (2025) 'noyb win: Microsoft 365 Education tracks school children', *noyb.eu*. Available at: https://noyb.eu/en/noyb-win-microsoft-365-education-tracks-school-children

OECD (2019) *TALIS 2018 Results (Volume I): Teachers and School Leaders as Lifelong Learners — England (UK) Country Note*. Paris: OECD Publishing. Available at: www.oecd.org/content/dam/oecd/en/about/programmes/edu/talis/talis2018participantnotes/isc1to3/TALIS2018TR_ISCED1_CN_ENG.pdf

OECD (2023) *PISA 2022 Results (Volume I): The State of Learning and Equity in Education*. Paris: OECD Publishing. Available at: https://doi.org/10.1787/53f23881-en

Okoruwa, D. (2024) 'Google Classroom's pandemic boom: How it scaled to 150M users', *LinkedIn Pulse*. Available at: www.linkedin.com/pulse/google-classrooms-pandemic-boom-how-scaled-150m-users-okoruwa-qsnsc/

Patrinos, H.A., Vegas, E. and Carter-Rau, R. (2022) 'An analysis of COVID-19 student learning loss.' *Policy Research Working Paper 10033*. Washington, D.C.: World Bank. Available at: https://openknowledge.worldbank.org/server/api/core/bitstreams/2f5687e1-25a0-5d2d-9e41-29aa5d172ae0/content

Public Sector Executive (2024) *Schools Report 2024*. Available at: www.publicsector.co.uk/SchoolsReport2024.pdf

Riley, T. (2022) 'Apps expose student data privacy', *CyberScoop*. Available at: https://cyberscoop.com/apps-expose-student-data-privacy/

Roberts, N. (2020) 'Google: England behind on EdTech at start of crisis', *TES*, 1 May. Available at: www.tes.com/magazine/archive/google-england-behind-edtech-start-crisis

See, B.H. (2024) 'Insights into UK teachers' wellbeing and workload during the COVID-19 pandemic lockdown: Testimonies from the silent voices and lessons learnt', *Education Sciences*, 14(4), 344. Available at: https://doi.org/10.3390/educsci14040344

Stuart, K. (2021) 'Microsoft education users grow from 7 million to over 100 million', *Business Insider*, January. Available at: www.businessinsider.com/microsoft-education-google-chromebooks-teams-2021-1

Sutton Trust (2021) *Remote Learning: The Digital Divide*. London: The Sutton Trust. Available at: www.suttontrust.com/our-research/remote-learning-the-digital-divide/

Thomson, D. (2024) *How Attainment Gaps in Literacy Change Over Time*. FFT Education Datalab, September. Available at: https://ffteducationdatalab.org.uk/2024/09/how-attainment-gaps-in-literacy-change-over-time/

UNESCO (2020) *Startling Digital Divides in Distance Learning Emerge*. *UNESCO*, 21 April. Available at: www.unesco.org/en/articles/startling-digital-divides-distance-learning-emerge

UNESCO (2021) *One Year into COVID-19 Education Disruption: Where Do We Stand?*. UNESCO, March. Available at: www.unesco.org/en/articles/one-year-covid-19-education-disruption-where-do-we-stand

UNICEF (2020) *National Education Responses to COVID-19*. UNICEF Data. Available at: https://data.unicef.org/resources/national-education-responses-to-covid19/

Watson, P. (2021) 'How the tech-savvy Estonians delivered education during Covid', *FutureScot*. Available at: https://futurescot.com/how-did-estonian-schools-become-the-most-digitally-advanced-in-europe/

Weale, S. (2021) 'Home schooling is widening attainment gap between rich and poor, finds report', *The Guardian*, 21 January. Available at: www.theguardian.com/education/2021/jan/21/home-schooling-is-widening-attainment-gap-between-rich-and-poor-finds-report

Whitaker, F. (2020a) 'Coronavirus: Oak National Academy delivers 2m lessons in first week', *Schools Week*, 27 April. Available at: https://schoolsweek.co.uk/coronavirus-oak-national-academy-delivers-2m-lessons-in-first-week/

Whitaker, F. (2020b) 'DfE broke pupil data protection laws, damning ICO audit reveals', *Schools Week*. Available at: https://schoolsweek.co.uk/dfe-broke-pupil-data-protection-laws-damning-ico-audit-reveals/

Whitaker, F. (2021) 'Retain teaching technologies and online parents' evenings after Covid, say NEU members', *Schools Week*. Available at: https://schoolsweek.co.uk/retain-teaching-technologies-and-online-parents-evenings-after-covid-say-neu-members/

Whitaker, F. (2022) 'DfE reprimanded after pupil data used by gambling firms', *Schools Week*. Available at: https://schoolsweek.co.uk/dfe-reprimanded-after-pupil-data-used-by-gambling-firms/

Winter, E., Costello, A., O'Brien, B. and Hickey, G. (2021) 'Teachers' use of technology and the impact of Covid-19', *Irish Educational Studies*, 40(2), 235–246. Available at: https://doi.org/10.1080/03323315.2021.1916559

World Bank, UNESCO and UNICEF (2021) *The State of the Global Education Crisis: A Path to Recovery*. Washington, D.C., Paris, New York: The World Bank, UNESCO, and UNICEF. Available at: www.unicef.org/media/111621/file

Hype versus Reality 4

AI EdTech Enters the Scene

INTRODUCTION

Artificial intelligence is now widely framed as the next transformative force in education. Policy documents, commercial platforms, and public discourse repeatedly promise personalised learning, improved attainment, and more efficient systems. Nevertheless, the empirical foundation for these claims remains far more limited than the rhetoric suggests.

Across multiple generations of educational technology, a consistent pattern emerges: innovation is adopted at speed, while evidence accumulates slowly, unevenly, and often retrospectively. Artificial intelligence does not break this pattern. It intensifies it. The result is a widening gap between what is promised and what can be substantiated.

This chapter examines that gap. Drawing on research on intelligent tutoring systems, adaptive learning platforms, and generative AI, it argues that while some technologies can support learning under specific conditions, the evidence remains mixed, context dependent, and frequently weaker than marketing claims imply. Case studies of widely adopted platforms, alongside documented failures such as the 2020 A-level grading algorithm and bias in proctoring and detection systems, illustrate how this gap can translate into real educational harm.

At the same time, these developments are unfolding within systems already shaped by inequality. Access to devices, connectivity, training, and institutional capacity remains uneven within schools, between schools, and across national contexts. Artificial intelligence is not entering a neutral environment. It is entering one in which

 DOI: 10.1201/9781003662945-4

advantages compound. In this context, the risks and benefits of AI are unlikely to be evenly distributed.

Before turning to the evidence itself, however, a more fundamental question must be addressed. What lines should not be crossed?

The technology sector has long operated according to a logic of rapid deployment followed by retrospective correction. The well-known ethos of "move fast and break things" captures a broader culture in which products are released, scaled, and monetised before their wider consequences are fully understood. In most sectors, this approach carries risk. In education, what is at stake is not only system performance or market share, but children's learning, their data, and, in some cases, their dignity and wellbeing.

Recent developments illustrate the pattern. AI-powered tools have been adopted at scale in classrooms with limited independent evaluation. Platforms have made ambitious claims about impact that are not supported by rigorous evidence. Earlier generations of educational technology followed similar trajectories, often with disappointing results once initial enthusiasm subsided.

This raises a question the sector has been slow to confront: where are the boundaries? What constitutes a non-negotiable in the design and deployment of AI systems for children?

One of the clearest attempts to articulate such limits comes from the *Safe AI for Children Alliance*, which identifies a small number of baseline prohibitions, including the creation of sexualised images of minors, the design of systems that foster emotional dependency, and the encouragement of self-harm (Safe AI for Children Alliance, 2025). The significance of these principles lies not only in their content, but in the fact that they need to be stated at all.

Beyond non-negotiables lie guardrails, the broader structures that guide how technology is developed and deployed. Gasser and Mayer-Schönberger, in their 2024 book *Guardrails: Guiding Human Decisions in the Age of AI*, argue that the critical innovation needed is not technological but social: societies must design the structures—laws, norms, incentives, and accountability mechanisms—that shape how AI-enabled decisions are made, rather than simply delegating those decisions to the technology itself (Gasser and Mayer-Schönberger, 2024). Their argument is that guardrails should empower individual choice while accounting for the social good, and should be flexible enough to adapt as circumstances change; principles with direct relevance to how schools procure and govern AI tools. In education, the guardrail question is particularly acute, because the people most affected by the decisions—children—are the least equipped to challenge them.

Some technology companies have sought to address these concerns by articulating their own internal guardrails. Anthropic, for example, published its "Claude Constitution" in 2025, setting out the values and behavioural constraints designed to guide its model, with an explicit prioritisation of safety, ethical behaviour, and helpfulness (Anthropic, 2025). Similarly, OpenAI's Charter, first published in 2018, commits the organisation to ensuring that artificial general intelligence benefits humanity and avoids uses that could cause harm or concentrate power (OpenAI, 2018).

These developments are notable. They represent an attempt by technology companies to make explicit the principles that govern their systems, and to do so in public. In that sense, they mark a shift towards greater transparency.

However, they also raise a fundamental problem. When the organisation that creates a system is also responsible for defining the limits of its use, governance remains internal. A constitution written by the developer, for the developer's product, is not equivalent to independent oversight. The history of technology regulation offers little reassurance that self-imposed constraints are sufficient, particularly where commercial incentives and rapid deployment are involved.

The distinction is not trivial. It reflects a deeper tension between corporate self-regulation and public accountability. In education, this tension is especially acute. Decisions about the use of AI systems affect children, yet the frameworks governing those systems are often defined without meaningful external scrutiny.

The tension that follows runs throughout this chapter. Artificial intelligence in education sits between rapid technological expansion and limited evidential grounding, between commercial incentives and public responsibility, and between innovation and protection. The sections that follow examine what the research actually shows, where the claims exceed the evidence, and what happens when systems are deployed before these questions are adequately resolved.

THE GAP BETWEEN HYPE AND EVIDENCE

As noted in earlier discussions of educational technology, the distance between promise and classroom reality has often been substantial. Artificial intelligence risks widening this gap rather than closing it.

Historically, the technologies that have had the most enduring impact on education have not been those designed explicitly for schools, but those developed for broader commercial use and later adapted to educational contexts. Calculators and personal computers are often cited examples. By contrast, technologies designed specifically for education have rarely demonstrated consistent, large-scale improvements in attainment.

This pattern is reflected in the research base. Hattie's synthesis of over 800 meta-analyses identifies an average effect size of 0.40, representing approximately one year's progress for a year's input (Hattie, 2009). While this benchmark is not without criticism, it remains a useful reference point. Many educational technologies, including those incorporating artificial intelligence, fall below this threshold or show highly variable results depending on context and implementation.

The challenge of evidencing impact has become more acute with the proliferation of products that incorporate "AI" as a feature rather than as a clearly defined intervention. At the 2026 BETT Show in London, a substantial proportion of technologies on display claimed some form of generative AI enhancement. Only a few years earlier, similar claims were made about mobile learning. The language has shifted, but the pattern remains.

Independent evaluations of AI-enabled tools tend to show modest effects at best, while documented cases of algorithmic failure and bias illustrate the risks of premature adoption. The 2020 A-level grading controversy in England demonstrated how algorithmic systems can encode and amplify existing inequalities when deployed in high-stakes contexts. More recent examples, including conversational systems producing historically inaccurate or harmful outputs, further underline the limitations of current models.

At the same time, institutional responses have not always kept pace with these developments. Guidance on the use of AI tools in assessment, for example, has in some cases continued to endorse detection systems whose reliability remains contested. The result is a landscape in which adoption is widespread, but the evidential and governance foundations remain uncertain.

The implications are not evenly distributed. Emerging data suggests that schools with greater resources are more likely to develop coherent strategies for AI adoption, invest in staff training, and integrate tools effectively (Latham and Montecute, 2025). By contrast, less well-resourced schools are more likely to encounter these technologies in fragmented and uncoordinated ways (techUK, 2025). In such contexts, students may experience the risks of AI before its potential benefits are realised.

The central issue, therefore, is not whether AI can contribute to education. It is whether the conditions required for that contribution are in place. Without careful implementation, robust evaluation, and appropriate oversight, there is a significant risk that the gap between promise and reality will continue to widen.

WHAT THE RESEARCH ACTUALLY SHOWS ABOUT AI IN EDUCATION

Before examining specific platforms and their claims, it is important to establish what the research base tells us about artificial intelligence in education. While the body of literature is growing, its findings are more cautious and more qualified than much of the surrounding discourse suggests.

One of the most frequently cited areas of evidence concerns intelligent tutoring systems. A meta-analysis by Ma et al. (2014), examining 107 effect sizes across 14,321 participants, found that the use of such systems was associated with improved learning outcomes when compared with teacher-led large group instruction, non-adaptive computer-based learning, and textbook-based approaches. These findings are often presented as evidence of the effectiveness of AI in education.

However, a critical qualification follows. The same study found no significant difference between learning from intelligent tutoring systems and learning from individualised human tutoring or small-group instruction. In other words, these systems can replicate aspects of effective teaching, but they do not exceed it.

More recent research broadly supports this pattern while introducing additional nuance. Reviews of adaptive learning systems suggest that while positive effects are often observed, these are highly dependent on implementation and context. In many cases, improvements appear to be driven by structured practice, feedback, and time-on-task rather than by the AI component itself.

This raises an important methodological point. Much of the research in this field relies on quasi-experimental designs, varies significantly in duration, and uses outcome measures that are not easily comparable across studies. As a result, while the overall direction of findings may be positive, the strength and generalisability of the evidence remain limited.

The picture becomes more uncertain when we turn to generative AI. Given the relative novelty of these tools, the evidence base is still emerging. Early studies and systematic reviews suggest a mixed picture. Some report increased student engagement and positive perceptions of usefulness, with students describing interactions with generative AI as helpful, confident, and enjoyable (Wu et al., 2025) and that interactions "enhance[s] their educational experience, either by optimizing the time spent studying or by providing quick access to personalized educational resources that facilitate their understanding of complex materials" (Vieriu and Petrea, 2025). At the same time, a consistent concern is over-reliance. Students may accept incorrect outputs without verification, and may use these tools in ways that reduce cognitive effort rather than deepen understanding (Chua, Zheng and Ling, 2025, Jose et al., 2025).

These concerns are increasingly reflected in classroom observations. Teachers report that some students use generative AI to bypass the effort required for learning, rather than engaging with the material itself. This raises questions about whether such tools support learning or simply change the way tasks are completed (Center for Democracy and Technology, 2025).

The limitations of the current evidence base are significant. Many studies rely on self-reported perceptions rather than objective measures of learning outcomes. Longitudinal studies are largely absent, making it difficult to determine sustained impact over time. This is not surprising given the speed with which these tools have been introduced into educational settings, but it does constrain the conclusions that can be drawn.

In primary and secondary education, the evidence is even thinner. Empirical studies in K–12 contexts remain limited, and those that do exist offer mixed or inconclusive results. Some early findings suggest potential negative effects on measures such as self-efficacy and depth of learning, though these results require further validation (Agyei, Roohr and Otieno, 2025).

Taken together, the research base points to a consistent conclusion. Artificial intelligence can support certain forms of learning under specific conditions. It can provide structured practice, feedback, and, in some cases, increased engagement. However, there is little evidence to suggest that it produces substantial improvements over well-established pedagogical approaches, particularly those involving skilled human instruction.

This does not mean that AI has no role in education. It does mean that its role must be understood within the limits of the current evidence. At present, those limits sit in tension with the scale and certainty of the claims being made.

THE NAMED PLATFORM EVIDENCE GAP: MARKETING OUTPACING RESEARCH

Anyone working closely in the AI and education space will quickly notice how often bold marketing claims are not matched by rigorous independent evidence. This gap has significant implications for school procurement, public trust, and policy. It is especially pronounced in the case of generative AI, where the recency of the technology makes long-term claims about sustained impact extremely difficult to substantiate. Any platform claiming major improvements in outcomes should therefore be treated with caution.

Century Tech provides a useful example. The company has claimed 'up to 10× the national average grade improvement' and a '30 per cent improvement in understanding', citing a UCL study (Century Tech, 2023; Century Tech, n.d.). However, that study was conducted in partnership with the company rather than as a fully independent evaluation. At the time of writing, Century has not been evaluated through an Education Endowment Foundation trial, despite the EEF's role in England as a key "What Works" body in education. Much of the evidence cited in support of the platform is company-funded or partnership-based, and there remains no independent randomised controlled trial establishing a causal relationship between platform use and improved learning outcomes. This does not mean that the platform has no value. It does mean that the scale of the claims currently exceeds the strength of the available evidence.

A similar pattern can be seen elsewhere. *Third Space Learning* has cited evidence of "7 months' progress in 14 weeks", yet the independent Education Endowment Foundation trial found no evidence that the intervention improved Key Stage 2 mathematics outcomes compared with business-as-usual teaching (Education Endowment Foundation, 2018). Teachers involved in the trial were broadly positive about aspects of the provision, particularly pupil confidence and verbal interaction, but the central attainment claim was not borne out. The company has since shifted towards its AI tutor, "Skye", but this too remains without robust independent validation. Sparx Maths presents a more mixed case: its strongest evidence comes from observational rather than experimental research, and while higher engagement appears associated with better outcomes, that is not the same as demonstrating that the platform itself is the cause of those gains (RAND, 2021a, 2021b).

Internationally, the picture is also uneven. Carnegie Learning's *MATHia* has one of the stronger research foundations in this field. A RAND Corporation cluster randomised controlled trial across 147 schools found a positive effect in the second year of implementation, equivalent to roughly eight percentile points (Pane et al., 2014). However, there were no significant effects in Year 1, suggesting that even where a platform is effective, benefits may depend on time, embedding, and implementation quality. This is an important corrective to the cycle of rapid adoption and abandonment that often characterises EdTech. Educational effects, where they exist, do not always appear immediately.

No current tool better exemplifies the gap between AI hype and educational evidence than Khanmigo, Khan Academy's GPT-powered tutor. Its development story is telling. Khan Academy's leadership has described how the organisation effectively abandoned its previous development roadmap after seeing GPT-4 demonstrated in 2022, moving from early concept to launch in just seven months. The pace of development reflected technological possibility more than established educational need.

Adoption has been rapid. Khanmigo grew from approximately 68,000 student and teacher users in 2023–24 to more than 700,000 in 2024–25, with projections of further expansion. Yet this growth has far outpaced independent evaluation. Khan Academy has publicly acknowledged that Khanmigo has not yet been tested through a randomised controlled trial, citing cost and practical constraints. This is striking. A tool now used by hundreds of thousands of learners has been scaled before its efficacy has been independently established.

Even Khan Academy's own reporting suggests a more complex picture than the public narrative of transformation implies. Kristen DiCerbo has acknowledged that one of the major challenges is meaningful student engagement (Schwartz, 2025). Some students use the tool productively, but others respond minimally or seek shortcuts rather than understanding. A pilot study conducted by Michigan Virtual reported similar concerns: teachers saw promise in the tool's ability to introduce concepts and support relevance, but students often struggled to formulate useful questions and at times used the system to arrive at answers without deeper learning (Michigan Virtual, 2025).

This matters. If a student's default interaction with a chatbot is to avoid cognitive effort, the technology may reduce friction, but it may also reduce learning. Skilled teachers do not simply provide answers. They interpret hesitation, recognise avoidance, encourage persistence, and adapt their responses in light of the learner in front of them. That is a very different pedagogical relationship from one in which a system responds fluently but cannot meaningfully judge the difference between confusion, disengagement, and strategic minimal effort.

Khan Academy has also acknowledged that *Khanmigo* can make mistakes, including in mathematics (Khan Academy, 2024a). This is not incidental. Generative AI systems remain probabilistic models, and for all their fluency they are still prone to error. Khan Academy's own efficacy page makes an important distinction here: the evidence it presents for improved outcomes relates primarily to the broader Khan Academy platform and its mastery model, not specifically to Khanmigo itself. Studies of Khanmigo's efficacy remain underway (Khan Academy, 2024b). The organisation deserves some credit for being explicit about that. But the central point remains: adoption has moved ahead of proof.

The earlier case of Knewton offers a cautionary parallel. Once heralded as one of the most ambitious and transformative adaptive learning ventures in education, Knewton raised around $180 million and promised a "robot tutor in the sky" capable of responding to individual student need (Westervelt, 2015). Nonetheless, the company ultimately failed to deliver on its promise and was sold at a fraction of its valuation (McKenzie, 2019). Critics at the time argued that what was being sold was less an educational breakthrough than an investment story, and that the company's real audience was venture capital rather than classrooms.

The lesson is not simply that hype can collapse. It is that educational technology succeeds, where it succeeds at all, under much more demanding conditions than technological rhetoric often admits. High quality content, sound pedagogy, meaningful teacher training, thoughtful implementation, and sustained institutional trust all matter. The current generation of AI vendors would do well to remember that. A polished interface layered over a frontier model is not, in itself, an educational solution.

Taken together, these cases illustrate a consistent pattern. The issue is not that every platform fails, nor that AI tools can never add value. It is that the strongest claims in the market are frequently made in advance of the strongest evidence. In a field as consequential as education, that order should concern us.

THE A-LEVEL ALGORITHM DISASTER: A UK CASE WITH GLOBAL LESSONS FOR AI GOVERNANCE

If the previous section illustrates how claims about AI in education can outpace evidence, the events surrounding the 2020 A-level grading process in England demonstrate something more consequential: what happens when algorithmic systems are deployed at scale, in high-stakes educational contexts, without sufficient scrutiny, transparency, or governance.

Although this case is rooted in the United Kingdom, its significance is not national but global. The conditions that produced it—rapid deployment, reliance on historical data, limited external oversight, and pressure to preserve system-level outcomes—are present in education systems worldwide. As AI tools become more deeply embedded in assessment, decision-making, and student evaluation, the lessons from this episode extend far beyond the specific policy context in which it occurred.

In response to the cancellation of examinations during the COVID-19 pandemic, Ofqual was tasked with producing a standardisation model that would maintain consistency with previous years' grade distributions. The resulting system, often referred to as the Direct Centre Performance Model, drew on a combination of historical school performance from 2017 to 2019, prior attainment data, and teacher-submitted rankings of students.

The intention was to prevent grade inflation. The outcome was markedly different

On results day, 13 August 2020, 39.1 per cent of A-level grades were downgraded. Of these, 35.6 per cent fell by one grade, 3.3 per cent by two grades, and 0.2 per cent by three grades. Approximately 280,000 students received lower grades than those predicted by their teachers (ITV, 2020). The algorithm's accuracy ranged from 27 per cent to 68 per cent depending on the subject.

The mechanism through which these outcomes were produced is central to understanding the failure. For subjects with cohorts of fifteen or more students, the model largely overrode teacher assessments in order to fit historical school grade distributions. For smaller cohorts, particularly those with fewer than five students, teacher-assessed grades were accepted with little or no adjustment.

This structural feature had predictable consequences. Students attending historically high-performing schools were more likely to retain strong grades. Those in lower-performing schools, often serving more disadvantaged communities, were more likely to be downgraded. Ofqual's own analysis showed that students from the lowest socio-economic backgrounds saw larger declines in attainment than their more advantaged peers (Gibbons, 2020).

Subject entry patterns amplified these effects. Smaller cohort subjects—often concentrated in independent schools—benefited disproportionately from the model's reliance on teacher assessment. For example, 97.4 per cent of Latin entries were effectively based on teacher-assessed grades, compared to just 28.8 per cent of Psychology entries, which are more commonly taken in state schools. UpReach analysis found that students in sixth form colleges were around 20 per cent more likely to have their grades downgraded than those in private schools (UpReach, 2020).

The logic of the system becomes clearer, and more troubling, when stated plainly. It worked by taking a school's historical grade distribution and fitting current students into it. This meant that a student's grade was determined not primarily by their own ability or their teacher's professional judgement, but by how previous cohorts at their school had performed. If a school had not historically produced top grades in a subject, the algorithm made it statistically unlikely that current students would do so, regardless of their actual attainment (Kolkman, 2020).

Technical weaknesses compounded these structural issues. As Kelly (2021) explains, the model's validation process relied on retrospective rankings generated from actual exam results. In effect, grades were checked against rankings derived from the same data, creating a circular test that gave a misleading impression of accuracy. The system appeared robust because it was, in part, validating itself.

Warnings existed but were not acted upon with sufficient weight. The Royal Statistical Society offered expert input but was not meaningfully integrated into the process (Trendall, 2020). Exam boards raised concerns about anomalous results. Appeals processes were initially limited and, in some cases, required payment, raising further equity concerns for disadvantaged students.

The public response was immediate and forceful. Students protested outside the Department for Education, legal challenges were initiated, and within days the government reversed course, awarding students the higher of their teacher-assessed or calculated grades. Senior officials resigned or were removed from their posts, including Ofqual's chief regulator and the Department for Education's permanent secretary (BBC, 2020).

It is important to be precise about where the failure lies. The issue was not the use of an algorithm in itself. Statistical moderation has long been part of assessment systems. The failure was in how the model was designed, tested, and deployed. Assumptions about fairness were embedded without sufficient scrutiny. Known limitations were not adequately mitigated. Most critically, the system was implemented at scale in a high-stakes context without mechanisms for meaningful challenge prior to impact.

The relevance of this case extends well beyond the UK. The A-level grading controversy did not involve generative AI. It did, however, reveal a broader truth about algorithmic systems in education. When decisions about students are derived from historical data, those systems risk encoding and amplifying existing inequalities. When those systems are opaque, their outcomes become difficult to challenge. When they are deployed rapidly, without independent validation, their consequences are felt before their limitations are understood. These conditions are not unique to one country. They are increasingly characteristic of AI adoption in education systems globally. The lesson is therefore not simply that a particular model failed. It is that without robust governance, transparency, and independent scrutiny, such failures are not exceptional. They are predictable.

BIAS IN PRACTICE: PROCTORING AND AI DETECTION SYSTEMS

If the A-level grading controversy demonstrates the risks of algorithmic decision-making in high-stakes contexts, the rapid expansion of AI-driven proctoring and detection systems illustrates a different but related problem: the normalisation of systems that embed bias, operate with limited transparency, and are often adopted in the absence of robust evidence.

While these technologies are frequently presented as solutions to academic integrity challenges, particularly in the context of remote and digital assessment, the evidence suggests that they introduce new forms of risk, many of which disproportionately affect already marginalised groups. Although many of the most widely documented cases originate in higher education, the tools themselves are increasingly marketed to schools, and the underlying issues are not context-specific. As with the A-level algorithm, the lessons extend far beyond the settings in which the problems first became visible.

The scale and consistency of these issues becomes clearer when examining documented cases across multiple national contexts.

One of the most widely criticised categories of tools is AI-based remote proctoring systems, which use facial recognition, eye tracking, and behavioural analysis to monitor students during examinations. These systems are often framed as neutral and objective. In practice, their performance has been shown to vary significantly across different groups of users.

Research has identified consistent disparities in how facial recognition systems operate across skin tones, with higher error rates for students with darker skin (Himes et al., 2022). Reports from students describe being repeatedly flagged for "suspicious behaviour" due to lighting conditions, camera positioning, or difficulty maintaining a fixed gaze, all of which can disproportionately affect students with disabilities or those working in less controlled environments (Asher-Schapiro, 2020). In some documented cases, students have been required to adjust their physical surroundings or even their appearance in order to be recognised by the system.

These issues are not merely technical. They raise fundamental questions about fairness, dignity, and the conditions under which students are assessed. The requirement to submit to continuous surveillance in one's own home, often under opaque conditions, represents a significant shift in the relationship between institutions and learners. As the Center for Democracy and Technology (2021) argues, such systems can disadvantage students with disabilities and create barriers to equitable participation.

Criticism has also focused on the broader assumptions embedded in these tools. Systems that attempt to infer attention, intent, or honesty from behavioural signals rely on contested psychological and technical premises. As Ogan (2019) notes, the idea that complex human states such as engagement or deception can be reliably inferred from observable signals remains highly uncertain. Yet these assumptions are operationalised in systems that make consequential judgements about students.

Alongside proctoring tools, a second category of systems has gained prominence: AI detection tools designed to identify text generated by large language models. These systems have been widely adopted by schools and universities seeking to address concerns about academic integrity. However, their reliability has been repeatedly questioned.

Empirical studies have shown that AI detection tools can exhibit systematic bias against non-native English speakers, whose writing may be more likely to be flagged as machine-generated (Liang et al., 2023). At the same time, false positives—cases in which human-written work is incorrectly identified as AI-generated—have been widely reported. OpenAI itself withdrew its own detection tool, citing a "low rate of accuracy" (Coldewey, 2023).

Institutional responses have often lagged behind these findings. In some cases, detection outputs have been treated as evidence of misconduct, triggering formal investigations or disciplinary processes. Reports from students and academic institutions indicate that such processes can be difficult to contest, particularly where the underlying systems are proprietary and their methods are not transparent (Sammy, 2023; Jordan, 2023).

The implications for fairness are significant. When a system produces a false positive, the burden of proof can shift to the student, who may be required to demonstrate that their own work is genuinely their own. For students already navigating linguistic, cultural, or educational barriers, this creates an additional layer of vulnerability.

China's classroom surveillance: The extreme end of deployment

To see where these tendencies can lead when scaled further, it is useful to look beyond proctoring and AI detection to the broader use of AI-enabled surveillance in educational settings. Developments in China provide an important, if extreme, example of how systems that claim to measure attention, engagement, or emotional state can move from experimentation to routine deployment.

In 2018, reports emerged that Hangzhou No. 11 High School was using Hikvision's "Smart Classroom Behaviour Management System" to scan students' faces every thirty seconds, classifying facial expressions such as happiness, anger, sadness, and surprise, alongside a set of classroom behaviours, in order to generate real-time attentiveness scores for teachers (Houser, 2018). Vice principal Zhang Guanchao defended the system on the grounds that students whose scores fell below a threshold were not paying sufficient attention in class.

The significance of this case lies not only in the technology itself, but in what it reveals about a wider educational logic: the assumption that attention, engagement, and even emotion can be rendered legible through data and monitored continuously in the name of performance. This is the same underlying logic that appears, in less extreme form, in some proctoring systems and classroom analytics tools elsewhere.

There was domestic backlash to the Hangzhou programme. On Weibo, critics questioned why such technology was not being used to measure enthusiasm in political lectures at universities, exposing the selective and coercive nature of the system's application (Mozur, 2018). In 2019, following criticism of a similar pilot at China

Pharmaceutical University, Lei Chaozi of China's Ministry of Education stated that classroom facial recognition should be curbed and regulated, warning that student data should not be collected unless strictly necessary (Futurism, 2019).

Yet regulatory caution did not prevent broader adoption. By 2021, 135 of China's 137 "double first-class" universities had incorporated facial recognition technology in some form, with the pandemic accelerating the spread of monitoring systems across campuses (Zhu, Wang and Li, 2024). What began as identity verification at gates and entrances expanded into behavioural monitoring and emotion inference inside educational environments, supported by the wider "smart campus" agenda (Sixth Tone, 2022).

Only in 2025 did the regulatory picture shift more decisively. China's Cyberspace Administration and Ministry of Public Security introduced the *Security Management Measures for the Application of Facial Recognition Technology*, which banned emotion recognition and classification by ethnicity, religion, or health status, imposed stricter consent requirements for minors under fourteen, and limited the use of facial recognition where less intrusive alternatives exist (Cyberspace Administration of China and Ministry of Public Security, 2025). Some of the systems that had once symbolised China's AI-in-education ambitions were now, at least in part, unlawful.

Even in a context where educational surveillance expanded rapidly, harms became sufficiently visible that regulatory intervention followed. The difficulty is that it followed only after such systems had already been deployed and normalised.

The human consequences are difficult to dismiss. One student, quoted in reporting on the Hangzhou system, described the experience of constant monitoring: "I don't dare be distracted," reflecting the sense of being continuously observed (Ogan, 2019). More extreme still was the use of brainwave-tracking headbands such as BrainCo's Focus1, marketed as a way of measuring student concentration and transmitting the results to teachers and parents (Li, 2022). Parental backlash was sharp, with some objecting that children were being treated as experimental subjects rather than learners.

The Chinese case should not be dismissed as an outlier with little relevance beyond its own context. Its significance lies in the way it clarifies the trajectory of data-intensive educational monitoring when few meaningful constraints are imposed at the outset. It illustrates what happens when the desire to quantify learning behaviour overtakes basic questions about dignity, proportionality, and the limits of acceptable surveillance.

It also provides a useful point of contrast. In Europe, regulatory frameworks such as the AI Act take a far more restrictive view of emotion inference in educational settings, reflecting a recognition that such systems raise fundamental concerns relating to privacy, autonomy, and freedom of thought. The Chinese example therefore does not sit outside the chapter's argument. It sharpens it. It shows where the same underlying assumptions can lead when they are taken to their logical conclusion.

The issue, once again, is not that data-driven technologies can never be useful. In controlled contexts, with appropriate safeguards, they may contribute to assessment processes. The problem is the speed and manner of their adoption. Tools with known limitations are being deployed in high-stakes environments, often without independent validation, clear standards for use, or effective mechanisms for redress.

Across both categories—proctoring and detection—a common pattern emerges. Systems are introduced in response to a genuine problem. They are framed as efficient, scalable solutions. Their limitations are acknowledged but downplayed. And their impacts are felt most acutely by those least able to challenge them.

The parallels with the A-level algorithm are not coincidental. In each case, the core issue lies not in the existence of the technology, but in the conditions under which it is deployed. Historical biases are encoded in data. Assumptions are embedded in models. Oversight is limited. And the individuals most affected have little visibility into, or control over, the systems that shape their outcomes.

For education systems globally, the lesson is increasingly clear. The risks associated with AI in education are not confined to rare or exceptional failures. They are visible in the routine operation of widely used tools. Without stronger governance, greater transparency, and more rigorous evidence, these risks are likely to persist—and, as adoption increases, to scale.

GLOBAL INEQUALITY AND THE DIGITAL DIVIDE: AI ENTERS AN UNEVEN SYSTEM

If the previous sections demonstrate that AI systems in education can reproduce bias and fail under conditions of weak governance, a further question follows: who is most exposed to these risks, and who is most likely to benefit?

Artificial intelligence is not entering a uniform educational landscape. It is being introduced into systems already marked by profound inequalities in access, infrastructure, institutional capacity, and educational outcomes. In this context, the impact of AI is unlikely to be neutral. It is more likely to follow, and in some cases intensify, existing lines of advantage and disadvantage.

This pattern is not new. Across earlier waves of educational technology, from computers to virtual learning environments, access has consistently been uneven. What distinguishes the current moment is the degree to which AI systems depend not only on access to devices, but on a broader ecosystem of conditions: reliable connectivity, high-quality data, institutional governance, and staff with the capacity to evaluate and implement tools effectively.

Emerging evidence suggests that these conditions are not evenly distributed. Schools with greater resources are more likely to invest in AI tools, provide staff training, and integrate technologies into coherent pedagogical strategies. By contrast, less well-resourced schools are more likely to encounter AI in fragmented ways, through isolated tools or externally imposed systems, without the supporting structures needed for effective use (Sutton Trust, 2025; techUK, 2025).

The consequence is not simply a difference in access, but a difference in outcomes. Where implementation is strategic and supported, AI tools may enhance aspects of teaching and learning. Where implementation is ad hoc, under-resourced, or poorly governed, the same tools may increase workload, introduce new risks, or fail to deliver meaningful benefit. In such contexts, students may experience the limitations of AI systems before they experience their potential advantages. The digital divide, therefore, is no longer only a question of access. It is increasingly a question of access to effective, well-governed, and pedagogically grounded uses of technology.

This distinction becomes particularly important in relation to data. AI systems rely on large volumes of data to function effectively. Schools with more advanced digital infrastructures are better positioned to generate, manage, and use such data, and are more likely to have governance frameworks capable of ensuring that data is used responsibly. In less resourced settings, data practices may be more limited, less consistent, or more dependent on external providers, raising additional concerns about privacy, control, and long-term use.

At a global level, these disparities are further amplified. Differences between national education systems in funding, regulatory capacity, teacher training, and digital infrastructure shape how AI is adopted and governed. In high-income contexts, the challenge may be one of oversight and coordination. In lower-income contexts, the challenge may be more fundamental: limited access to devices, unreliable connectivity, and competing priorities within already stretched education systems.

International organisations have begun to highlight these risks. UNESCO (2023; 2025) has emphasised that the introduction of AI in education must be aligned with the protection of learners' rights, particularly in contexts where regulatory frameworks are still developing. Without such alignment, systems developed in one context may be deployed in another without adequate consideration of local conditions, needs, or safeguards.

The result is a form of asymmetry. Technologies are developed in well-resourced environments, trained on data that reflects particular populations, and then deployed globally. The benefits and risks of those systems are not evenly shared.

And underpinning all of this is the digital divide. The available evidence should be read as a warning. Schools with the greatest resources are best positioned to realise the potential benefits of AI, while those with the least are often most exposed to its risks. This is not simply a question of technology. It is an equity problem with a technological accelerant.

CONCLUSION: FROM PROMISE TO PROOF

If AI becomes embedded in core educational functions such as assessment, feedback, and progression, then differences in how these systems are implemented will translate into differences in educational opportunity. Students in well-resourced systems may encounter AI as a tool that supports learning. Students in less resourced systems may encounter it as a system that constrains or misrepresents their abilities. The implications extend beyond individual classrooms. They speak to the role of education in shaping future opportunity.

Across the cases examined in this chapter, a consistent pattern emerges. AI systems are introduced into education with ambitious claims and uneven evidence. Their impacts are shaped by the contexts in which they are deployed, and those contexts are not equal. The risk is not only that AI fails to deliver on its promises. It is that, in doing so, it reinforces the very inequalities education systems are intended to address.

None of this means that AI has no place in education. That would be the wrong conclusion to draw. The question is not whether AI will form part of education's future, but whether institutions will repeat the familiar pattern of previous technology cycles: adopting first, evaluating later, and recognising the harms only once they have become entrenched.

Avoiding that outcome requires a shift that is as much institutional as it is technical. It requires honesty about what is not yet known, rigour in how tools are evaluated, governance structures capable of keeping pace with deployment, and a clear insistence that educational technology remains accountable to the learners it is intended to serve.

The measure of any educational technology is not how advanced or efficient it appears, but whether it demonstrably improves outcomes for students, particularly those who have the most to gain. That is the standard against which AI in education must be judged. On the evidence available so far, it is a standard the field has yet to consistently meet.

REFERENCES

Agyei, E., Roohr, K. and Oticno, C. (2025) 'Generative AI use in K-12 education: A systematic review', *Frontiers in Education*, 10, 1647573. Available at: https://doi.org/10.3389/feduc.2025.1647573

Anthropic (2025) *Claude's Constitution*. Available at: www.anthropic.com/constitution

Asher-Schapiro, A. (2020) 'Online exams raise concerns of racial bias in facial recognition', *Christian Science Monitor*, 17 November. Available at: www.csmonitor.com/Technology/2020/1117/Online-exams-raise-concerns-of-racial-bias-in-facial-recognition

BBC News (2020) 'Top DfE civil servant Jonathan Slater sacked', *BBC News*, 26 August. Available at: www.bbc.co.uk/news/uk-politics-53920146

Center for Democracy and Technology (2021) *How Automated Test Proctoring Software Discriminates against Disabled Students.* CDT. Available at: https://cdt.org/insights/how-automated-test-proctoring-software-discriminates-against-disabled-students/

Center for Democracy and Technology (2025) *Schools' Embrace of AI Connected to Increased Risks*. Washington, D.C.: CDT. Available at: https://cdt.org/insights/hand-in-hand-schools-embrace-of-ai-connected-to-increased-risks-to-students/

Century Tech (n.d.) 'About CENTURY', *HundrED*. Available at: https://hundred.org/en/innovations/century-tech

Century Tech (2023) 'Ufi VocTech Project: Using artificial intelligence to improve further education resits results', *Century Tech News*. Available at: www.century.tech/news/ufi-voctech-project-using-artificial-intelligence-to-improve-further-education-resits-results/

Chua, H.W., Zheng, Y. and Ling, L. (2025) 'A systematic review of responses, attitudes, and utilization behaviors on generative AI for teaching and learning in higher education', *Education Sciences*, 15(4), 505. Available at: https://pmc.ncbi.nlm.nih.gov/articles/PMC12023922/

Coldewey, D. (2023) 'OpenAI scuttles AI-written text detector over "low rate of accuracy"', *TechCrunch*, 25 July. Available at: https://techcrunch.com/2023/07/25/openai-scuttles-ai-written-text-detector-over-low-rate-of-accuracy/

Cyberspace Administration of China and Ministry of Public Security (2025) *Security Management Measures for the Application of Facial Recognition Technology* [人脸识别技术应用安全管理办法]. Promulgated 13 March, effective 1 June 2025. Available at: www.chinalawtranslate.com/en/facial-rec-2025/

Education Endowment Foundation (2018) *Affordable Maths Tuition.* Available at: https://educationendowmentfoundation.org.uk/projects-and-evaluation/projects/affordable-maths-tuition

Futurism (2019) 'Surprise move: China to curb use of facial recognition in schools', *Futurism*, 6 September. Available at: https://futurism.com/the-byte/china-curb-facial-recognition-schools

Gasser, U. and Mayer-Schönberger, V. (2024) *Guardrails: Guiding Human Decisions in the Age of AI.* Princeton: Princeton University Press. doi: 10.1515/9780691256351

Hattie, J. (2009) *Visible Learning: A Synthesis of Over 800 Meta-Analyses Relating to Achievement.* London: Routledge.

Himes, D., Ravert, R.D., Lim, E. and Trede, T. (2022) 'Remote proctoring and racial disparities in facial recognition', *Frontiers in Education*, 7, 881449. doi: 10.3389/feduc.2022.881449. Available at: www.frontiersin.org/journals/education/articles/10.3389/feduc.2022.881449/full

Houser, K. (2018) 'A Chinese school is using facial recognition to monitor how attentive students are', *Futurism*, 17 May. Available at: https://futurism.com/smart-eye-china-facial-recognition

ITV News (2020) 'Ofqual forced into downgrades by "implausible" teacher predictions', *ITV News*, 14 August. Available at: www.itv.com/news/2020-08-14/ofqual-forced-into-downgrades-by-implausible-teacher-predictions

Jordan, A. (2023) 'Lancaster SU calls on uni to stop using Turnitin over fears it falsely detects ChatGPT use', *The Tab*, 29 June. Available at: https://thetab.com/2023/06/29/lancaster-su-calls-on-uni-to-stop-using-turnitin-over-fears-it-falsely-detects-chatgpt-use

Jose, B., Cherian, J., Verghis, A.M., Varghise, S.M. and Joseph, S. (2025) 'The cognitive paradox of AI in education: Between enhancement and erosion', *Frontiers in Psychology*, 16, 1550621. Available at: www.frontiersin.org/journals/psychology/articles/10.3389/fpsyg.2025.1550621

Kelly, A. (2021) 'The great algorithm fiasco', *British Educational Research Association Blog*. Available at: www.bera.ac.uk/blog/the-great-algorithm-fiasco

Khan Academy (2024a) 'Khan Academy efficacy results', *Khan Academy Blog*, November. Available at: https://blog.khanacademy.org/khan-academy-efficacy-results-november-2024

Khan Academy (2024b) 'Why we're deeply invested in making AI better at math tutoring and what we've been up to lately', *Khan Academy Blog*. Available at: https://blog.khanacademy.org/why-were-deeply-invested-in-making-ai-better-at-math-tutoring-and-what-weve-been-up-to-lately

Kolkman, D. (2020) 'F**k the algorithm: What the world can learn from the UK's A-level grading fiasco', *LSE Impact Blog*, 26 August. Available at: https://blogs.lse.ac.uk/impactofsocialsciences/2020/08/26/fk-the-algorithm-what-the-world-can-learn-from-the-uks-a-level-grading-fiasco/

Laird, E., Dwyer, M. and Quay-de la Vallee, H. (2025) 'Hand in Hand: Schools' Embrace of AI Connected to Increased Risks to Students', *Center for Democracy and Technology*. Available at: https://cdt.org/insights/hand-in-hand-schools-embrace-of-ai-connected-to-increased-risks-to-students/

Latham, K. and Montacute, R. (2025) *Artificial Advantage?.* London: The Sutton Trust. Available at: www.suttontrust.com/our-research/artificial-advantage/

Li, J. (2022) 'A mind-reading headband is facing backlash in China', *Quartz*. Available at: https://qz.com/1742279/a-mind-reading-headband-is-facing-backlash-in-china

Liang, W., Yuksekgonul, M., Mao, Y., Wu, E. and Zou, J. (2023) 'GPT detectors are biased against non-native English writers', *Patterns*, 4(7), 100779. doi: 10.1016/j.patter.2023.100779. Available at: https://pmc.ncbi.nlm.nih.gov/articles/PMC10382961/

Ma, W., Adesope, O.O., Nesbit, J.C. and Liu, Q. (2014) 'Intelligent tutoring systems and learning outcomes: A meta-analysis', *Journal of Educational Psychology*, 106(4), 901–918.

McKenzie, L. (2019) 'Wiley buys Knewton adaptive learning technology company', *Inside Higher Ed*, 7 May. Available at: www.insidehighered.com/digital-learning/article/2019/05/07/wiley-buys-knewton-adaptive-learning-technology-company

Michigan Virtual (2025) *AI in Education: A 2025 Snapshot of Trust, Use, and Emerging Practices*. Available at: https://michiganvirtual.org/research/publications/ai-in-education-a-2025-snapshot-of-trust-use-and-emerging-practices/

Mozur, P. (2018) 'In China, classroom cameras scan student faces for emotion, stoking fears of new form of state monitoring', *The Globe and Mail*, 26 May. Available at: www.theglobeandmail.com/world/article-in-china-classroom-cameras-scan-student-faces-for-emotion-stoking/

Ogan, A. (2019) 'Reframing classroom sensing: Promise and peril', *Interactions*. Available at: https://interactions.acm.org/archive/view/november-december-2019/reframing-classroom-sensing

OpenAI (2018) *OpenAI Charter*. Available at: https://openai.com/charter/

Pane, J.F., Griffin, B.A., McCaffrey, D.F. and Karam, R. (2014) *Effectiveness of Cognitive Tutor Algebra I at Scale*. Research Brief RB-9746. Santa Monica, CA: RAND Corporation. Available at: www.rand.org/pubs/research_briefs/RB9746.html

RAND Europe and University of Cambridge (2021a) *Independent Analysis of the Relationship between Sparx Maths and Maths Outcomes: Key Findings*. Cambridge: RAND Europe. Available at: www.educ.cam.ac.uk/research/programmes/sparx/SparxKeyFindings.pdf

RAND Europe and University of Cambridge (2021b) *Independent Analysis of the Relationship between Sparx Maths and Maths Outcomes: Technical Report*. Cambridge: RAND Europe. Available at: www.educ.cam.ac.uk/research/programmes/sparx/SparxTechnicalReport.pdf

Safe AI for Children Alliance (2025) *Non-Negotiables for Children's AI Safety*. Available at: www.safeaiforchildren.org/non-negotiables-campaign/

Sammy, K. (2023) 'Universities doubtful about Turnitin's new AI detection tool', *Techzine*. Available at: www.techzine.eu/news/applications/104118/universities-doubtful-about-turnitins-new-ai-detection-tool/

Schwartz, S. (2025) '3 Questions for K-12 leaders to consider amid the AI tutoring boom', *K-12 Dive*, 25 August. Available at: www.k12dive.com/news/3-questions-for-k-12-leaders-to-consider-amid-the-ai-tutoring-boom/757314/

Sixth Tone (2022) 'Chinese school faces backlash over use of facial recognition scanners', *Sixth Tone*, 14 January. Available at: www.sixthtone.com/news/1009712/chinese-school-faces-backlash-over-use-of-facial-recognition-scanners

Sutton Trust (2025) *Artificial Advantage? A First Look at How AI Is Being Used by Schools and Teachers in the Classroom*. London: The Sutton Trust. Available at: www.suttontrust.com/our-research/artificial-advantage/

techUK (2025) *Bridging the Gaps: AI in Education and the Urgent Call for Inclusion*. Available at: www.techuk.org/resource/bridging-the-gaps-ai-in-education-and-the-urgent-call-for-inclusion.html

Trendall, S. (2020) 'Ofqual hits back as statisticians' row over five-year NDA intensifies', *PublicTechnology*, 26 August. Available at: www.publictechnology.net/2020/08/26/education-and-skills/ofqual-hits-back-statisticians-row-over-five-year-nda-intensifies/

Ubell, R. (2019) 'Explaining the shakeout in the adaptive learning market', *Inside Higher Ed*, 12 June. Available at: www.insidehighered.com/digital-learning/views/2019/06/12/explaining-shakeout-adaptive-learning-market-opinion

UNESCO (2023) *Guidance for Generative AI in Education and Research.* Paris: UNESCO. Available at: www.unesco.org/en/articles/guidance-generative-ai-education-and-research

UNESCO (2025) *AI and Education: Protecting the Rights of Learners.* Paris: UNESCO. Available at: www.unesco.org/en/articles/ai-and-education-protecting-rights-learners

upReach (2020) *Ofqual Algorithm Research.* 17 August. Available at: https://cms.upreach.org.uk/uploads/up_Reach_Ofqual_Algorithm_Research_17_Aug_2020_08dd382464.pdf

Vieriu, A.M. and Petrea, G. (2025) 'The impact of artificial intelligence (AI) on students' academic development', *Education Sciences*, 15(3), 343. Available at: https://doi.org/10.3390/educsci15030343

Westervelt, E. (2015) *Meet the mind-reading robo tutor in the sky.* NPR, 13 October. Available at: www.npr.org/sections/ed/2015/10/13/437265231/meet-the-mind-reading-robo-tutor-in-the-sky

Wu, F., Dang, Y. and Li, M. (2025) 'A systematic review of responses, attitudes, and utilization behaviors on generative AI for teaching and learning in higher education', *Behavioral Sciences*, 15(4), 467. doi: 10.3390/bs15040467. Available at: www.mdpi.com/2076-328X/15/4/467

Zhu, H., Wang, X. and Li, Y. (2024) 'Exploring college students' risk perception and acceptance intention of facial recognition technology in China', *Telematics and Informatics*, 93, 102169. Available at: www.sciencedirect.com/science/article/abs/pii/S0736585324000972

AI Ethics in Practice

Building a Human-Centred Classroom

5

PART I: THE TOOLS WERE ALREADY HERE

When schools began talking about “AI” in 2023, they were several decades late to the conversation.

Google Search entered the classroom without a press release. So did predictive text, grammar checkers, plagiarism detectors, recommendation engines, and early alert systems that promised to spot “risk” before a teacher ever could. By the time ChatGPT arrived, many schools were already living inside automated judgment, surrounded by AI driven systems that ranked, filtered, scored, and steered. We just had not attached the label that would have forced a serious public debate. That silence mattered. Because by the time ethics entered the room, the room was full.

To understand why today’s AI ethics crisis feels so sudden, we have to name the long runway that produced it. Education did not jump straight from chalkboards to generative models. It moved through decades of digitalisation that normalised data capture as the price of participation and treated commercial platforms as infrastructure rather than as curriculum. UNESCO’s 2023 Global Education Monitoring Report puts it plainly: *the terms of technology use in education are not neutral. They carry costs, trade-offs, and power relationships that are often underestimated, particularly when systems adopt tools faster than they build the governance capacity to manage them* (UNESCO, 2023). That point matters because the ethics we now debate in relation to “AI” are not new ethical questions. They are intensified hyperspeed versions of older ones that were never resolved.

DOI: 10.1201/9781003662945-5

The earliest digital tools in education were framed as practical aids. Search would expand knowledge. Spellcheck would reduce barriers. Learning management systems would "streamline" teaching and alleviate administrative burdens. These claims were not entirely wrong, but they were incomplete. They ignored the deeper shift: schooling was becoming datafied. Teaching and learning were being translated into measurable traces. Attendance became a dataset, engagement became a metric, writing became a score, and behaviour became a dashboard. And when social life is translated into numbers, the numbers begin to govern the social life. That is the central argument of scholarship on the datafication of education, which highlights how the availability of data and algorithms introduces new forms of measurement, surveillance, and control inside educational institutions (Jarke and Breiter, 2019; Williamson et al., 2020).

This is the point at which the story becomes less about tools and more about authority.

Search engines, for example, did not simply provide answers. They shaped how students ask questions, which sources are treated as credible, and what "research" looks like under time pressure. Search is an epistemic instrument. It ranks knowledge, privileges certain forms of text and images, and nudges inquiry toward what is already popular, well-linked, or commercially optimised. Yet for years, many school systems treated search literacy as optional, even as search became core to classroom practice. There is a difference between teaching students to find information and teaching students to understand the system that decides what information they see first. The second is an ethical requirement because it is about agency.

The same pattern appeared in automated writing tools. Grammar checkers and writing assistants altered the feedback loop between teacher and student by inserting a third voice into the process, one that speaks with confidence and claims objectivity. In many contexts, automated writing evaluation has shown measurable effects on revision behaviours and writing outcomes, particularly for second-language learners, but the literature also records tensions around over-reliance, narrowed definitions of quality, and the risk that students learn to write for the tool rather than for meaning (Fu et al., 2024). When students internalise machine feedback as the standard of correctness, schools should ask what language norms are being privileged and what forms of voice are being penalised. This is less a technical footnote, and more a question about who decides which language counts as "good".

Plagiarism detection systems created another shift: the movement from trust-based pedagogy to suspicion-based surveillance. Tools such as *Turnitin* are often framed as integrity supports, but critical scholarship has long argued that they also function as compliance mechanisms that reshape the relationship between student and institution (Bruton and Childers, 2016). This matters in school contexts because the logic of these systems is not simply "detect copying." It is "treat all writing as potentially illicit until verified by a system the student cannot interrogate." Once normalised, that logic becomes cultural. It changes how students experience assessment and how teachers experience their role. It also raises questions about data ownership and long-term retention, especially when student writing is stored in proprietary databases and used to train detection models without meaningful negotiation about rights.

At the same time, schools increasingly adopted learning analytics and early warning systems to predict student risk. The idea was seductive: identify disengagement early, intervene quickly, reduce dropout. The research base shows that such systems can achieve predictive accuracy in controlled settings, and early work in learning analytics describes large-scale institutional efforts to mine student data for risk indicators (Jayaprakash et al., 2014). But as the field matured, so did its ethical critique. Scholars of learning analytics have identified recurring issues that map directly onto safeguarding: duty to act, informed consent, data ownership, equality and justice, and the dangers of categorising students in ways that may become self-fulfilling (Ferguson, 2019). Once a child is labelled "at risk" by an algorithm, the label may follow them. Teachers may unconsciously lower expectations. Students may internalise the classification. None of that requires malicious intent. It requires only a system that confuses prediction with truth.

This is why the ethical foundation for AI in schools cannot begin with generative AI. It must begin with the long normalisation of digital decision-making. Systems that suggest, score, rank, track, and recommend did not arrive yesterday. They arrived gradually and often invisibly, as a function of procurement. They entered as "free" services, both convenient and efficient.

Consider the platformisation of the classroom through major corporate ecosystems. Google's education suite became a default stack in many schools, particularly where budgets were tight and procurement teams were under pressure. Google itself stated in 2018 that 80 million teachers and students relied on G Suite for Education (Google, 2018). By 2017, more than 30 million U.S. K to 12 students were using Google education apps (Axios, 2017; Vox, 2020). Scholars have challenged the assumption that such adoption is purely benign. Krutka, Smits and Willhelm describe how the embrace of Google in schools occurred with limited debate and argue that the educational consequences cannot be separated from broader questions of corporate power, data extraction, and democratic accountability (Krutka, Smits and Willhelm, 2021). This is as much a governance decision as it is a privacy discussion. When a platform becomes the environment of schooling, it shapes pedagogy, communication, and administrative practice in ways that rarely pass through democratic oversight (Axios, 2020).

What makes this especially consequential is that platforms are not merely tools used inside schools. They become the operating conditions for schooling. They reshape what teachers can do, what students can do, and what becomes legible to the institution. The platform decides what is measurable, what is flagged, what is stored, what is easy, what is hard, what is possible, and what becomes routine. In that sense, infrastructure becomes policy.

And because these systems were framed as infrastructure rather than instruction, they rarely faced the scrutiny applied to curriculum or assessment. In many jurisdictions, no national body reviewed whether they distorted learning or exposed students to risk. No ethics committee approved them. No professional standard guided their use. The governance gap was structural. It was built into how education systems purchase technology, how they evaluate "innovation," and how they distribute responsibility.

This is then where the damage becomes predictable. Most school systems adopted digital tools without building the professional capacity to govern them. Teachers were not taught how algorithmic systems work. They were not given time or training to ask what data is collected, how it is processed, where it is stored, and what rights families retain. Research on digitalisation repeatedly highlights that technology policy often outpaces teacher preparation, leaving educators to manage complex systems without the knowledge needed to recognise harms or insist on safeguards (UNESCO, 2023;

OECD, 2021; Selwyn, 2019). Selwyn's work is useful here because it punctures the comforting myth that educational technology is a simple add-on. He argues that the question is never only what technology can do, but what values it advances, what labour it displaces, and what forms of teaching it redefines (Selwyn, 2019). When schools adopt automated decision systems without building ethical literacy, teachers are set up as operational users rather than informed professionals.

The result is a familiar pattern. Students from marginalised backgrounds are more likely to be misread by systems trained on normative data. Children with disabilities are more likely to be flagged as underperforming in contexts where the system cannot interpret difference. Students who speak in dialect, who code-switch, who write in hybrid forms, who learn asynchronously, who do not present as "standard," become more vulnerable to misclassification. And teachers, undertrained and time-poor, can drift into deference. The dashboard begins to feel like a second opinion. Over time, it can become the first.

This is where ethics breaks down: not because schools are reckless, but because the technologies were introduced with no ethical infrastructure to match. There is often no protocol for redress, no shared language for transparency, no clear accountability chain when the tool harms a child. Ethics cannot operate as a private feeling held by a thoughtful teacher. It must operate as a public system that shapes procurement, training, oversight, and student protection.

At this point, it is tempting to say that the COVID-19 pandemic changed everything. It did accelerate adoption, but it did not invent the problem. Investigations into pandemic-era education technology showed how quickly schools and governments could endorse tools that enabled tracking and data exploitation at scale, often without meaningful consent or the possibility of refusal (Human Rights Watch, 2022). What mattered was not only the surveillance itself, but the governance conditions that allowed it: urgency, lack of capacity, and the framing of technology as the only route to continuity. When schooling is treated as impossible without a vendor platform, children's rights become negotiable.

And so we arrive at the present moment. AI is not new. What is new is that we have finally named it loudly enough that ministers, regulators, and school boards have to respond.

Ethics in AI begins when we stop pretending the system is neutral—when we ask what decisions are being made, who is being shaped by them, and who is accountable when they fail. The rest of this chapter offers the tools to answer.

What happens when data systems designed for efficiency become systems of judgment, and when predictive logics enter institutions built on professional discretion and human development? The research record over the past decade shows that when algorithmic systems are layered onto fragile governance structures, they do not simply assist decision-making. They restructure it. Part 2 turns to that record.

PART II: WHERE ETHICS BREAK DOWN

Ethics in education becomes visible in institutional failure: when a student is flagged by a system and no adult in the building can explain the criteria, or when automated grading tools override teacher judgment. It is visible when predictive analytics are introduced under the language of early intervention but operate without scrutiny of how risk is constructed.

This section reflects documented breakdown across multiple jurisdictions and research domains.

Surveillance as educational infrastructure

The contemporary classroom operates within what scholars describe as the datafication of education: the transformation of learning processes into quantifiable, extractable, and governable data (Jarke and Breiter, 2019; Williamson, 2017). More than being collected, data becomes the basis for classification, evaluation, and intervention. Once this occurs, educational governance shifts from relational judgment to informational control.

The scale of this shift became visible during pandemic remote learning. In 2021, Human Rights Watch examined 164 education technology products used across 49 countries. Of the total, 89 per cent engaged in data practices that risked or directly infringed children's rights, including third-party tracking, behavioral profiling, and persistent identifiers extending beyond educational use (Human Rights Watch, 2022). In many cases, schools and ministries endorsed these tools without conducting formal data protection impact assessments or negotiating meaningful contractual limits.

The ethical issue here is structural asymmetry. Schools lack the technical and legal capacity of multinational vendors. Under conditions of urgency, procurement prioritises continuity over scrutiny, and once implemented, platforms become infrastructural—withdrawal appears destabilising. Over time, the governance deficit stops looking like a deficit and starts looking like the norm.

Prediction, classification, and structural reproduction

As has already been highlighted, the Ofqual grading algorithm in the United Kingdom in 2020 remains one of the clearest demonstrations of algorithmic reproduction of inequality. The statistical standardisation model adjusted teacher assessments using historical institutional performance. Approximately 39 per cent of grades were downgraded. Students from historically lower-performing schools were disproportionately affected (Ofqual, 2020).

The system encoded prior attainment patterns as corrective baselines. In doing so, it operationalised structural inequality as statistical stability.

This pattern aligns with established research in algorithmic fairness. Systems trained on historically stratified datasets replicate stratification unless explicitly counterweighted. In educational environments where attainment correlates strongly with socioeconomic status, race, disability, and geography, predictive models risk entrenching disadvantage under the appearance of neutrality.

Learning analytics scholarship has repeatedly identified classification as an ethical fault line. Ferguson (2019) highlights duty to act, informed consent, and justice as core challenges once risk profiling begins. Slade and Prinsloo (2013) earlier warned that predictive systems can reposition students from autonomous learners to managed subjects, shifting power from professional discretion to statistical governance.

The core issue is more about authority than accuracy. When a system labels a student "at risk," that classification alters expectation. Expectation influences opportunity. Opportunity shapes outcome. The predictive loop becomes self-reinforcing.

Personalisation and normative encoding

Adaptive learning systems and automated writing tools are frequently framed as individualised supports. Empirical evidence shows modest gains in surface-level revision or practice efficiency in certain contexts, particularly among second-language learners (Fu et al., 2024). However, the same literature documents narrowed definitions of quality and alignment to dominant linguistic norms.

Algorithmic systems encode standards derived from training data. If that data reflects normative grammar, dominant dialects, or historically privileged performance patterns, deviation becomes error. What appears as personalisation is often standardisation under a different label.

Research in educational data systems further demonstrates disproportionate flagging in behavioral prediction tools when disciplinary history is included as a feature. If disciplinary records reflect racialised or disability-linked bias, predictive outputs amplify that bias rather than neutralise it. This phenomenon has been widely documented in algorithmic governance research beyond education and is directly applicable within school analytics environments.

Implementation context intensifies these effects. Williamson and Eynon (2023) show that schools serving disadvantaged populations are more likely to implement intensive data systems under accountability pressure. In such environments, adaptive platforms can move from supplementary tools to structural substitutes for human support. In wealthier schools, similar tools remain bounded by teacher oversight and parental scrutiny.

Thus the same technical system produces divergent ethical consequences depending on institutional capacity. This is not a tool problem alone. It is a governance capacity problem.

Professional authority and algorithmic deference

Ethical fragility increases when professional capacity lags behind technological adoption.

A 2025 GMB survey in the United Kingdom reported that 84 per cent of school staff had received no formal training in AI or digital governance (GMB, 2025). In the United States, RAND's 2023 survey found that more than half of teachers had experimented with AI tools, yet fewer than 15 per cent had received formal guidance on ethical deployment or bias mitigation (RAND, 2023).

This training deficit has implications beyond skill acquisition. It reshapes professional authority. When teachers are presented with predictive dashboards, automated scoring, or behavioural alerts, a second epistemic actor enters the classroom. Without structured training in interpretability, override protocols, and bias recognition, educators may default to algorithmic deference.

Research in automation bias demonstrates that humans tend to over-rely on automated outputs even when contradictory evidence is available, particularly under time pressure. In school environments characterised by workload stress, this tendency is amplified. The system's output can begin to appear more objective than professional intuition.

Governance mechanisms often fail to compensate. Procurement decisions are frequently centralised, driven by vendor narratives emphasising efficiency and compliance. Independent audits of algorithmic systems are rare in K to 12 contexts. Students are rarely consulted on technology implementation or governance, and data protection impact assessments are unevenly enforced. In many ways this is more governance by acquisition than by deliberation.

Democratic deficit and student voice

The final breakdown concerns participation.

International child rights frameworks emphasise the right of children to be heard in matters affecting them. Yet algorithmic systems in schools are usually deployed without meaningful consultation with students or families. Students are profiled before they are informed and parents notified after contracts are signed. Appeal processes for algorithmic decisions are opaque or informal. This produces a democratic deficit within the educational institution. Governance shifts from visible human deliberation to embedded technical systems whose logic is rarely accessible to those subject to it.

Ethical collapse, therefore, is not an isolated malfunction: it is a systemic condition produced by the convergence of:

1. Normalised data extraction as infrastructure
2. Predictive models trained on stratified historical data
3. Uneven institutional capacity across school contexts
4. Inadequate professional preparation and oversight
5. Absence of participatory governance

Under these conditions, AI could be seen to reorganise educational decision-making as much as it offers assistance. Equity requires more than technological access. It requires structural capacity, interpretive literacy, and enforceable accountability. When those are absent, breakdown is almost guaranteed.

If Part 2 demonstrates anything, it is this: ethical failure in AI is as much institutional as it is technical. Systems do not collapse because code is malicious. They collapse because governance is thin, training is absent, participation is excluded, and power is left unexamined.

Schools will use AI. There is no question of that. But in order to do so, they must redesign the ethical architecture that must accompany it. Once that is accepted, the task becomes clearer: to reconstruct, rather than retreat. This will be the focus of Part III.

PART III: BUILDING BACK WITH PURPOSE

Ethics in education is so much more than a checklist on a clipboard. It should be seen more as an operating system, structuring procurement, pedagogy, professional development, safeguarding, and accountability. Without that integration, AI governance becomes symbolic compliance rather than institutional practice.

Global frameworks already exist.

The OECD: From economic policy to educational governance

The OECD's Recommendation of the Council on Artificial Intelligence, adopted in 2019 by more than forty member and partner countries, was the first intergovernmental standard on AI. Its origin lies not in education but in economic governance. The concern was that AI systems, if left unregulated, could destabilise labour markets, undermine democratic institutions, and exacerbate inequality. The Recommendation therefore established five value-based principles: inclusive growth and sustainable development, human-centred values and fairness, transparency and explainability, robustness and security, and accountability.

In education, these principles translate directly into institutional obligations. Fairness requires that predictive learning systems be routinely audited for disparate impact across socioeconomic, racial, linguistic, and disability groups. Accountability requires named oversight structures within school systems, including documented review processes and appeal pathways for students affected by automated decisions. Transparency requires that algorithmic decision criteria be explainable to teachers and parents, not hidden behind vendor claims of proprietary protection.

Human oversight requires that automated outputs remain advisory rather than determinative, particularly in high-stakes decisions such as grading, placement, or behavioural escalation. At school level, implementation means integrating data impact assessments into procurement, establishing AI governance committees that include educators, safeguarding leads and data protection officers, and mandating override authority for trained professionals. The OECD framework is a structural demand that public institutions retain democratic control over AI deployment.

UNESCO: Artificial intelligence as a human rights question

UNESCO's (2021) Recommendation on the Ethics of Artificial Intelligence marked a significant expansion of the AI debate into human rights law and global governance. Unlike the OECD, whose emphasis began with economic coordination, UNESCO explicitly grounded its framework in international human rights instruments, including the Universal Declaration of Human Rights and the Convention on the Rights of the Child

(United Nations, 1948, 1989). Its principles include proportionality and do no harm, safety and security, fairness and non-discrimination, transparency and explainability, privacy and data governance, human oversight and determination, and responsibility and accountability.

In education, this reframing is decisive. It positions AI not as a productivity tool but as a rights-sensitive intervention in childhood. Fairness becomes a requirement to prevent algorithmic discrimination in assessment and support systems. Accountability requires traceable decision chains when AI influences educational outcomes. Transparency obliges schools to communicate clearly how student data is processed and shared. Human rights demand data minimisation and meaningful consent, especially for minors. Human oversight requires that educators remain the final decision-makers in matters affecting student progression or wellbeing.

At school level, UNESCO's framework can be operationalised through child-rights impact assessments prior to AI adoption, explicit consent protocols for families, mandatory data retention limits, and inclusion of AI literacy within citizenship education. The key shift is conceptual: AI governance becomes an extension of child safeguarding rather than an IT function (Council of International Schools, 2024). This is not the responsibility of the IT network manager.

IEEE ethically aligned design: Human flourishing as design constraint

The IEEE's Ethically Aligned Design initiative, first published in 2019 and developed through global expert consultation, differs in origin and tone. Emerging from engineering communities rather than intergovernmental negotiation, it frames AI ethics around human wellbeing and human agency. Its emphasis on transparency, accountability, awareness of misuse, competence, and human oversight is explicitly design-oriented. Systems should be built to support human autonomy rather than diminish it.

In educational contexts, this principle has profound implications. Fairness requires that system designers actively test for representational bias in training datasets used for educational applications. Accountability requires auditability of system outputs and version histories. Transparency requires explainable interfaces that allow teachers to interrogate recommendations. Human rights considerations demand avoidance of manipulative design patterns or covert behavioural nudging in learning platforms.

Human oversight requires that educational AI systems be architected with human-in-the-loop mechanisms, including override, review, and iterative correction. At school level, applying IEEE's design lens means refusing black-box deployments, requiring vendor documentation of bias testing procedures, and embedding explainability tools directly into teacher dashboards. It also means building internal capacity to question system outputs rather than accepting them as authoritative. The IEEE contribution is methodological: ethics must be engineered into systems before they reach the classroom.

The OECD's AI Principles (2019), UNESCO's Recommendation on the Ethics of Artificial Intelligence (2021), and IEEE's Ethically Aligned Design (2019) converge on core obligations: fairness, accountability, transparency, human rights, and human oversight. These documents are so much more than abstract moral statements: they are governance blueprints. What they lack is translation into school-level implementation. Translation *is* the work, and it must be a core focus of leadership teams the world over.

Fairness in school context means more than statistical parity. It requires explicit examination of whether training data reflects historical inequality, whether predictive models incorporate biased proxies, and whether system outputs disproportionately affect protected groups. It requires routine bias audits and public reporting. It requires capacity to pause deployment when patterns of harm emerge.

Accountability means that algorithmic systems must have named institutional stewards. Someone must be responsible for oversight, review, appeal, and redress. If a student is misclassified, there must be a documented pathway for challenge. If a predictive tool influences intervention decisions, the basis for that influence must be transparent and reviewable.

Transparency requires more than publishing vendor documentation. It requires explainability at the point of use. Teachers must understand what variables inform a recommendation. Students must know when automated systems are shaping their learning pathway. Parents must have access to clear information about data collection, storage, and third-party sharing. Transparency without accessibility is not transparency.

Respect for human rights demands that AI deployment in schools be treated as a child protection issue. Data minimisation, purpose limitation, consent, and the right to withdraw are not optional features. They are conditions of legitimacy. This is where the safeguarding frame becomes essential.

Schools already operate with safeguarding protocols for physical safety, psychological wellbeing, and abuse prevention. AI governance must be integrated into that architecture.

That means:

- ➢ Every AI deployment requires a documented impact assessment prior to implementation.
- ➢ Safeguarding leads must be involved in procurement decisions.
- ➢ Staff training must include algorithmic bias, automation bias, and interpretability literacy.
- ➢ Students must have structured participation in digital governance through advisory panels or councils.
- ➢ Override authority must remain with trained educators in every high-stakes decision.

These are minimum structural safeguards—they must not be aspirational.

The academic literature on AI governance makes this point with increasing clarity. Floridi et al. (2018), in the *AI4People framework*, argued that ethical principles such as beneficence, non-maleficence, autonomy, justice, and explicability must be embedded within institutional design rather than treated as abstract virtues. Jobin, Ienca and Vayena's comparative analysis of eighty-four global AI ethics guidelines demonstrates substantial convergence around fairness, accountability, transparency, and human oversight, yet they also warn that convergence at the level of principle does not guarantee convergence at the level of enforcement (Jobin, Ienca and Vayena, 2019).

Mittelstadt (2019) goes further, cautioning that principle-based AI ethics risks becoming rhetorically powerful but operationally weak if not paired with concrete governance mechanisms. Cath et al. (2018) similarly observe that translating ethical commitments into policy requires institutional capacity, legal clarity, and oversight infrastructures capable of monitoring compliance and addressing harm. In other words, the gap between ethical declaration and ethical protection is structural. In educational systems, that gap becomes particularly consequential because children lack the bargaining power, legal literacy, and institutional leverage to contest algorithmic decisions independently. The lesson from the broader AI ethics literature is unequivocal: principles must be institutionalised or they remain symbolic. In schooling, symbolic ethics is insufficient.

SCHOOL-LEVEL GOVERNANCE: FROM PRINCIPLE TO ENFORCEABLE PRACTICE

If AI governance is to move beyond aspiration, schools require a structured policy architecture that translates global principles into enforceable daily practice. The European Union's *AI Act* provides a useful reference point representing the most developed attempt to regulate AI as behaviour rather than simply as product classification (European Union, 2024; OECD, 2023). The Act distinguishes systems by risk category, but more importantly, it imposes obligations on providers and deployers regarding documentation, human oversight, transparency, data governance, and accountability. It is, fundamentally, a behavioural regulation: it governs how AI is used, by whom, under what supervision, and with what safeguards. Schools, regardless of jurisdiction, can draw from this model.

First, communication must be institutionalised. Parents and students should receive clear, accessible disclosure of every AI system that materially affects learning, assessment, or wellbeing. Disclosure must specify: the purpose of the system, the categories of data processed, retention periods, whether third parties receive data, and the mechanism for contesting decisions. Communication cannot be buried in a generic privacy notice. It must be proactive and comprehensible.

Second, every school should maintain a public AI register. This document should list deployed systems, their function, risk level, oversight owner, and review date. Under the EU AI Act, high-risk systems require documentation, data governance measures, and human oversight protocols (European Union, 2024). Even where national law does not require this level of rigour, schools can voluntarily adopt similar internal standards. Doing so reframes AI deployment as a matter of institutional accountability rather than technological convenience.

Third, opt-out and appeal mechanisms must be operational rather than symbolic. For systems influencing assessment, placement, or behavioural escalation, families should have a defined pathway to request human review. That pathway should include time-bound response requirements and a named decision-maker. No consequential educational decision should be fully automated. This is consistent with emerging regulatory norms that prohibit solely automated decisions with significant effects without human intervention.

Fourth, procurement contracts must contain enforceable clauses addressing data minimisation, purpose limitation, model retraining boundaries, subcontractor transparency, and audit rights. Schools often lack negotiating leverage individually, but consortia and ministries can standardise contract language. If AI is behavioural infrastructure, vendor relationships must be governance relationships.

Fifth, professional training must be mandatory. Not optional workshops, but structured literacy in algorithmic bias, automation bias, interpretability, and override protocols. The EU AI Act's emphasis on human oversight highlights that supervision is not passive observation; it requires competence (European Union, 2024). An educator cannot meaningfully supervise a system they do not understand.

Sixth, safeguarding frameworks must explicitly incorporate digital risk. AI systems capable of profiling, behavioural prediction, or emotional inference should be assessed through the same lens as any intervention affecting child wellbeing. The question is not only whether the system functions accurately, but whether it alters power relations or exposes vulnerability.

Sample ethical AI policy framework for schools

The following language, drawing on established international AI governance principles (OECD, 2019; UNESCO, 2021; IEEE, 2019), illustrates how global AI principles can be translated into enforceable institutional commitments at school level.

Purpose and scope

This institution recognises that artificial intelligence systems are not neutral tools but decision-support infrastructures that may influence student learning, assessment, wellbeing, and opportunity. The purpose of this policy is to ensure that any AI system deployed within the school operates in a manner consistent with fairness, accountability, transparency, human rights, and meaningful human oversight.

This policy applies to all AI-enabled systems used in instructional delivery, assessment, student monitoring, behavioural analytics, administrative decision-making, and communication.

Human oversight and final authority

No AI system shall make or materially determine consequential educational decisions without meaningful human review.

All high-impact outputs, including grading adjustments, placement recommendations, risk classifications, or behavioural flags, must be reviewed and, where appropriate, modified or overridden by a qualified staff member.

Human oversight requires active supervision, not passive acceptance, consistent with emerging prohibitions on solely automated decisions with significant effects (UNESCO, 2021). Staff responsible for reviewing AI outputs must receive documented training in system functionality, potential bias, and override procedures.

Fairness and non-discrimination

Prior to deployment, all AI systems must undergo an institutional impact assessment, reflecting documented concerns regarding algorithmic reproduction of inequality (Ferguson, 2019; Slade and Prinsloo, 2013). This should include evaluating potential disparate effects on students across race, ethnicity, gender, disability, language background, and socioeconomic status.

Where predictive or classification systems are used, the school shall:

- Conduct periodic bias audits using disaggregated data.
- Review model outputs for disproportionate impact.
- Suspend or modify deployment if patterns of structural inequity are identified.

AI systems shall not be used to automate exclusionary or disciplinary decisions without heightened review safeguards.

Transparency and explainability

The school shall maintain a publicly accessible AI Register listing:

- The name and function of each AI system.
- The categories of data processed.
- The purpose of processing.
- The retention period.
- The designated oversight officer.
- The date of last review.

Students and families shall receive clear notification when AI systems materially influence instructional or evaluative processes.

Where feasible, systems must provide explainable outputs that allow educators to understand the basis of recommendations.

Data governance and privacy

AI deployment shall adhere to principles of data minimisation and purpose limitation. Only data strictly necessary for the educational objective shall be processed.

The school shall:

- Prohibit secondary use of student data for unrelated commercial model training without explicit institutional approval.
- Specify retention periods in vendor contracts.
- Require transparency regarding subcontractors and cross-border data transfers.
- Conduct data protection impact assessments for systems involving profiling or behavioural inference.

Students and families shall have the right to access, correct, and request deletion of personal data in accordance with applicable law.

Opt-out and appeal mechanisms

Students and parents shall have the right to request human review of AI-influenced decisions.

For designated high-impact systems, families may request alternative instructional pathways where feasible.

Appeals shall be handled by a named staff member within a defined response timeframe.

Procurement and vendor accountability

All procurement contracts involving AI systems must include clauses addressing:

- Transparency of system functionality.
- Audit rights.
- Data ownership and retention.
- Incident notification requirements.
- Prohibition of undisclosed model retraining on student data.

Where possible, procurement decisions shall include consultation with safeguarding leads, instructional staff, and student representation bodies.

Professional capacity and ongoing review

The institution shall provide mandatory professional development on AI literacy, including:

- Algorithmic bias and fairness.
- Automation bias and overreliance.
- Interpretability and explainability.
- Ethical red flags and escalation protocols.

All AI systems shall undergo annual review assessing educational impact, equity outcomes, and compliance with this policy.

Student participation

Recognising students as rights-bearing participants, the school shall establish mechanisms for student input regarding digital systems that affect their learning experience.

Student advisory panels may review proposed AI deployments and contribute to policy revision.

Safeguarding integration

AI governance shall be integrated into existing safeguarding and wellbeing frameworks.

Any system capable of profiling, behavioural prediction, or emotional inference shall undergo enhanced safeguarding review prior to deployment.

Why this matters.

This language reflects a core principle emerging from the strictest regulatory approaches globally: AI governance is behavioural. It governs how systems are used, supervised, documented, and challenged. It does not merely classify risk. It assigns responsibility.

Schools that adopt such policy language move from passive technology consumption to active institutional stewardship. These measures are minimum structural safeguards, transforming AI from an ambient technology into a governed educational practice.

ILLUSTRATIVE BEST PRACTICE SCENARIOS

The following scenarios are structured examples designed to demonstrate how artificial intelligence can be deployed in ways that advance inclusion while remaining anchored in governance, human oversight, and rights protection.

Case 1: Adaptive language support for multilingual learners

A secondary school serving a linguistically diverse population implemented an artificial intelligence enabled writing assistant to support students acquiring the language of instruction. The tool was selected for formative feedback on vocabulary range, sentence structure, and cohesion. Crucially, deployment followed a documented impact assessment.

Before adoption, the school tested the system on anonymised historical writing samples from students representing multiple dialects and language backgrounds. Teachers examined whether the tool disproportionately flagged nonstandard dialect as error. Where bias appeared, configuration settings were adjusted to reduce prescriptive correction of dialect features unrelated to academic clarity.

The system was positioned explicitly as advisory. All summative assessments remained human evaluated. Students were informed that the tool provided suggestions rather than judgments, and classroom instruction included lessons on how automated feedback systems are trained and where they may reflect dominant linguistic norms. An opt out pathway was built into the platform. Students who preferred human only feedback could request alternative support. Data retention was limited contractually to instructional purposes, with no secondary model training permitted.

Within one academic year, English language learners demonstrated measurable improvement in drafting fluency and revision frequency. More importantly, student surveys reported increased confidence in experimenting with complex sentence structures. The improvement was not attributable to automation alone. It was attributable to structured oversight, explicit bias testing, and a pedagogical framing that preserved student agency.

This model illustrates that artificial intelligence can support language inclusion when it is treated as scaffolding rather than authority.

Case 2: Assistive AI for neurodiverse learners

A middle school piloted an artificial intelligence enabled reading interface designed to support students with diagnosed dyslexia and processing speed differences. The system provided adjustable pacing, text to speech, visual chunking, and real time comprehension prompts.

Prior to implementation, the school convened a review panel including special education specialists, parents, and student representatives. The panel evaluated whether the system's comprehension prompts risked narrowing interpretive thinking by privileging literal responses. Modifications were made to ensure prompts invited inferential reasoning rather than only surface recall.

Human oversight was embedded at every stage. Teachers reviewed system generated progress reports weekly, contextualising them against classroom observation. No student placement decisions were made solely on automated data. The system was explicitly categorised internally as a support tool, not a diagnostic instrument. To protect dignity, the interface was universal rather than segregated. All students could access its features, preventing the stigmatisation of those requiring additional scaffolding. Data from usage patterns was anonymised before aggregate analysis, and no behavioural profiling features were activated.

Over two terms, students previously reluctant to participate in extended reading tasks demonstrated increased engagement time and voluntary reading frequency. Parents reported reduced frustration during homework completion. Teachers reported improved classroom inclusion, not because the system replaced professional judgment, but because it reduced cognitive load barriers that had previously impeded participation.

The success of this scenario lies not in technological sophistication, but in governance discipline. The school resisted the temptation to treat the system as diagnostic authority. It invested in oversight, transparency, and universal design principles.

Case 3: Ethics in practice

There is real-world precedent for this level of redesign.

A 2024 study commissioned by the Dutch Ministry of Education and discussed by the Netherlands Institute for Human Rights warned that adaptive learning algorithms risk reinforcing socioeconomic and migration-based inequalities when insufficiently tested across diverse student populations (Netherlands Institute for Human Rights, 2024). The report highlighted particular concerns for students from lower income backgrounds, students with migration histories, and learners with conditions such as dyslexia or attention deficit disorders. It called for stronger evaluation standards, transparency requirements, and clearer accountability structures before such systems are embedded in classrooms.

In response to similar concerns emerging in school contexts, some institutions have begun pausing pilots of adaptive platforms in order to conduct structured bias reviews in partnership with academic experts. In these cases, student feedback has been incorporated into system audits, content tagging has been revised, explainability features strengthened, and opt out mechanisms formalised prior to reimplementation. The lesson is not that artificial intelligence must be abandoned, but that trust must be built through documented oversight and participatory governance.

What matters here is not a single institution, but the posture it represents. Pausing deployment, inviting external scrutiny, incorporating student voice, and revising systems before reimplementation reflects institutional maturity. It signals a refusal to treat artificial intelligence as a neutral product to be consumed and instead recognises it as shared infrastructure requiring shared responsibility.

The larger challenge is scaling that posture. Governance redesign cannot depend on isolated acts of caution or individual leadership. It must become structural and global. If trust is to anchor artificial intelligence in schools, oversight must be embedded. AI governance must move from reactive correction to anticipatory design. That requires building institutional capacity before harm occurs, allocating budget for both software *and* oversight, and resisting vendor narratives that frame adoption as inevitable and delay as obstruction. Most critically, it requires restoring professional authority. Teachers must be trained not simply as users of AI systems, but as interpreters and challengers of those systems. Professional development must include critical data literacy, bias detection, and structured override protocols. When machine output conflicts with professional judgment, the professional must prevail.

Students must also be educated as rights-bearing participants. AI literacy in schools must focus on both tool use and critical inquiry into how systems are built, who they benefit, and what trade-offs they embed. A human-centred classroom is one in which students understand that systems are designed, and therefore contestable. This is not anti-technology. It is pro-democracy.

The human-centred classroom is one in which:

- Data serves learning rather than ranking.
- Prediction supports care rather than categorisation.
- Automation reduces administrative burden without displacing professional judgment.
- Transparency is embedded at the point of interaction.
- Student dignity is treated as non-negotiable.

Ethics, in this sense, is the condition under which innovation is legitimate, rather than being seen as a brake. The alternative is clear. Without structural redesign, AI becomes a mechanism for accelerating existing inequality, diffusing responsibility, and eroding trust. With redesign, it can support more responsive, inclusive, and reflective schooling. The choice is institutional. The technology is already here. Governance must catch up.

CONCLUSION

The evidence leaves little room for ambiguity. Artificial intelligence does not enter schools as a neutral tool. It enters as a governing infrastructure. It ranks, predicts, classifies, and nudges. It shapes which students are noticed, which are flagged, which are accelerated, and which are redirected. When that infrastructure is adopted without redesigning the ethical architecture of the institution, it does not simply assist schooling. It reorganises it.

We have now seen enough to abandon the fiction of technological innocence. Data systems trained on unequal histories reproduce unequal futures. Predictive models alter expectation. Automated scoring reshapes standards. Platform infrastructures normalise surveillance as participation. None of this requires malicious intent—only institutional passivity.

The question is no longer whether AI will shape education. It already does. The question is whether public education systems will exercise sovereignty over that shaping, or whether they will outsource it to commercial architectures optimised for scale rather than justice.

If ministries treat AI adoption as procurement rather than public governance, they erode democratic accountability at the very site where citizenship is formed. If school leaders accept algorithmic outputs without building interpretive capacity and redress mechanisms, they weaken professional authority. If safeguarding frameworks fail to incorporate digital oversight, they leave children exposed not only to data extraction, but to silent categorisation that can shadow opportunity. Neutrality is not available here.

To deploy AI in schools without enforceable bias audits, transparent decision pathways, human override authority, and participatory governance is to accept structural risk as collateral damage. And collateral damage in education is not abstract. It is measured in diminished expectations, narrowed pathways, and constrained futures. The alternative demands discipline.

- It demands that algorithmic impact assessments precede adoption, not follow controversy.
- It demands named institutional accountability for every system influencing student outcomes.
- It demands that teachers be trained as critical interpreters, not passive operators.
- It demands that students be treated as rights-bearing participants, not data subjects.
- It demands that human judgment remain sovereign in consequential decisions.

When those conditions are met, AI can serve education. Not because the technology is inherently ethical, but because the institution is.

Education is a public trust. Childhood is not an experimental environment for unexamined systems. Ethical AI in schools is not innovation management. It is the defense of democratic equality at the point where it is most fragile. The tools are already here. The governance must rise to meet them. And history will record which institutions understood that in time.

REFERENCES

Axios (2017) *Google Launches News Literacy Program.* Axios, 6 June. Available at: www.axios.com/2017/12/15/google-launches-news-literacy-program-1513302787

Axios (2020) *New Mexico Accuses Google of Violating Kids' Privacy with Data Collection.* Axios, 20 February. Available at: www.axios.com/2020/02/20/new-mexico-google-lawsuit-children-data

Bruton, S. and Childers, D. (2016) 'The ethics and politics of policing plagiarism: a qualitative study of faculty views on student plagiarism and Turnitin®', Assessment & Evaluation in Higher Education, 41(2), pp. 316–330. https://doi.org/10.1080/02602938.2015.1008981.

Cath, C., Wachter, S., Mittelstadt, B., Taddeo, M. and Floridi, L. (2018) 'Artificial intelligence and the "good society": The US, EU, and UK approach', *Science and Engineering Ethics*, 24(2), 505–528. https://doi.org/10.1007/s11948-017-9901-7

Council of International Schools (2024) 'Generative AI: A whole school approach to safeguarding children', *CIS Perspectives Blog*, 1 May. Available at: www.cois.org/about-cis/perspectives-blog/blog-post/~board/perspectives-blog/post/generative-ai-a-whole-school-approach-to-safeguarding-children

European Union (2024) Regulation (EU) 2024/1689 of the European Parliament and of the Council of 13 June 2024 laying down harmonised rules on artificial intelligence (Artificial Intelligence Act). Available at: https://eur-lex.europa.eu/eli/reg/2024/1689/oj/eng

Ferguson, R. (2019) 'Ethical challenges for learning analytics', *Journal of Learning Analytics*, 6(3), 25–30. https://doi.org/10.18608/jla.2019.63.5

Floridi, L., Cowls, J., Beltrametti, M., Chatila, R., Chazerand, P., Dignum, V., Luetge, C., Madelin, R., Pagallo, U., Rossi, F., Schafer, B., Valcke, P. and Vayena, E. (2018) 'AI4People—An ethical framework for a good AI society', *Minds and Machines*, 28(4), 689–707. https://doi.org/10.1007/s11023-018-9482-5

Fu, Q.-K. et al. (2024) 'A review of AWE feedback: types, learning outcomes, and implications', Computer Assisted Language Learning, 37(1–2), pp. 179–221. Available at: www.tandfonline.com/doi/full/10.1080/09588221.2022.2033787

GMB (2025) *AI in 1 in 5 Schools—But Staff not Trained.* GMB, 28 April. Available at: www.gmb.org.uk/news/artificial-intelligence-in-1-in-5-schools-but-staff-have-no-training and to pdf: www.gmb.org.uk/assets/components/pdf/artificial-intelligence-in-1-in-5-schools-but-staff-have-no-training.pdf

Google (2018) 'Tools for every school: G Suite for Education updates', *Google Blog*, 23 January.

Human Rights Watch (2022) *"How Dare They Peep into My Private Life?" Children's Rights Violations by Governments That Endorsed Online Learning during the COVID-19 Pandemic.* New York: Human Rights Watch.

IEEE (2019) *Ethically Aligned Design: A Vision for Prioritizing Human Wellbeing with Autonomous and Intelligent Systems.* 1st edn. IEEE. Location: New York, NY, USA. Available at: https://standards.ieee.org/wp-content/uploads/import/documents/other/ead1e.pdf

Jarke, J. and Breiter, A. (2019) 'The datafication of education', *Learning, Media and Technology*, 44(1), 1–6. https://doi.org/10.1080/17439884.2019.1573833

Jayaprakash, S.M., Moody, E.W., Lauría, E.J.M., Regan, J.R. and Baron, J.D. (2014) 'Early alert of academically at-risk students: An open source analytics initiative', *Journal of Learning Analytics*, 1(1), 6–47. https://doi.org/10.18608/jla.2014.11.3

Jobin, A., Ienca, M. and Vayena, E. (2019) 'The global landscape of AI ethics guidelines', *Nature Machine Intelligence*, 1(9), 389–399. https://doi.org/10.1038/s42256-019-0088-2

Krutka, D.G., Smits, R.M. and Willhelm, T.A. (2021) 'Don't be evil: Should we use Google in schools?', *TechTrends*, 65(4), 421–431.

Mittelstadt, B.D. (2019) 'Principles alone cannot guarantee ethical AI', *Nature Machine Intelligence*, 1(11), 501–507. https://doi.org/10.1038/s42256-019-0114-4

Morrison, S. (2020) *Google's Education Tech Has a Privacy Problem.* Vox, 21 February. Available at: www.vox.com/recode/2020/2/21/21146998/google-new-mexico-lawsuit-children-data-privacy-g-suite-education

Netherlands Institute for Human Rights (2024) *Government, help schools prevent digital systems from treating students unequally*. Available at: www.mensenrechten.nl/actueel/nieuws/2024/05/13/overheid-help-scholen-te-voorkomen-dat-digitale-systemen-hun-leerlingen-ongelijk-behandelen discussion from research report by Smeets, E., Geurts, R. and Van Helvoirt, D. with Van Zuijdam, B. (2024) *Algoritmen in het onderwijs: Een onderzoek in opdracht van het College voor de Rechten van de Mens*. Nijmegen: KBA Nijmegen and ResearchNed.

OECD (2019) *Recommendation of the Council on Artificial Intelligence (OECD/LEGAL/0449).* Available at: https://legalinstruments.oecd.org/en/instruments/oecd-legal-0449

OECD (2021) *OECD Digital Education Outlook 2021: Pushing the Frontiers with Artificial Intelligence, Blockchain and Robots*. Paris: OECD Publishing.

OECD (2023) *OECD Framework for the Classification of AI Systems: A Risk-Based Approach to Trustworthy AI.* Paris: OECD Publishing.

Ofqual (2020) *Awarding GCSE, AS and A Levels in Summer 2020: Interim Report.* London: Office of Qualifications and Examinations Regulation. www.gov.uk/government/publications/awarding-gcse-as-a-levels-in-summer-2020-interim-report

RAND Corporation (2023) *Educator Perspectives on Artificial Intelligence in U.S. Schools.* Santa Monica, CA: RAND.

Selwyn, N. (2019) *Should Robots Replace Teachers? AI and the Future of Education.* Cambridge: Polity.

Slade, S. and Prinsloo, P. (2013) 'Learning analytics: Ethical issues and dilemmas', *American Behavioral Scientist*, 57(10), 1510–1529. https://doi.org/10.1177/0002764213479366

UNESCO (2021) *Recommendation on the Ethics of Artificial Intelligence*. Paris: UNESCO.

UNESCO (2023) *Global Education Monitoring Report 2023: Technology in Education: A Tool on Whose Terms?.* Paris: UNESCO. Available at: www.hapsc.org/wp-content/uploads/2023/10/2023-Global-Education-Monitoring-Report.pdf

United Nations (1948) *Universal Declaration of Human Rights*. New York: United Nations.

United Nations (1989) *Convention on the Rights of the Child.* New York: United Nations.

Williamson, B. (2017) *Big Data in Education: The Digital Future of Learning, Policy and Practice*. London: Sage.

Williamson, B., Bayne, S. and Shay, S. (2020) 'The datafication of teaching in higher education: Critical issues and perspectives', *Teaching in Higher Education*, 25(4), 351–365. https://doi.org/10.1080/13562517.2020.1748811

Williamson, B. and Eynon, R. (2020) 'Historical threads, missing links, and future directions in AI in education', *Learning, Media and Technology*, 45(3), 223–235. https://doi.org/10.1080/17439884.2020.1798995

AI Governance Frameworks for Schools

6

It usually begins with a purchase order.

A platform promising adaptive support. A dashboard offering predictive insights. A writing assistant that claims to reduce marking time by half. The sales language is fluent in efficiency. The procurement form is short. The demonstration is impressive. The decision feels technical.

It is not.

When a school adopts an artificial intelligence system, it is not merely acquiring software. It is redistributing authority. It is deciding which judgments may be automated, which classifications may be normalised, and which forms of data will become actionable. It is determining whether professional discretion remains sovereign or becomes advisory to statistical output. Governance enters the picture late, if at all. Too often, it arrives only when something goes wrong.

International policy frameworks have been warning against this pattern for several years. The Organisation for Economic Co-operation and Development's Recommendation on Artificial Intelligence places accountability and human-centred values at the core of AI deployment, explicitly requiring organisations to ensure that responsibility for system outcomes is identifiable and enforceable (OECD, 2019). The United Nations Educational, Scientific and Cultural Organisation extends this principle further, grounding artificial intelligence governance in human rights law and calling for oversight, impact assessment, and participatory safeguards across the full lifecycle of AI systems (UNESCO, 2021).

These are not abstract declarations. They are institutional instructions. Yet, in many school systems, artificial intelligence enters through procurement channels designed for textbooks and furniture. It is evaluated for cost, compatibility, and usability. It is rarely

DOI: 10.1201/9781003662945-6

evaluated for epistemic authority, distributive impact, or child rights implications. The result is a governance inversion: the technology scales before the oversight does. This chapter argues that such inversion is unsustainable.

Artificial intelligence in education must be governed at multiple levels simultaneously. It cannot be delegated to an information technology coordinator, nor absorbed into generic data protection policy. It requires a defined architecture of responsibility spanning classroom practice, school leadership, government oversight, vendor accountability, and participatory engagement with parents and students. Why? Because artificial intelligence alters decision structures.

Research examining global AI ethics guidelines demonstrates convergence around principles of fairness, transparency, accountability, and human oversight (Jobin, Ienca and Vayena, 2019). What remains inconsistent is implementation. As Mittlestadt (2019) cautions, principles without institutional embedding risk becoming symbolic rather than protective. In educational settings, symbolism is insufficient. Children cannot litigate algorithmic harm. Teachers cannot override systems they are not trained to interpret. Parents cannot contest decisions they do not understand. Governance must therefore be designed in advance, not improvised after controversy. The task before schools is not to slow innovation. It is to constitutionalise it.

To constitutionalise artificial intelligence in education is to answer several foundational questions before deployment begins:

- ➢ Who is responsible when a predictive model misclassifies a student?
- ➢ Who has authority to override automated recommendations?
- ➢ Who evaluates disparate impact across socioeconomic or linguistic groups?
- ➢ Who ensures that data collected for learning support is not repurposed for behavioural profiling?
- ➢ Who hears the student's voice when the system's output conflicts with lived experience?

If no one can answer these questions clearly, governance is absent.

A multi-level framework does not multiply bureaucracy. It clarifies responsibility. Teachers supervise operational use. Principals steward institutional alignment. School systems enforce structural safeguards and contractual standards. Parents and students participate in oversight mechanisms that legitimise deployment. Vendors are held to documented transparency and risk management obligations. Each layer performs a distinct function, and each layer is accountable to the others.

The European Union's Artificial Intelligence Act illustrates the direction of regulatory travel. It does not regulate artificial intelligence solely by what it is, but by *how it is used* and *by whom*. It imposes obligations on deployers (schools) as well as providers (tech companies), requiring documentation, risk management, human oversight, and accountability structures for high-risk systems (European Union, 2024). The message is clear: responsibility cannot be outsourced to code. Schools, as public institutions, cannot afford to wait for external enforcement to define their governance architecture. They must build it internally. This chapter sets out that architecture.

It begins by defining role-based responsibilities across classroom, leadership, and system levels. It then proposes concrete governance instruments: oversight committees, data protection impact assessments, structured procurement protocols, and participatory advisory mechanisms. Finally, it addresses the necessity of iterative feedback loops, ensuring that artificial intelligence use is not static but continuously evaluated against educational outcomes and rights-based standards. The goal is not to create fear of artificial intelligence. It is to create capacity:

Capacity to question.
Capacity to supervise.
Capacity to correct.
Capacity to refuse.

If the previous chapter demonstrated how ethics breaks down in the absence of structure, this chapter constructs the structure itself. If Chapter 5 established that ethical failure in artificial intelligence is institutional rather than technical, Chapter 6 must now demonstrate how institutional design prevents that failure. Artificial intelligence will remain in schools. The question is whether it will remain governed.

PART I: WHAT AI GOVERNANCE IS AND WHAT IT IS NOT

If artificial intelligence is infrastructure, governance is architecture. It determines who holds the weight.

The term "AI governance" is often misunderstood in school contexts. It is often conflated with digital literacy, cybersecurity, data protection, or information technology management. These domains overlap, but they are not interchangeable. A school can teach students how to use generative tools responsibly and still lack governance. It can install firewalls, comply with data protection regulations, and still fail to address how algorithmic systems shape educational judgment. AI governance is not about tool proficiency. It is about power, responsibility, and institutional design.

At the international level, governance is defined not by technical configuration but by *behavioural obligations*. The Organisation for Economic Co-operation and Development describes AI governance in terms of accountability, human-centred values, transparency, robustness, and oversight across the lifecycle of systems (OECD, 2019). The United Nations Educational, Scientific and Cultural Organisation frames governance as a human rights obligation, requiring impact assessment, participation, and redress mechanisms where AI systems may affect individuals or communities (UNESCO, 2021). The European Union's Artificial Intelligence Act further clarifies that obligations attach not only to providers but to deployers. It regulates how systems are used, supervised, documented, and reviewed (European Union, 2024). These frameworks converge on a central principle: governance concerns conduct.

In school settings, that distinction matters profoundly. Information technology departments manage infrastructure. Cybersecurity teams protect networks. Data protection officers oversee compliance with privacy law. AI literacy initiatives teach students and teachers how to use tools critically and safely. All of these are necessary. None of them alone constitute governance. Governance begins when an institution asks: who is authorised to rely on this system's output? Under what conditions? With what safeguards? And with what consequences if harm occurs?

Consider the difference between literacy and governance. AI literacy equips a teacher to understand how a large language model generates text, what biases may arise from training data, and how to prompt responsibly. AI governance determines whether that model may be used for assessment feedback, whether outputs must be reviewed before influencing grades, whether student data may be retained by the vendor, and how disputes will be resolved. Literacy is individual competence. Governance is institutional accountability.

The distinction mirrors established safeguarding practice. Schools do not address child protection through awareness sessions alone. They embed safeguarding into policy, reporting structures, designated leads, and mandatory procedures. Every staff member is trained, but responsibility is tiered and traceable. There are clear escalation pathways. Documentation is required. Oversight is continuous. AI governance demands a similar posture.

Artificial intelligence systems increasingly influence educational classification, recommendation, and evaluation. Predictive analytics may flag attendance risk. Adaptive platforms may steer curriculum pace. Automated scoring tools may shape formative feedback. These are not trivial functions. They affect opportunity structures. When such systems operate without clearly defined oversight roles, institutional accountability becomes diffuse.

Research on algorithmic governance highlights this risk. Jobin, Ienca and Vayena (2019) demonstrate that while global AI ethics guidelines widely endorse accountability and fairness, implementation mechanisms remain inconsistent. Mittlestadt (2019) argues that principles alone cannot guarantee ethical outcomes without enforceable processes. In educational institutions, where decisions carry developmental consequences, the absence of structured oversight amplifies that vulnerability.

For professors and teachers unfamiliar with AI governance terminology, the distinction can be clarified through three contrasts. First, governance is not the same as cybersecurity. Cybersecurity protects systems from external intrusion. Governance regulates internal decision authority. A school may have exemplary network security while simultaneously allowing automated systems to influence high-stakes decisions without review. Second, governance is not equivalent to compliance. Compliance ensures adherence to legal requirements such as data protection statutes. Governance extends beyond minimum legal thresholds to address fairness, transparency, and professional responsibility. The European Union's regulatory approach illustrates this distinction by requiring documented risk management and human oversight for certain categories of AI systems, not merely lawful data processing (European Union, 2024). Third, governance is not a one-time approval process. It is iterative. The OECD explicitly calls for ongoing monitoring and evaluation across the lifecycle of AI systems (OECD, 2019). Systems evolve. Data distributions shift. Context changes. Governance must adapt accordingly. This is why AI governance is inseparable from culture.

When a school adopts artificial intelligence tools without clarifying supervisory authority, it subtly reorders professional norms. Teachers may begin to treat algorithmic outputs as neutral evidence rather than probabilistic suggestions. Students may perceive automated classifications as objective truth. Administrators may default to vendor documentation in place of institutional judgment. Governance interrupts that drift. It reasserts that systems are designed artefacts embedded in social contexts. It requires explicit conversation about how authority is distributed and retained.

In practice, this involves cultural commitments as much as procedural ones. Staff must feel authorised to question system outputs. Leadership must resist the assumption that automation equates to objectivity. Procurement processes must incorporate ethical review alongside budgetary assessment. Students and parents must have channels through which concerns can be raised without reputational risk.

The analogy to safeguarding is not rhetorical flourish. Safeguarding evolved precisely because institutions recognised that vulnerability cannot be managed informally. It requires designated leads, documented procedures, mandatory training, and clear reporting lines. Artificial intelligence, as decision-support infrastructure affecting children, warrants equivalent seriousness. AI governance therefore represents a whole-school commitment. It is distributed across classrooms, leadership offices, district oversight structures, and community engagement mechanisms. It is concerned with behaviour as much as technology. It defines who may rely on automated outputs, how those outputs are supervised, and what happens when they conflict with human judgment. The remainder of this chapter translates that conceptual distinction into operational design. Governance must be visible, traceable, and embedded. Otherwise, artificial intelligence will shape institutional practice by default rather than by design.

A governance blueprint for everyday practice

If governance is to mean anything in schools, it must be legible in ordinary institutional life. It must appear not only in principles, but in meeting structures, staff expectations, family communication, and the practical terms under which technology is allowed to enter the school at all. A useful governance blueprint therefore begins with three linked questions: who reviews artificial intelligence before it is used, under what conditions may it be used, and how do educators learn to question it well?

The first requirement is a standing oversight structure that is small enough to function and broad enough to see institutional risk clearly. In most schools, this need not be a large new bureaucracy. A workable committee can bring together senior leadership, safeguarding, data protection or legal oversight where available, curriculum expertise, and at least one classroom practitioner. Its value lies in composition as much as mandate. Artificial intelligence systems do not affect only infrastructure. They affect teaching, assessment, wellbeing, and trust. Oversight must therefore reflect the school as a whole rather than a single technical office.

The second requirement is a clear user agreement architecture. Schools often require students, parents, and staff to accept technology terms they did not write and may not fully understand. That is inadequate where artificial intelligence is concerned. Institutional user agreements should specify, in plain language, what forms of AI use are permitted, what forms require disclosure, what forms are prohibited, and what rights users retain if they wish to question or challenge AI mediated outcomes. These agreements should not read like legal disclaimers imported from vendors. They should function as civic documents that translate institutional values into intelligible expectations.

Third, educator preparation must move beyond basic tool familiarity. The crucial professional skill is not simply using AI, but reading it critically. Teachers need structured opportunities to examine where outputs appear persuasive but rest on weak inference, where confidence is mistaken for accuracy, and where apparently neutral recommendations may carry embedded assumptions about ability, behaviour, or language. AI critical thinking in schools means cultivating professional habits of interrogation: What is this system actually doing? What evidence supports this output? What may it be missing? Who might be disadvantaged if we accept it too quickly?

This blueprint also requires more disciplined collaboration with providers. Schools should expect clear lines of accountability, meaningful explanation of how systems reach outputs, and credible evidence that foreseeable risks have been tested rather than merely acknowledged. A provider that offers efficiency without transparency is not offering partnership. It is asking for trust without scrutiny.

Finally, governance must build in correction. Schools should create routine channels through which staff, students, and families can report concerns, ambiguities, or unintended effects. Those observations should not sit at the margins. They should feed directly into review, revision, and, where necessary, withdrawal. A governance framework earns legitimacy when it proves capable of learning from its own use.

PART II: FROM ETHICAL COMMITMENT TO INSTITUTIONAL DESIGN

Most educational organisations do not lack technological goodwill. They lack structure.

When school leaders say, “We need AI governance,” what they usually mean is that they need clarity. Many do not yet know where governance begins. They do not know whether it sits with IT, with safeguarding, with curriculum leadership, or with legal counsel. They do not know whether governance requires a new committee, a new policy, or simply better teacher training. The uncertainty is structural, not intellectual. Artificial intelligence governance, properly understood, is an institutional coordination problem rather than a bolt-on to an existing digital policy.

Educational institutions are layered organisations. Authority flows vertically from governing boards or ministries to principals to teachers. Responsibility flows horizontally across safeguarding, curriculum, assessment, data protection, and professional development. Artificial intelligence intersects all of these domains simultaneously. Without deliberate design, it exploits the gaps between them. The first step in building AI governance, therefore, is not drafting a policy. It is mapping institutional authority.

Step one: institutional role delineation

Before any system is deployed, the school must define—explicitly and in writing—where decision authority resides at each level of AI use.
This requires distinguishing four distinct categories of responsibility:

1. Operational Supervision: Who oversees the day-to-day use of AI tools in classrooms?
2. Institutional Approval: Who authorises adoption and ensures alignment with safeguarding and assessment integrity?
3. Structural Oversight: Who monitors systemic risk, vendor compliance, and equity impact across the institution?
4. Participatory Accountability: Who represents student and parent interests in reviewing AI deployment?

Without this delineation, responsibility becomes implied rather than assigned. Implied responsibility collapses under pressure. International governance instruments consistently emphasise accountability as traceable and assignable (OECD, 2019; UNESCO, 2021).

For schools beginning on Monday morning, the practical starting point is a short institutional memorandum that answers a simple but profound question:

If an AI system produces harm, who is responsible for investigating and responding?

That document becomes the spine of governance.

Step two: Classifying AI use by decision impact

Not all AI use requires identical oversight. Governance must be proportionate.

The European Union's Artificial Intelligence Act introduces a risk-based approach, distinguishing between minimal, limited, and high-risk systems, and attaching obligations accordingly (European Union, 2024). While schools outside the European Union may not be legally bound by this regulation, the logic is instructive. Schools should classify AI systems according to the degree to which they influence consequential educational decisions.

For example:

- ➢ Low-impact systems: AI tools used for brainstorming, drafting assistance, or non-evaluative classroom support.
- ➢ Moderate-impact systems: Adaptive learning systems influencing pacing or practice pathways.
- ➢ High-impact systems: Systems affecting grading, placement, behavioural classification, or eligibility for support.

This classification exercise is not bureaucratic. It is epistemic. It forces institutions to confront the level of authority they are delegating. High-impact systems require formal impact assessment, documented human oversight protocols, and structured review cycles. Low-impact systems may require lighter supervision but still demand transparency. The act of classification itself builds institutional literacy.

Step three: Establishing a governance body with mandate

Many schools have technology committees. Few have governance committees with defined authority. AI governance requires a formally constituted body with a written mandate. This body must operate at the school or government level depending on institutional size.

Its responsibilities should include:

- ➢ Reviewing proposed AI deployments prior to implementation.
- ➢ Evaluating documented impact assessments.
- ➢ Monitoring incident reports related to AI systems.
- ➢ Conducting annual reviews of high-impact systems.
- ➢ Recommending suspension where significant risk emerges.

The committee's authority must be clear. It is not advisory theatre. It must have the power to delay or reject deployment. Scholarly analyses of AI ethics frameworks consistently emphasise that oversight must be institutionalised to avoid principle drift (Jobin, Ienca and Vayena, 2019; Mittlestadt, 2019). In schools, institutionalisation means standing structures, recorded minutes, and procedural continuity. Governance is visible when it leaves documentation.

Step four: Embedding human oversight as a professional obligation

Human oversight cannot mean passive review of automated output. It requires competence and authority. Research on automation bias demonstrates that individuals frequently defer to algorithmic systems even when contradictory evidence exists, particularly in high-workload contexts (Parasuraman and Riley, 1997). In educational settings, this risk is amplified by time pressure and data abundance. Governance must therefore formalise override authority.

Teachers must retain final decision-making power in all consequential educational determinations. This authority must be written into policy. It must be accompanied by training in interpretability and bias awareness. It must be protected against subtle organisational pressure to "follow the data." Professional autonomy is not threatened by AI. It is threatened by the absence of governance around AI.

Step five: Aligning governance with safeguarding architecture

Schools already possess a governance model capable of handling risk: safeguarding.

Safeguarding frameworks operate through designated leads, mandatory reporting pathways, documentation requirements, and annual review cycles. They recognise that vulnerability cannot be managed informally. AI governance should be integrated into this existing architecture rather than constructed in isolation.

This means:

- ➢ Designated AI oversight leads, analogous to safeguarding leads.
- ➢ Mandatory reporting of AI-related incidents affecting students.
- ➢ Inclusion of AI risk in annual safeguarding reviews.
- ➢ Clear escalation pathways where automated systems intersect with wellbeing concerns.

UNESCO's Recommendation explicitly frames AI governance within a human rights paradigm, emphasising do-no-harm, accountability, and participatory safeguards (UNESCO, 2021). Integrating AI oversight into safeguarding aligns institutional practice with this global normative framework.

Step six: Drafting governance as behavioural policy

AI governance policy must regulate behaviour, not merely define technology. A well-drafted policy answers:

- ➢ Under what conditions may AI influence assessment?
- ➢ What documentation is required before adoption?
- ➢ How is consent obtained where applicable?
- ➢ What rights do students and parents have to contest AI-influenced decisions?
- ➢ What review cycle governs continued use?

Policy must be operational. It must contain procedural triggers. For example:

- ➢ No high-impact AI system may be deployed without a completed impact assessment approved by the governance committee.
- ➢ All high-impact systems undergo annual review.
- ➢ Families may request human review of AI-influenced decisions within a defined timeframe.

These clauses transform ethical aspiration into enforceable practice.

Step seven: Building iterative review and feedback loops

Governance is not static. AI systems evolve. Vendors update features. Data distributions shift. The OECD emphasises lifecycle governance, requiring ongoing monitoring and evaluation of AI systems (OECD, 2019). Schools must mirror this approach.

At minimum:

- ➢ Maintain an AI register documenting all deployed systems.
- ➢ Conduct annual equity impact reviews for high-impact systems.
- ➢ Collect teacher and student feedback on system usability and perceived fairness.
- ➢ Establish sunset clauses for pilot programmes requiring reauthorisation.

Without iterative review, governance degrades into initial compliance followed by institutional drift.

This is where schools can begin on Monday morning: Not with a vendor demonstration or training workshop, but with institutional mapping, risk classification, and role assignment. When authority is clarified, oversight is documented, and review cycles are embedded, artificial intelligence becomes governed practice. And that is the threshold schools must cross if they intend to remain custodians of educational judgment rather than passive hosts to algorithmic influence.

VENDOR GOVERNANCE AND CONTRACTUAL ACCOUNTABILITY

Artificial intelligence governance in schools extends into procurement, contractual architecture, and technical documentation. Schools do not build most of the systems they deploy. They inherit them. Governance therefore requires structured engagement with actors whose incentives are not identical to educational mandates. The asymmetry is obvious. Technology providers possess technical expertise, proprietary code, and legal infrastructure. Schools possess responsibility for children. Without contractual clarity, that asymmetry resolves in favour of the provider.

International governance frameworks converge on a central principle: accountability attaches not only to system design but to system deployment (OECD, 2019; European Union, 2024). The European Union Artificial Intelligence Act is explicit in distinguishing between providers and deployers and assigning obligations to both. While schools are usually deployers rather than providers, they remain responsible for ensuring that systems are used in accordance with fundamental rights and institutional obligations. This distinction is essential. Governance is not outsourced by procurement.

Due Diligence Prior to Adoption

Before entering contractual agreement with an AI vendor, institutions must require structured documentation. At minimum, providers should supply:

- A clear statement of system purpose and intended educational function.
- A description of the categories of data used for training and operation.
- Known limitations, including contexts in which performance degrades.
- Documentation of bias testing procedures and mitigation strategies.
- Data retention timelines and deletion protocols.
- Disclosure of subcontractors or third-party data processors.

These requirements align with transparency and documentation obligations embedded in international AI governance standards (OECD, 2019; UNESCO, 2021) and in regulatory regimes such as the EU AI Act (European Union, 2024). In practice, this means that procurement processes must evolve from price comparison exercises into governance evaluations. If a vendor cannot explain how a system generates a recommendation, that is not a technical inconvenience. It is a governance failure.

Contractual safeguards

Contracts must formalise behavioural constraints. At minimum, agreements should include clauses addressing:

- Prohibition of secondary use of student data for unrelated model training without explicit institutional authorisation.
- Clear allocation of liability in cases of data breach or demonstrable harm.
- Mandatory notification of substantial system updates affecting functionality.
- Audit rights permitting independent review where feasible.
- Defined data retention limits consistent with educational necessity.

Data protection regimes such as the General Data Protection Regulation (GDPR) in the European Union and the Lei Geral de Proteção de Dados in Brazil already require purpose limitation and data minimisation (European Union, 2016; Lei Geral de Proteção de Dados Pessoais (LGPD), 2018). However, AI-specific clauses are often absent from school-level contracts. Governance requires explicit integration.

Where institutions lack negotiating leverage individually, government-level or consortium procurement models can standardise expectations. Governance is strengthened when institutions negotiate collectively.

Transparency beyond marketing

Vendors frequently frame systems as "explainable" or "ethical." Governance requires verification. Explainability in an educational context does not require disclosure of proprietary source code. It requires functional intelligibility. Teachers must be able to understand:

- What variables influence a recommendation.
- Whether outputs are probabilistic or deterministic.
- What data inputs materially affect results.
- How to override or correct outputs.

Without interpretability at the point of use, human oversight is nominal.

Scholarly analysis of AI ethics repeatedly warns that principle-based commitments without operational enforceability risk becoming symbolic (Mittlestadt, 2019; Jobin, Ienca and Vayena, 2019). In procurement contexts, symbolism is often embedded in marketing language. Governance requires separating representation from demonstrable capability.

Continuous monitoring and vendor relationship management

Governance does not conclude at contract signature. AI systems are dynamic. Models are retrained. Features are updated. Interfaces shift. Institutions must therefore implement:

- Annual vendor review meetings assessing system performance and equity outcomes.
- Documentation of any significant algorithmic modifications.
- Reassessment of risk classification when functionality expands.
- Clear communication to staff and families when changes occur.

The OECD emphasises lifecycle governance, requiring ongoing evaluation rather than static compliance (OECD, 2019). Schools must adopt the same posture. Vendor relationships must be treated as governance partnerships rather than service subscriptions. AI governance in schools is partly a procurement reform project, but without contractual discipline, institutional governance collapses under commercial pressure.

PROFESSIONAL CAPACITY AND CULTURAL TRANSFORMATION

Artificial intelligence governance will fail in schools that treat it as nothing more than a compliance exercise or technical upskilling problem. Governance succeeds only when professional judgment is strengthened rather than displaced. Schools are communities of professionals, deep with pedagogical expertise, subject knowledge, and an understanding of context. When AI systems enter these institutions, they introduce a further decision logic: probabilistic inference derived from historical data. Governance must mediate between these competing logics. If it does not, the danger is that standard practice is absorbed into an overreliance on algorithmic decision-making and text generation.

Early research on automation bias demonstrates that humans systematically over-rely on algorithmic outputs, particularly in complex environments and under workload pressure (Parasuraman and Riley, 1997). Subsequent research in decision sciences confirms that algorithmic recommendations often acquire an aura of objectivity, even when users know they are imperfect. This is exacerbated by these outputs becoming further polished as AI tools increase in sophistication. In schools, where teachers manage high cognitive and emotional loads, the temptation to treat dashboards as authoritative is predictable. Governance, therefore, must do more than instruct educators to "be critical." It must build structured interpretive competence.

Algorithmic literacy as professional practice

AI literacy for students is widely discussed. AI literacy for educators is less clearly defined. Yet governance depends on it. Professional AI literacy should include:

- Understanding the difference between correlation and causation in predictive systems.
- Recognising proxy variables that may encode socioeconomic or demographic bias.
- Identifying the limits of model generalisation across populations.
- Distinguishing between decision-support and decision-automation.

The OECD Recommendation emphasises that actors involved in AI systems must possess adequate understanding to ensure accountability (OECD, 2019). UNESCO similarly highlights the need for capacity-building to enable meaningful human oversight (UNESCO, 2021). Without interpretive literacy, oversight becomes ceremonial. In practice, this means structured professional development programmes that go beyond tool demonstrations. Educators must examine real system outputs, simulate override scenarios, and analyse case-based ethical dilemmas. Governance training must be experiential.

Preserving professional authority

Governance must also address a subtler cultural risk: erosion of professional confidence. If institutional discourse frames AI as more objective than human judgment, teachers may begin to internalise a secondary status. Over time, institutional deference to algorithmic output can become habitual. The system becomes the arbiter; the educator becomes the implementer. This inversion undermines both accountability and legitimacy. Policy must therefore codify a principle: in all consequential educational decisions, human judgment prevails.

This principle aligns with regulatory approaches that restrict fully automated decision-making in high-impact contexts (European Union, 2024). It also resonates with established professional ethics in education, which place responsibility for student welfare and assessment with qualified educators. Codification matters. When override authority is written into policy, it is protected from cultural drift.

Embedding AI governance in existing professional structures

Governance documents can be written in a week. Culture takes years. But cultural transformation accelerates when governance aligns with familiar institutional mechanisms. Schools already operate through:

- Curriculum review cycles
- Safeguarding audits
- Assessment moderation processes
- Continuing professional development requirements

AI governance should integrate into these structures rather than create parallel bureaucracies.

For example:

- AI-influenced assessment tools should be reviewed during moderation meetings.
- Safeguarding training should incorporate digital profiling risks.
- Curriculum committees should examine AI use within subject delivery.
- Annual performance reviews should include reflection on digital tool governance.

This integration reinforces the message that AI governance is part of professional responsibility.

Student and parent literacy as governance reinforcement

Professional capacity alone is insufficient. Governance becomes robust when transparency extends outward. The Convention on the Rights of the Child affirms the right of children to participate in decisions affecting them (United Nations, 1989). In the context of AI, this right translates into informational transparency and structured participation.

Students should be informed when AI systems materially influence learning pathways or assessment processes. Age-appropriate explanation builds trust and democratic awareness. Parent communication must be proactive rather than reactive. When students understand that systems are designed and contestable, institutional accountability strengthens.

From training to norm formation

The ultimate goal of professional capacity building is about the formation of norms, rather than merely accumulating knowledge.

Governance becomes durable when:

- Questioning algorithmic output is normalised.
- Pausing deployment is seen as prudent rather than resistant.
- Documenting uncertainty is valued rather than concealed.
- Ethical review precedes innovation rather than follows controversy.

The literature on organisational governance emphasises that formal structures are necessary but insufficient without cultural internalisation (Cath, 2018). In schools, culture shapes daily behaviour more powerfully than policy documents. Therefore, governance training must be continuous, evolving with system deployment and reinforced through leadership messaging and peer discourse.

ITERATIVE REVIEW AND ADAPTIVE GOVERNANCE

No governance framework survives contact with technological change unless it is designed to revise itself. Artificial intelligence systems are not static instructional materials. They are adaptive, updateable, and frequently retrained. Vendors refine models. Data distributions shift. User behaviour changes. Regulatory standards evolve. A governance structure that treats deployment as a one-time approval event will decay quietly. The question is not whether systems change. It is whether institutional oversight keeps pace.

Lifecycle governance rather than one-off approval

The Organisation for Economic Co-operation and Development emphasises that trustworthy artificial intelligence requires continuous monitoring, evaluation, and adjustment across the system lifecycle (OECD, 2019). Governance, therefore, must extend beyond pre-deployment assessment into sustained supervision. For schools, this requires formal review cycles.

High-impact systems should be subject to:

- Annual impact reassessment, including equity analysis.
- Documentation of any material functionality changes introduced by the provider.

- Review of incident reports or complaints associated with the system.
- Confirmation that human oversight mechanisms remain operational and understood.

Moderate-impact systems may follow a lighter review cadence, but they must not disappear into infrastructural invisibility. The act of scheduled review does more than ensure compliance—it preserves institutional memory. Without it, responsibility disperses as staff change roles and attention shifts elsewhere.

Institutional memory and documentation

Educational institutions experience high turnover in leadership, teaching staff, and governance bodies. AI systems often outlast the individuals who authorised them. Adaptive governance requires documentation structures that survive personnel change. At minimum, institutions should maintain:

- An AI Register documenting all deployed systems, their purpose, risk classification, oversight lead, and review date.
- A decision log recording approval rationale and conditions of deployment.
- An incident and escalation record detailing system failures, override decisions, or reported harms.
- Archived versions of vendor documentation and contractual amendments.

Documentation means traceability, and therefore accountability. Scholarly analyses of AI governance frameworks repeatedly emphasise that accountability requires the ability to reconstruct decision pathways (Jobin, Ienca and Vayena, 2019). In a school context, that reconstruction must be possible years after initial deployment.

Structured feedback loops

Governance cannot rely solely on formal committees. It must incorporate lived experience. Teachers, students, and parents interact with AI systems daily. Their observations often surface issues long before formal audits detect them. Institutions should therefore embed structured feedback mechanisms, such as:

- Anonymous staff reporting channels for AI-related concerns.
- Student surveys assessing perceived fairness or clarity of AI-influenced processes.
- Parent consultation forums following major deployments.
- Formal review sessions during curriculum or safeguarding audits.

Feedback must be documented and reviewed by the governance body. It must not dissolve into informal conversation. Participatory governance aligns with human rights-based frameworks that emphasise inclusive stakeholder involvement in AI oversight (UNESCO, 2021). In educational institutions, participation strengthens legitimacy.

Sunset clauses and reauthorisation

Perhaps the most underutilised governance mechanism in schools is the sunset clause. Pilot programmes frequently become permanent by inertia. Adaptive learning tools remain embedded long after their initial justification has faded. Adaptive governance requires expiration by default. High-impact AI systems should be authorised for defined periods, after which reapproval is required. Reauthorisation should depend on:

- Evidence of educational benefit.
- Absence of documented disparate impact.
- Ongoing compliance with data governance requirements.
- Continued staff competence in oversight.

This mechanism transforms governance from passive continuation to active choice. It also mitigates vendor lock-in, which can distort institutional decision-making over time.

Escalation and suspension protocols

Governance must include the capacity to pause. If equity analysis reveals disproportionate impact, if a data breach occurs, or if system behaviour deviates materially from documentation, institutions must have authority to suspend deployment pending review. The European Union's regulatory model reflects this principle by empowering supervisory authorities to restrict or withdraw non-compliant systems (European Union, 2024). While schools are not regulators, they can mirror this logic internally. Suspension authority should be explicit within policy. Without it, institutions become procedurally obligated to continue using systems even when doubt arises. Pausing is not failure: it is governance functioning as intended.

Adaptive governance as cultural commitment

Iterative review mechanisms only operate when institutional culture values revision. Educational institutions are accustomed to curriculum reform, assessment moderation, and safeguarding audits. AI governance must be treated with equivalent seriousness. When staff understand that system review is routine rather than exceptional, defensive postures diminish. Transparency increases. Concerns surface earlier. Trust deepens. Governance, in this sense, becomes anticipatory rather than reactive.

CLOSING THE FRAMEWORK

At this stage, the architecture is complete. Artificial intelligence governance in schools requires:

- Clear delineation of responsibility across institutional layers.
- Risk classification proportional to decision impact.
- A formally mandated oversight body.
- Contractual discipline in vendor relationships.
- Professional capacity that protects human judgment.
- Iterative review mechanisms that preserve accountability over time.

None of these elements is radical. Together, they are transformative. The absence of governance does not produce neutrality. It produces default rule by system design. The presence of governance restores institutional agency.

Educational institutions most often exist to cultivate human judgment, democratic participation, and equitable opportunity. Artificial intelligence will intersect with each of these missions. The question is whether that intersection is supervised or incidental. AI governance frameworks do not constrain innovation. They legitimise it.

INSTITUTIONAL CODES OF CONDUCT AND BEHAVIOURAL PROTOCOLS

Governance structures without behavioural norms remain fragile. Oversight committees can be formed. Registers can be drafted. Contracts can be negotiated. Yet if everyday conduct is undefined, artificial intelligence seeps into practice through informal habit rather than deliberate choice. Institutions require both structural governance and behavioural clarity.

Educational systems already operate under professional codes of conduct governing safeguarding, assessment integrity, and academic honesty. Artificial intelligence introduces new behavioural ambiguities that those codes were not designed to anticipate. Without explicit integration, ethical expectations remain implicit and therefore inconsistently applied. The first governance task at this level is definitional. Institutions must articulate where artificial intelligence use intersects with core professional obligations. Three domains are particularly sensitive.

First, assessment. If educators use generative systems to design assessment criteria, generate feedback, or suggest grades, what level of disclosure is required? If predictive tools influence placement decisions, at what point must human reasoning be documented? Assessment is not merely administrative—it can significantly shape life chances. Behavioural norms must therefore clarify that final evaluative authority rests with qualified professionals and that any AI-assisted assessment must be reviewable and defensible independent of system output. There is too much at stake to think otherwise.

Second, data interpretation. When dashboards flag students as "at risk," what constitutes responsible professional response? Governance must define that algorithmic classification triggers an inquiry rather than jumping to conclusions. A flagged status must never substitute for engaging with the people involved. Professional codes should require documentation when algorithmic recommendations are followed or overridden in high-impact decisions. Such documentation protects both students and staff by ensuring decision-making is auditable.

Third, student use of artificial intelligence. Many institutions focus narrowly on plagiarism or academic integrity. Governance requires a broader frame. Students must understand not only when AI use is permitted but under what conditions it aligns with learning objectives. Banning AI simply pushes it underground. At the other extreme, unrestricted acceptance erodes the development of vital skills. Behavioural codes should therefore distinguish between formative assistance, collaborative ideation, and full substitution. Transparency norms, including disclosure where appropriate, cultivate ethical literacy rather than adversarial enforcement. Carrots are always better than sticks when it comes to creating a healthy educational climate.

The development of such behavioural codes should not occur in isolation. They must be aligned with existing professional ethics frameworks and institutional missions. Where codes conflict with pedagogical philosophy, revision must be explicit rather than assumed.

Importantly, behavioural governance should not be written in punitive language. Its purpose is not surveillance but clarity. Research on institutional ethics consistently demonstrates that cultures grounded in articulated norms exhibit higher levels of internal accountability than those reliant solely on sanctions. When expectations are transparent, professional autonomy is strengthened rather than constrained.

Codes of conduct must also address disclosure obligations. Where artificial intelligence materially shapes learning pathways or assessment processes, students and families should be informed. The right of children to participate in decisions affecting them, articulated in international child rights instruments, extends to digital mediation of their educational experience. Transparency at the behavioural level operationalises that right.

Finally, behavioural governance requires internal review mechanisms. Codes must not be static declarations. They should be revisited annually, informed by incident reports, technological developments, and community feedback. This iterative revision ensures that norms evolve alongside practice rather than trailing behind it.

When institutional conduct is clarified, governance ceases to be abstract. It becomes daily practice. Artificial intelligence in education is not governed solely by committees or contracts. It is governed by what teachers choose to accept, question, override, or disclose in the course of ordinary work. Codes of conduct transform those choices from individual improvisation into collective discipline. Without behavioural protocols, structural governance is porous. With them, governance becomes cultural.

VERTICAL COORDINATION AND ESCALATION PATHWAYS

Artificial intelligence governance in schools cannot rely on horizontal agreement alone. It must function vertically. Concerns raised in classrooms must move upward with clarity. Decisions taken at government or board level must move downward with accountability. Without defined pathways, governance becomes fragmented. Educational institutions are stratified systems. Teachers operate at the point of contact. School leaders manage institutional alignment. Government officials or governing boards negotiate procurement and compliance obligations. Artificial intelligence cuts across all three layers simultaneously. If communication flows only informally, responsibility dissolves between them.

The first requirement is a documented escalation protocol. When a teacher identifies a potential issue with an AI system, whether a suspected bias in output, a malfunction affecting grading, or a concern raised by a student, there must be a clear reporting pathway. This pathway should specify:

- To whom the concern is reported at school level.
- The timeframe within which acknowledgement is required.
- The conditions under which the matter is elevated to the governance committee.
- The threshold for school system or board notification.

The absence of such clarity produces two predictable outcomes. Minor concerns accumulate without review. Major concerns trigger reactive crisis management. Neither reflects institutional maturity. Escalation pathways should mirror safeguarding protocols. When safeguarding concerns arise, educators do not deliberate privately. They report through designated channels. Artificial intelligence systems influencing assessment, classification, or behavioural monitoring warrant comparable seriousness. This is more than a metaphor. In both cases, potential harm to students is shaped through institutional practice.

Vertical coordination also requires downward accountability. School systems or boards frequently approve procurement decisions affecting multiple schools. If an issue is identified at one site, information must flow laterally and vertically. A flagged bias in one school's deployment may signal systemic risk. Governance bodies at system level should therefore maintain cross institutional incident logs and ensure that lessons learned in one context inform others.

The European Union's regulatory framework emphasises deployer responsibility, meaning that entities using AI systems retain obligations even when systems are procured externally (European Union, 2024). For educational institutions, this reinforces that approval at system level does not absolve classroom level responsibility, nor does classroom level concern negate institutional accountability."

Clear documentation supports this coordination. Each escalation should generate a record containing:

- Description of the issue.
- Immediate action taken.
- Determination of risk level.
- Decision regarding continuation, modification, or suspension.
- Follow-up review date.

Such documentation is not designed to assign blame. It creates institutional learning.

Escalation pathways must also define authority to pause deployment. If a system is suspected of causing significant inequity or operational harm, the governance structure must empower designated leaders to suspend its use pending review. Without this authority, escalation becomes symbolic. The institution recognises risk yet continues operation. This is the point at which governance either functions or fails.

Vertical coordination further extends to communication with families. Where an incident materially affects students, transparent communication must occur at the appropriate level. The instinct to minimise disclosure in order to avoid reputational risk undermines trust. Governance requires proportionate transparency.

Importantly, escalation protocols must not create deterrents to reporting. Teachers should not fear professional repercussions for questioning system outputs. Students should not fear academic penalty for raising concerns about automated decisions. Institutional culture must signal that reporting strengthens governance rather than threatens it.

Coordination also requires periodic review of the escalation system itself. Annual audits should examine whether concerns were resolved within defined timeframes, whether patterns of issue recurrence exist, and whether additional safeguards are required. Governance becomes robust when it examines its own processes.

Finally, vertical integration must operate in both directions. Policy revisions at governance or board level must be communicated clearly to classroom educators. Professional development updates should accompany significant policy shifts. Governance cannot reside in leadership documents alone. It must reach practice.

Artificial intelligence spreads decision-making across different levels of an institution. Without clear coordination, responsibility becomes unclear and accountability weakens. Where escalation pathways are clear, institutions respond proportionately. Where they are absent, institutions react defensively. Governance is measured not by the absence of problems but by the clarity of response when problems arise.

GOVERNANCE CAPACITY ACROSS UNEQUAL CONTEXTS

Artificial intelligence governance cannot be designed only for well-resourced institutions. Educational systems operate under radically different material conditions. Some schools have dedicated compliance officers and legal teams. Others rely on a single principal balancing administrative, pedagogical, and safeguarding duties simultaneously. Governance must therefore be principled yet scalable.

The risk of inequity operates in two directions. On one side, under-resourced schools may adopt AI systems precisely because they promise efficiency. Predictive dashboards, automated grading tools, and adaptive tutoring platforms are often marketed as solutions to staffing shortages. Where governance capacity is limited, these systems may become substitutes for human support rather than supplements to it. Research on digitalisation in education consistently demonstrates that technological systems are most intensively deployed in contexts under accountability pressure (Williamson, 2017). Without structured oversight, such deployment risks entrenching inequality rather than alleviating it. On the other side, governance frameworks that demand extensive audits, complex documentation, and specialised expertise may be unattainable in low-capacity environments. If governance becomes administratively burdensome, well-resourced institutions will comply while others default to informal practice. The answer is not to lower standards. It is to clarify minimum viable governance. Every institution, regardless of context, can implement three foundational measures.

First, visible responsibility. Even in small schools, one designated individual must hold oversight responsibility for AI deployment. This need not be a new role. It may be assigned to an existing leader. What matters is clarity. Second, risk awareness. Institutions should conduct a simple classification of AI systems according to decision impact. Even without formal legal instruments, schools can identify which systems influence grading, placement, or behavioural categorisation. High-impact systems warrant heightened caution irrespective of jurisdiction. Third, documentation of concern. A basic incident log recording AI-related issues establishes traceability. It requires minimal resources, yet signals institutional seriousness.

Beyond these foundational steps, governance can scale proportionally. Governance-level consortia may centralise vendor review to reduce duplication of effort. Ministries may issue template impact assessment frameworks. Universities can partner with local schools to conduct bias analysis as part of research collaboration. Regional cooperation reduces individual burden while preserving the integrity of any oversight.

Global regulatory trajectories reinforce the importance of this scalable approach. The European Union's risk-tier model assigns obligations proportionate to system impact (European Union, 2024). Brazil's Lei Geral de Proteção de Dados establishes rights-based data governance without prescribing identical procedural burdens across sectors (ANPD, 2024, 2025; Brazil, 2018). In the United States, state-level initiatives such as Colorado's Artificial Intelligence Act similarly emphasise deployer responsibility while recognising contextual variation (Colorado General Assembly, 2024). These frameworks demonstrate that governance can be differentiated without being diluted.

The deeper issue, however, is cultural rather than procedural. Institutions with limited resources often possess strong relational cultures. Teachers know students personally. Decision-making remains human-centred by necessity. Governance frameworks must preserve this strength. Artificial intelligence should not displace relational knowledge under the guise of efficiency. In low-capacity environments, human judgment is often the institution's most valuable asset.

Conversely, highly resourced institutions face a different risk: overreliance on technical sophistication. Advanced analytics may create the illusion of comprehensive oversight while obscuring interpretive complexity. Governance in these contexts requires restraint and critical scrutiny rather than expansion.

In both cases, proportional governance rests on the same core principle: artificial intelligence must not exceed any institution's ability to supervise it. This principle is not anti-innovation. It is common sense. Educational systems that adopt technologies beyond their oversight capacity expose themselves to structural vulnerability. Governance maturity, therefore, should precede high-impact deployment. Where maturity is developing, pilot programmes with sunset clauses and limited scope offer responsible experimentation.

Finally, global equity requires knowledge-sharing networks. Ministries and professional associations can facilitate exchange of governance practices across regions. International organisations have already begun articulating AI ethics frameworks. The next phase must focus on practical institutional translation that respects contextual variation while preserving rights-based standards. Artificial intelligence governance in schools is not a competition in regulatory sophistication. It is a commitment to safeguarding institutional integrity across diverse conditions. When governance is scaled thoughtfully, it strengthens rather than fragments educational systems. When capacity is ignored, innovation becomes uneven and trust erodes.

CONCLUSION: BUILDING GOVERNANCE AS INSTITUTIONAL PRACTICE

Artificial intelligence governance in schools is a developmental process. No institution begins fully formed. Schools do not wake up with perfect oversight structures, fully trained staff, and aligned vendor contracts. They begin where they are. Every educational institution shares the same structural starting point: professional commitment to students, layered authority, and evolving digital practice. From that shared foundation, governance maturity develops over time.

Leadership development is part of that maturation. School leaders must learn to interpret technological claims with discernment, to ask structured questions about data and oversight, and to recognise when institutional capacity is outpaced by system complexity. That learning is iterative. It cannot be downloaded in a workshop. It must be cultivated through reflective practice and peer exchange.

Staff development follows a similar pattern. Educators will not become algorithmic specialists, nor should they. What they require is confidence in questioning, clarity in overriding authority, and familiarity with institutional pathways for concern. When questioning becomes normal rather than exceptional, governance becomes cultural.

Institutions benefit profoundly from collective learning. Building communities of practice across schools, school governance bodies, and universities allows governance experience to circulate. One school's incident report becomes another's preventative insight. Regional networks can share impact assessment templates, procurement clauses, and professional development resources. Collaborative governance reduces duplication of effort and mitigates resource inequality.

Partnerships with higher education institutions can also strengthen oversight capacity. Universities frequently possess research expertise in data ethics, algorithmic fairness, and educational technology evaluation. Structured collaboration allows schools to access analytical depth without internal expansion of administrative burden.

Ministries and professional associations play an enabling role here. By providing model frameworks, shared documentation standards, and guidance notes, they reduce fragmentation and reinforce coherence across institutions. Governance does not require uniformity, but it does benefit from shared language.

It is important to emphasise that governance development is cumulative. Institutions move through stages. Initial inventory leads to role clarity. Role clarity supports structured review. Structured review enables cultural confidence. Cultural confidence sustains adaptive refinement.

At no point is perfection required. What is required is visible commitment. Artificial intelligence will continue to integrate into educational systems across jurisdictions and resource levels. Institutions that approach governance as a learning process rather than a compliance burden build resilience. They retain professional authority. They preserve trust.

The next chapter turns to the regulatory frameworks that increasingly shape this terrain. Legal obligations matter. They provide minimum thresholds and formal rights protections. Yet law operates most effectively where institutions have already clarified their own responsibilities. Governance, in that sense, precedes compliance.

Educational institutions have navigated curricular reform, safeguarding transformation, and digital integration before. Artificial intelligence is not the first systemic shift they have encountered. It is the latest. With deliberate structure, collaborative learning, and sustained reflection, schools and universities can shape this transition responsibly. The work takes time. And it begins, as governance always does, with clarity.

REFERENCES

ANPD (2024) *Tratamento de dados pessoais de crianças e adolescentes*. Brasília: Autoridade Nacional de Proteção de Dados. Available at: www.gov.br/anpd/pt-br/acesso-a-informacao/participacao-social/outras-acoes/documentos/ts_04_24_corrigido.pdf

ANPD (2025) *Regulatory Agenda for the 2025–2026 biennium*. Brasília: Autoridade Nacional de Proteção de Dados. Available at: www.gov.br/anpd/pt-br/acesso-a-informacao/institucional/atos-normativos/regulamentacoes_anpd/agenda_regulatoria_25_26___ingles___revisada_final_fev25.pdf

Brazil (2018) *Lei No. 13.709, de 14 de agosto de 2018: Lei Geral de Proteção de Dados Pessoais (LGPD)*. Brasília: Presidência da República. Available at: www.planalto.gov.br/ccivil_03/_ato2015-2018/2018/lei/l13709.htm

Cath, C. (2018) 'Governing artificial intelligence: Ethical, legal and technical opportunities and challenges', *Philosophical Transactions of the Royal Society A*, 376(2133), 20180080.

Colorado General Assembly (2024) Consumer Protections for Artificial Intelligence (SB24-205). 2024 Regular Session. Denver, CO: Colorado General Assembly. Available at: https://leg.colorado.gov/bills/sb24-205

European Union (2016) 'Regulation (EU) 2016/679 of the European Parliament and of the Council of 27 April 2016 on the protection of natural persons with regard to the processing of personal data and on the free movement of such data (General Data Protection Regulation)', *Official Journal of the European Union*, L119, 1–88. Available at: https://eur-lex.europa.eu/eli/reg/2016/679/oj

European Union (2024) 'Regulation (EU) 2024/1689 of the European Parliament and of the Council laying down harmonised rules on artificial intelligence (Artificial Intelligence Act)', *Official Journal of the European Union*. Available at: https://eur-lex.europa.eu/eli/reg/2024/1689/oj

Jobin, A., Ienca, M. and Vayena, E. (2019) 'The global landscape of AI ethics guidelines', *Nature Machine Intelligence*, 1(9), 389–399. https://doi.org/10.1038/s42256-019-0088-2

Lei Geral de Proteção de Dados Pessoais (LGPD) (2018) Law No. 13,709/2018 (Brazil). Available at: www.planalto.gov.br/ccivil_03/_ato2015-2018/2018/lei/l13709.htm

Mittlestadt, B.D. (2019) 'Principles alone cannot guarantee ethical AI', *Nature Machine Intelligence*, 1(11), November 2019, 501–507 doi: 10.1038/s42256-019-0114-4

OECD (2019) *Recommendation of the Council on Artificial Intelligence (OECD/LEGAL/0449).* Paris: OECD Publishing. Available at: https://legalinstruments.oecd.org/en/instruments/oecd-legal-0449

Parasuraman, R. and Riley, V. (1997) 'Humans and Automation: Use, Misuse, Disuse, Abuse', *Human Factors*, 39(2), 230–253. Available at: https://web.mit.edu/16.459/www/parasuraman.pdf

UNESCO (2021) *Recommendation on the Ethics of Artificial Intelligence.* Paris: UNESCO. Available at: https://unesdoc.unesco.org/ark:/48223/pf0000386693

United Nations (1989) *Convention on the Rights of the Child.* New York: United Nations.

Williamson, B. (2017). *Big Data in Education: The Digital Future of Learning, Policy and Practice.* London: SAGE. Available at: doi:10.4135/9781529714920

Regulatory Landscape

Privacy Laws, EU AI Act, COPPA, and Beyond

7

PART I: EXISTING REGULATORY ARCHITECTURE AND ETHICS GOVERNING AI IN EDUCATION

Regulation as historical response

Regulation rarely precedes technological transformation. It consolidates after power has shifted. It is said that regulation always trails innovation.

Modern data protection law did not arise because societies anticipated digital saturation. It emerged because the aggregation of personal information at scale destabilised previously informal boundaries of informational restraint. Alan Westin's early articulation of privacy as the claim to control personal information (Westin, 1967) captured an anxiety that would later crystallise into formal legal doctrine. By the 1970s, concerns over centralised computerised records led to the articulation of Fair Information Practice Principles, which became foundational to both European and international data protection regimes (Department of Health, Education, and Welfare Advisory Committee, 1973).

The trajectory from principle to statute culminated, in Europe, in the General Data Protection Regulation (Regulation (EU) 2016/679). The GDPR formalised limits once institutional asymmetries became too significant to ignore. Artificial intelligence regulation follows a similar arc. For decades, algorithmic systems shaped discrete domains

DOI: 10.1201/9781003662945-7

without sustained public scrutiny. Yet as predictive analytics, machine learning classification systems, and generative models began influencing high-stakes decisions, credit allocation, hiring, welfare eligibility, policing, admissions, grading, the ethical stakes intensified.

The publication of Safiya Noble's *Algorithms of Oppression* (2018) and Cathy O'Neil's *Weapons of Math Destruction* (2016) crystallised a public understanding that algorithmic systems are not neutral calculators but sociotechnical infrastructures capable of amplifying structural inequality. Ruha Benjamin's *Race After Technology* (2019) further demonstrated how automated systems can reproduce racial hierarchies under the guise of objectivity. Virginia Eubanks' *Automating Inequality* (2018) traced the entanglement of algorithmic governance and welfare policy, illustrating how predictive tools can entrench disadvantage. These works exposed a pattern: *automated systems, when deployed without oversight, tend to reflect and intensify historical stratification.*

As artificial intelligence entered education, through automated grading, predictive risk scoring, behavioural monitoring, and generative assistance, the same concerns migrated into schooling. Explored in Chapter 3, the Ofqual grading controversy in the United Kingdom in 2020 revealed how statistical standardisation can encode prior inequality into present outcomes. Investigations into pandemic-era educational technologies documented invasive surveillance and data exploitation affecting millions of children (Human Rights Watch, 2022). Regulation, in this context, is not reactionary overreach. It is governance catching up to infrastructural transformation.

The European Union Artificial Intelligence Act (Regulation (EU) 2024/1689) represents the most comprehensive attempt to date to legislate algorithmic systems through a risk-tier model. Its emergence is historically consistent: as algorithmic decision-making systems expand their reach into domains affecting fundamental rights, formal boundary setting intensifies.

Ethical foundations: Power, children, and the public character of education

Regulation is not merely administrative. It expresses moral judgment about where power should be limited. Artificial intelligence systems reconfigure power in subtle ways. They convert probabilistic correlations into decision signals. They translate historical data into predictive categories. They embed optimisation logics that prioritise efficiency, accuracy, or engagement over deliberative judgment.

Political philosopher Langdon Winner argued that technologies can embody forms of power and authority that shape social order (Winner, 1980). Algorithmic systems exemplify this claim. They operationalise categories that distribute opportunity and risk.

In education, this redistribution carries particular weight. Education is not simply a service market. It is a constitutional institution responsible for cultivating democratic agency, mobility, and intellectual development. Decisions made within educational systems shape life trajectories. When algorithmic systems influence those decisions, they alter the architecture of opportunity.

Danielle Citron (2008) warned that automated administrative systems can produce "technological due process" failures when opacity and scale combine to undermine procedural fairness. Subsequent scholarship on algorithmic fairness and accountability has demonstrated how predictive systems may encode bias through proxy variables and training data limitations (Barocas and Selbst, 2016; Selbst et al., 2019).

For minors, the ethical stakes intensify. Children lack bargaining power, legal literacy, and institutional leverage. They are subject to data extraction and automated categorisation without meaningful consent. UNESCO's 2021 *Recommendation on the Ethics of Artificial Intelligence* explicitly situates AI governance within a human rights framework, emphasising proportionality, do-no-harm, and the protection of vulnerable populations.

The ethical case for AI regulation in education rests on three interlocking commitments:

1. Protection of fundamental rights, including privacy, equality, and procedural fairness.
2. Preservation of democratic accountability in public institutions.
3. Prevention of structural harm produced by opaque optimisation systems.

Regulation is therefore not antagonistic to educational innovation. It is the democratic articulation of boundaries around power in domains affecting children.

Why there is no global AI regulator

Despite growing normative convergence, there is no global artificial intelligence authority.

The absence is structural rather than accidental. Education largely remains constitutionally embedded within nation states. Data governance reflects territorial sovereignty. Legal systems differ in their treatment of administrative authority, corporate responsibility, and individual rights. Economic strategies diverge between jurisdictions seeking to promote technological competitiveness and those prioritising consumer protection. The result is regulatory pluralism.

The European Union has adopted a comprehensive risk-tier framework through the Artificial Intelligence Act. The United States regulates children's data primarily through sectoral statutes such as the Children's Online Privacy Protection Act, alongside emerging state-level AI legislation. Brazil's Lei Geral de Proteção de Dados embeds rights-based data governance, including provisions relevant to automated decision-making. Singapore's Personal Data Protection Act and Model AI Governance Framework emphasise accountability and explainability within a flexible governance model (Personal Data Protection Act (PDPA), 2012).

At the multilateral level, the OECD Recommendation on Artificial Intelligence (2019) and UNESCO's Recommendation (2021) articulate global normative principles without binding enforcement power. Fragmentation, however, does not imply normative vacuum. There is emerging convergence around core themes: fairness, transparency, accountability, human oversight, and risk-based proportionality (Jobin, Ienca and Vayena, 2019). What differs is enforcement architecture and institutional design.

For schools and universities operating across jurisdictions, this produces layered compliance complexity. Governance must therefore be institutionally grounded before it can be jurisdictionally navigated.

Regulatory acceleration and compounding educational risk

Regulatory activity is intensifying because educational risk is compounding. First, scale. Generative AI systems have entered classrooms at unprecedented speed. Adoption has often outpaced policy formation. Second, infrastructural embedding. AI functionalities are now integrated into learning management systems, grading platforms, analytics dashboards, and admissions tools. Third, harm visibility. Litigation and investigative reporting have increased public awareness of algorithmic bias and surveillance in educational contexts. Cases involving automated proctoring, discriminatory admissions screening, and data misuse have shifted debate from theoretical critique to legal scrutiny. Fourth, rights framing. International human rights bodies increasingly recognise digital mediation of education as a rights-sensitive domain. The convergence of these factors produces legislative acceleration.

Innovation vs. regulation: A false dichotomy

The claim that regulation undermines innovation is historically fragile. Regulatory clarity often stabilises innovation by defining permissible boundaries. The GDPR structured data governance across the European Union without halting digital development. Financial regulation stabilised banking after systemic crisis.

In education, regulatory clarity reduces institutional uncertainty. When schools understand obligations regarding automated decision-making, data retention, and human oversight, they can innovate within defined parameters rather than retreat in fear of liability. The more accurate distinction is not innovation versus regulation, but extractive innovation versus accountable innovation. Accountable innovation aligns technological development with rights protection, public trust, and institutional legitimacy. In education, where the subjects of innovation are minors and the consequences are life-shaping, accountable innovation is not optional. Regulation, at its best, disciplines more than suppresses educational transformation.

PART II: EUROPEAN REGULATION

The general data protection regulation and the protection of children's data

The General Data Protection Regulation is frequently described as a 2016 reform. In reality, it is the culmination of more than two decades of European data protection development. The GDPR replaced Directive 95/46/EC, which had already embedded data protection obligations into European institutional life since the mid-1990s. For schools across the European Union and the United Kingdom, data protection compliance is not new. It has been structurally integrated into administrative practice for over 20 years.

What changed in 2018 was not the existence of data governance, but its intensity and enforceability. The GDPR elevated data protection from administrative compliance to constitutional significance within the European legal order. Article 8 of the Charter of Fundamental Rights of the European Union recognises the protection of personal data as a distinct fundamental right. The GDPR operationalises that right through binding obligations: lawfulness, fairness, transparency, purpose limitation, data minimisation, accuracy, storage limitation, integrity, and accountability (European Union, 2016).

For schools, these principles shape daily practice. Attendance registers, safeguarding records, behavioural logs, assessment data, and health information all constitute personal data. Where educational technology vendors process that data, they do so as processors on behalf of institutional controllers. The school retains legal responsibility for ensuring lawful processing. This is the first point educators must understand clearly: outsourcing infrastructure does not outsource accountability.

Extraterritorial reach

The GDPR's territorial scope extends beyond Europe. Article 3 applies the Regulation not only to organisations established within the European Union, but also to entities outside the Union that offer goods or services to individuals within it, or monitor their behaviour.

In practical terms, a school in Brazil using a United States based AI writing platform that stores or analyses data relating to an EU student may trigger GDPR obligations. Similarly, a European school adopting a generative AI tool hosted outside the EU must ensure that cross border data transfers comply with Chapter V of the Regulation, including adequacy decisions or standard contractual clauses. Educational institutions operating internationally cannot assume that local geography defines their regulatory exposure.

Lawful basis in educational contexts

Under Article 6, all personal data processing requires a lawful basis. In schools, the most common bases are:

- performance of a task carried out in the public interest
- compliance with a legal obligation
- legitimate interests
- consent

Consent, while intuitively appealing in educational settings, is legally fragile. The GDPR emphasises that consent must be freely given, specific, informed, and unambiguous. In hierarchical environments such as schools, the voluntariness of student consent is questionable, particularly where participation in digital platforms is structurally required.

This issue becomes acute with generative AI systems. If a teacher uploads identifiable student essays into a generative model for feedback assistance, what is the lawful basis? Public task? Legitimate interest? Explicit consent? Each carries doctrinal implications. The European Data Protection Board has repeatedly cautioned that controllers must be able to demonstrate *necessity and proportionality* in relation to the chosen basis. For teachers, the operational translation is clear: uploading student work into external AI systems is a regulated act requiring legal justification.

Data minimisation and generative systems

The principle of data minimisation requires that personal data be adequate, relevant, and limited to what is necessary in relation to the purposes for which they are processed (Article 5(1)(c)). Generative AI complicates this principle.

Traditional educational software processes defined datasets for defined purposes. Generative systems, by contrast, may retain inputs for model improvement, safety tuning, or content moderation. The opacity of training and retraining cycles raises legitimate questions about whether student data remains within the originally specified purpose.

Anonymisation is often proposed as a solution. Yet European jurisprudence has clarified that true anonymisation requires irreversible de-identification. Pseudonymised or partially redacted text may remain personal data if re-identification is reasonably possible. A teacher who removes a student's name from an essay before uploading it to an AI system has not necessarily anonymised the data. Writing style, contextual details, or embedded references may permit indirect identification. From a legal perspective, this remains personal data processing. For schools, this means that anonymisation is not a pedagogical shortcut. It is a technical and legal threshold.

Automated decision-making and Article 22

Article 22 of the GDPR provides individuals with the right not to be subject to a decision based solely on automated processing, including profiling, which produces legal or similarly significant effects.

In education, automated assessment systems, predictive risk scoring, or AI-driven placement recommendations may fall within this scope if they materially affect student progression or opportunity. Even where Article 22 is not directly triggered, the broader principles of fairness and transparency apply. Controllers must provide meaningful information about the logic involved in automated processing and the significance and envisaged consequences of such processing (Articles 13–15). For educators, this translates into a governance requirement: if an algorithm materially shapes a decision affecting a student, that decision must remain reviewable, explainable, and contestable.

The right to erasure and model training

The so-called "right to be forgotten" under Article 17 permits individuals to request erasure of personal data under defined conditions. Generative AI raises novel tensions here.

If student data has been incorporated into a model training corpus, can it truly be erased? Technical research on machine unlearning suggests that removing specific data from trained models is complex and not always feasible at scale. The legal and technical communities are actively debating how erasure rights apply in contexts where data influences parameter weights rather than remaining as discrete records. For schools, this means contractual vigilance. Vendor agreements must specify whether student data is used for model training, whether it is segregated, and whether deletion requests can be honoured in meaningful form. The doctrinal question is evolving. The compliance obligation is not.

Safeguarding as data governance

The GDPR's Recital 38 recognises that children merit specific protection with regard to personal data because they may be less aware of risks and consequences. In educational settings, data protection is therefore inseparable from safeguarding. Behavioural analytics systems that profile engagement patterns, emotional states, or disciplinary histories are not merely technical tools. They implicate fundamental rights.

For a teacher, the practical question is deceptively simple: if this data were disclosed publicly, would it alter a child's dignity or future opportunity? If the answer is yes, the processing must withstand heightened scrutiny.

GDPR in the era of generative AI

The GDPR was not drafted with large-scale generative models in mind. Yet its architecture remains adaptable because it regulates behaviour rather than specific technologies.

The shift introduced by generative AI is interpretive rather than structural. Questions of lawful basis, purpose limitation, minimisation, transparency, and erasure must now be applied to systems whose internal logic is probabilistic and whose outputs are synthetic. Legal scholarship since 2018 has emphasised that data protection law alone cannot resolve algorithmic accountability, but it provides foundational procedural safeguards (Barocas and Selbst, 2016; Selbst et al., 2019). In education, GDPR compliance is therefore the floor, not the ceiling, of AI governance.

For teachers and leaders, the translation is this:

If you would hesitate to photocopy and publicly display a student's data, you should hesitate before uploading it into an opaque generative system.

GDPR is not an administrative inconvenience. It is the legal articulation of a moral claim: children's data is not raw material for institutional experimentation. And as artificial intelligence systems expand within education, that claim becomes more, not less, relevant.

The European Union Artificial Intelligence Act: Risk, responsibility, and educational deployment

If the General Data Protection Regulation regulates how data is processed, the European Union Artificial Intelligence Act regulates how algorithmic systems are designed, deployed, supervised, and governed. Adopted in 2024, Regulation (EU) 2024/1689 represents the first comprehensive legislative framework to classify artificial intelligence systems according to risk level and to attach corresponding obligations. Its significance lies not only in scope but in structure. It moves beyond general principles and establishes enforceable compliance requirements tied to use cases.

For schools and universities, the crucial point is this: the AI Act regulates behaviour in context. It does not simply assess what an AI system is. It regulates how it is used, by whom, and for what purpose.

The risk-tier model

The AI Act categorises systems into four broad tiers:

1. Prohibited systems
2. High-risk systems
3. Limited-risk systems
4. Minimal-risk systems

Most educational AI applications will not fall into the prohibited category, which includes practices such as certain forms of manipulative subliminal influence or social scoring.

The relevant category for education is *high-risk.*

Annex III of the Act explicitly includes AI systems intended to be used for:

- determining access or admission to educational institutions
- evaluating learning outcomes
- assessing appropriate educational levels
- monitoring and detecting prohibited behaviour during tests

This classification is not symbolic. High-risk systems are subject to stringent requirements regarding data governance, technical documentation, risk management, human oversight, transparency, and post-market monitoring. Schools using such systems are not passive consumers. They are "deployers" under the Regulation, and deployers carry defined obligations.

Providers and deployers: Shared but distinct duties

The AI Act distinguishes between providers, importers, distributors, and deployers. EdTech vendors that develop AI systems are providers. Schools implementing them are deployers. Deployers must:

- use systems in accordance with instructions
- ensure human oversight
- monitor performance
- suspend use where risks emerge
- maintain logs and documentation

In other words, compliance does not end at procurement. It begins there.

For school leaders, this reframes adoption. Introducing an AI grading system or predictive analytics tool is not simply a pedagogical decision. It is a regulatory act that triggers institutional duties.

Human oversight: Legal requirement, not ethical preference

The AI Act mandates that high-risk systems be designed and used in such a way that they can be effectively overseen by natural persons. This provision aligns with Article 22 GDPR but extends beyond it. Human oversight is not limited to avoiding solely automated decisions. It requires meaningful capacity to intervene, override, and interpret outputs.

For example, if an AI system flags a student as at risk of academic failure, the institution must ensure that staff can:

- understand the basis of the flag
- contextualise it with professional judgment
- correct or override it
- document the reasoning

Human oversight under the Act is active supervision, not passive acknowledgment. In classroom terms, this means a teacher cannot simply rely on an AI-generated grade adjustment without professional review. The legal architecture insists that pedagogical authority remain intact (Parasuraman and Riley, 1997).

Data governance and bias mitigation

High-risk systems must use training, validation, and testing data sets that are relevant, representative, and free of errors as far as possible. This requirement is legally significant in educational contexts where historical attainment patterns correlate strongly with socioeconomic status, race, disability, or migration background. The Act does not demand perfection. It demands documented risk management and bias mitigation procedures.

For schools, this introduces a new expectation: they must inquire into vendor bias testing and demand documentation. Procurement without due diligence is no longer defensible once the system is classified as high risk. In practical terms, a school adopting an AI admissions screening tool should request evidence of:

- representational diversity in training data
- disparate impact testing
- mitigation protocols
- ongoing monitoring procedures

Failure to do so may expose the institution to regulatory liability.

Transparency obligations

The AI Act imposes specific transparency duties for systems that interact with individuals. Users must be informed when they are interacting with AI unless this is obvious from the context. In education, this may apply to generative tutoring systems or automated feedback engines. Transparency in this context is not marketing disclosure. It is a rights-based notification. Students must know when their learning pathway is being shaped by algorithmic systems.

This requirement intersects directly with the governance structures described in Chapter 6. Institutional AI registers, documented oversight roles, and disclosure policies are not merely best practice. They are preparatory compliance mechanisms.

Generative AI and general-purpose systems

The AI Act introduces special provisions for general-purpose AI systems and foundation models. While providers bear primary obligations for these systems, deployers remain responsible for ensuring lawful use in context.

For schools, this raises specific interpretive questions:

- If teachers input identifiable student data into generative systems, are they introducing high-risk use?
- If generative AI influences assessment outcomes, does the use become functionally high-risk even if the system itself is general-purpose?

These questions are still being clarified through implementing guidance and regulatory interpretation. However, the direction is clear: the functional impact of AI in context determines regulatory classification. Schools must therefore evaluate use cases, not merely software labels.

Post-market monitoring and institutional duty

Under the AI Act, compliance does not end at procurement. High-risk AI systems must be monitored after they are introduced into practice to ensure that they continue to operate safely, lawfully, and fairly. Providers are expected to collect and analyse information about system performance over time, while schools, as deployers, must keep records, report serious incidents, and respond when harms or distortions become visible.

This is important because many risks only emerge in context. A system that appears acceptable on paper may behave differently once used with real students in real institutional conditions. If an AI behavioural monitoring system begins disproportionately flagging students from a particular demographic group, the school cannot treat that pattern as incidental. It must investigate, document the issue, and, if necessary, suspend use. The point of post market monitoring is simple: high risk AI must be actively supervised after deployment, not merely approved in advance.

The educational implication

The AI Act does not require schools to become technology laboratories. It requires them to become conscious institutional stewards. Where GDPR secures the protection of personal data, the AI Act secures the procedural integrity of automated decision-making. Together, they establish a layered architecture of public protection:

- Data must be processed lawfully.
- Automated systems must be risk-classified.
- High-risk systems must be documented, supervised, and monitored.
- Human authority must remain operative.

For educators, the translation is not abstract. If an AI system affects admission, grading, progression, discipline, or access to opportunity, the institution must be able to explain, justify, and, where necessary, override its operation.

The AI Act signals a broader shift in European governance philosophy. Artificial intelligence is not treated as a neutral tool. It is treated as an infrastructural actor whose integration into public institutions requires democratic oversight. Education, as a domain affecting minors and life trajectories, sits squarely within that protective frame.

Interpreting Risk in Practice: Four Educational Scenarios

Risk classification under the AI Act is not determined by how sophisticated a system appears. It is determined by function, context, and consequence. The same tool may fall into different categories depending on how it is deployed. What follows are four educational scenarios. The question for each is not merely "what is the technology?" but "what is the institutional impact?"

Scenario A: Automated admission ranking

A selective secondary school introduces an AI system to screen incoming applications. The system analyses prior grades, attendance history, postcode, extra-curricular participation, and teacher comments to generate a ranked shortlist for human review.

Risk tier? High-risk.
Annex III of the AI Act explicitly includes AI systems used to determine access or admission to educational institutions. The system influences entry into an opportunity-structuring environment. Even if final decisions are made by a human committee, the ranking materially shapes outcomes.

What must the school do?

- ➔ Verify that the provider has conducted conformity assessment.
- ➔ Ensure human oversight is meaningful, not symbolic.
- ➔ Document bias testing procedures.
- ➔ Maintain logs of decision adjustments.
- ➔ Establish appeal mechanisms.
- ➔ Mandatory staff AI literacy training.

If leaders are unsure whether a system is high-risk, they should ask a simple question: does this system materially affect who gains or loses educational opportunity? If the answer is yes, assume heightened obligations.

Scenario B: Generative AI writing assistant used in class

A teacher allows students to use a generative writing assistant to brainstorm essay outlines. The system does not automatically grade, rank, or store identifiable data under institutional control. It functions as an optional tool, and teachers review all final submissions independently.

Risk tier? Likely minimal or limited risk, depending on configuration.

If the system is general-purpose and does not materially determine assessment outcomes, it may not qualify as high-risk. However, transparency obligations still apply. Students must know they are interacting with AI. Data protection duties remain operative under GDPR.

The key distinction here is consequentiality. The system supports learning but does not autonomously determine progression or classification. Still, leaders must ask:

- ➔ Are student inputs retained for model training?
- ➔ Is personal data processed?
- ➔ Does reliance on the system reshape assessment integrity?

Minimal regulatory classification does not eliminate governance responsibility.

Scenario C: AI behavioural monitoring during exams

A school deploys an AI-powered proctoring system that uses webcam analysis to detect suspicious behaviour during examinations. The system flags students for potential cheating and automatically escalates cases to administrators.

Risk tier? High-risk.
Annex III includes systems intended to detect prohibited behaviour during tests. The system directly influences disciplinary outcomes and potentially academic records.

Beyond classification, additional ethical dimensions arise. Behavioural inference systems may disproportionately flag students based on neurodiversity, cultural expression, or environmental factors.

The institution must therefore:

- ➔ Ensure human review before disciplinary action.
- ➔ Assess bias risk in facial and behavioural recognition.
- ➔ Provide students with contestation pathways.
- ➔ Document monitoring procedures.

If a system observes, profiles, and escalates in contexts with reputational consequences, it should be treated as high-risk.

Scenario D: Emotional state prediction dashboard

A vendor proposes an AI tool that analyses typing speed, attendance patterns, and engagement metrics to estimate students' emotional wellbeing. The system produces risk scores visible to teachers.

Risk tier? Potentially high-risk, and possibly approaching prohibited territory depending on implementation.

If the system performs profiling related to psychological states and materially influences interventions, it may fall under high-risk provisions related to education and potentially intersect with prohibitions on manipulative or exploitative practices targeting vulnerable groups. The legal classification depends on functionality. Does it merely assist teachers in noticing patterns? Or does it autonomously categorise and trigger interventions?

School leaders must evaluate:

- ➔ Is there scientific validity supporting the inference?
- ➔ Does the system risk discriminatory profiling?
- ➔ Are students aware and able to challenge outputs?

Where psychological inference is involved, proportionality scrutiny intensifies.

Scenario E: AI that assigns seating arrangements to optimise collaboration

A classroom tool analyses prior performance and suggests seating plans to improve peer learning dynamics. The teacher remains free to modify or ignore recommendations.

Risk tier? Minimal risk.
The system does not determine access, progression, grading, or disciplinary status. It suggests an organisational arrangement subject to full human discretion.

Nonetheless, transparency remains important. Students should know when algorithmic tools influence classroom structure.

How schools determine risk

Risk classification is not intuitive. It requires legal advice and functional analysis. School leaders should ask five diagnostic questions:

1. Does the system influence admission, grading, progression, discipline, or access to opportunity?
2. Does it profile or categorise students in ways that may have lasting consequences?
3. Does it operate autonomously or with meaningful human review?
4. Does it process sensitive or behavioural data?
5. Would an erroneous output materially affect a student's educational trajectory?

If multiple answers are affirmative, assume high-risk classification and proceed accordingly. Contact the legal department for advice. Risk is not a measure of technological sophistication. It is a measure of institutional consequence.

PART III: AI GOVERNANCE ACROSS JURISDICTIONS: WHY CONTEXT MATTERS

Artificial intelligence governance in schools does not unfold in a vacuum. It is shaped by national regulatory regimes, regional legal cultures, and varying levels of state capacity. A governance model that is appropriate in one jurisdiction may be legally insufficient or politically infeasible in another. For educators and university faculty operating globally, understanding this variation is not optional. It is foundational.

International convergence exists at the level of principle. The OECD Recommendation on Artificial Intelligence (OECD, 2019) and UNESCO's Recommendation on the Ethics of Artificial Intelligence (UNESCO, 2021) articulate fairness, accountability, transparency, and human oversight as universal norms. Yet implementation diverges significantly across regions.

AI governance in the European regulatory sphere and its influence

Although this chapter focuses beyond Europe, it is important to note that the European Union's Artificial Intelligence Act represents the most comprehensive binding AI regulation currently in force (European Union, 2024). It imposes obligations on both providers and deployers of high-risk AI systems, including documentation, risk management, data governance, and human oversight requirements. For schools operating within the European Union, governance is not optional. If an AI system used in education qualifies as high risk, deployers must ensure appropriate human oversight, maintain technical documentation, and implement risk mitigation processes. The Act regulates behaviour. It governs how systems are used and supervised, not merely how they are designed. This behavioural regulatory model is increasingly influencing governance conversations outside Europe.

AI governance in the United Arab Emirates

The United Arab Emirates has positioned itself as one of the most proactive states globally in the governance and strategic development of artificial intelligence. This trajectory began with the UAE National Strategy for Artificial Intelligence 2031, launched in 2017, which articulated a national ambition to integrate AI across government services, economic sectors, and education systems (UAE Government, 2018). The strategy established artificial intelligence as a core pillar of national development and introduced ministerial oversight through the Ministry of Artificial Intelligence, Digital Economy and Remote Work Applications, signalling a centralised governance approach uncommon in many Western jurisdictions.

Unlike the European Union, where regulatory authority is distributed across supranational institutions and member states, AI governance in the UAE is strongly coordinated through executive leadership and national policy frameworks. The country's governance model reflects a vertically integrated administrative structure in which national strategy, regulatory bodies, and sector-specific initiatives are aligned under federal direction.

Data governance within this system is primarily structured through Federal Decree-Law No. 45 of 2021 on the Protection of Personal Data (PDPL), which established the UAE's first comprehensive federal data protection regime (United Arab Emirates, 2021). The law introduces requirements concerning lawful data processing, consent, purpose limitation, and cross-border data transfers. While conceptually comparable to elements of the European GDPR, the PDPL operates within a different institutional environment, with greater emphasis on regulatory guidance and executive oversight rather than decentralised enforcement through independent supervisory authorities.

In 2026, the UAE further expanded its regulatory architecture with the introduction of the UAE Artificial Intelligence Act, a national framework establishing a risk-based classification system for AI systems operating within the country (United Arab Emirates, 2026). The emerging UAE Artificial Intelligence regulatory framework introduces four tiers of AI risk: minimal, limited, high, and critical and it imposes graduated compliance obligations ranging from transparency requirements to mandatory algorithm audits, incident reporting, and human oversight provisions for higher-risk systems (Dubai Digital Authority, 2026). The Act also created the UAE AI Authority, responsible for maintaining a national registry of AI systems, accrediting algorithm auditors, and coordinating enforcement and guidance across sectors.

Although the UAE AI Act conceptually resembles the European Union's risk-tier model, it is embedded within a more centralised regulatory ecosystem. Governance emphasises national alignment with strategic priorities such as smart-city infrastructure, financial services innovation, and digital public services. For educational institutions, this framework signals an emerging expectation that AI systems affecting learning outcomes, student data, or institutional decision-making will be subject to structured oversight and audit mechanisms.

In parallel, the UAE has introduced legislation addressing children's digital environments more directly. Federal Decree-Law No. 26 of 2025 on Child Digital Safety, which entered into force in January 2026, establishes legal responsibilities for parents, guardians, digital platforms, and service providers to ensure the safe digital participation of minors (United Arab Emirates, 2025). The law requires parental supervision of children's online activity, mandates the availability of parental control tools from digital service providers, and places restrictions on access to age-inappropriate digital environments. While primarily framed as a child protection measure, the legislation has implications for educational technology platforms and AI-enabled digital learning environments by emphasising the protection of children's privacy, dignity, and psychological wellbeing.

Taken together, these developments illustrate a governance model that differs structurally from both European and American approaches. Rather than emerging primarily through judicial interpretation or market regulation, AI governance in the UAE is articulated through coordinated national policy, strategic investment, and sector-specific legislation.

For schools operating within the UAE, including international schools following external curricula, this regulatory environment creates a hybrid governance obligation. Institutions must align with national regulatory frameworks governing data protection, artificial intelligence deployment, and child digital safety while simultaneously maintaining international safeguarding and educational standards expected by global accreditation bodies.

The result is a governance environment in which AI policy is shaped not only by institutional practice but by a national vision of technological development embedded within state-led strategy.

AI governance in Brazil

Brazil offers a rights-based but still transitional model of AI governance. Its most important binding instrument remains the Lei Geral de Proteção de Dados Pessoais (LGPD), enacted in 2018 and enforced from 2020, which established a comprehensive national framework for personal data protection (Brazil, 2018). Article 20 of the LGPD is particularly significant in AI contexts because it grants data subjects the right to request review of decisions made solely on the basis of automated processing when those decisions affect their interests (Brazil, 2018). In educational settings, this has direct implications for systems used in classification, assessment, behavioural profiling, or allocation of support. If an automated process materially shapes a student's educational pathway, the student or guardian may request human review.

What distinguishes Brazil from jurisdictions that already have dedicated AI legislation is that its broader AI regulatory framework remains in formation. The most developed proposal, PL 2338/2023, was approved by the Federal Senate in December 2024 and forwarded to the Chamber of Deputies in 2025, where it remained under legislative review and committee consideration through 2025 (Federal Senate, 2024; Chamber of Deputies, 2025a). The bill adopts a rights-based and risk-sensitive approach, grounded in human dignity, non-discrimination, transparency, accountability, and due process. In that respect, it sits conceptually closer to the European model than to the more fragmented United States approach. At the same time, as of the 2025–2026 period, it is still more accurate to describe Brazil as operating under a data protection regime with an emerging AI governance framework, rather than a fully settled AI statute.

This transition is reinforced by the work of the Autoridade Nacional de Proteção de Dados (ANPD). In its 2025–2026 Regulatory Agenda, the ANPD identified artificial intelligence as a priority area, including the development of interpretative parameters for Article 20 of the LGPD and guidance on the treatment of personal data in the training and use of AI systems (ANPD, 2024; ANPD, 2025). The ANPD has also placed increased emphasis on the protection of children and adolescents' data in digital environments, making Brazil especially relevant to any discussion of AI in education (ANPD, 2024).

For schools, the practical implication is that governance cannot wait for final legislative closure. Brazilian institutions must already align educational AI use with LGPD principles, especially purpose limitation, transparency, data minimisation, and the right to review automated decisions. This is particularly important in a federated educational system where state and municipal actors may adopt digital systems unevenly and where institutional interpretation may vary. In this context, school level clarity becomes essential. Governance must compensate for legal transition. Where statutory AI law is still consolidating, institutional design carries even greater responsibility. Brazil therefore illustrates a crucial governance lesson for education: where statutory AI regulation is still emerging, schools cannot postpone responsibility until legislation is complete.

AI governance in the USA

The United States regulates artificial intelligence through a fragmented and sectoral legal structure rather than a single comprehensive federal statute. This reflects constitutional federalism, a tradition of domain-specific privacy regulation, and a policy culture historically oriented toward technological innovation. For educational institutions, this means AI governance is shaped by overlapping layers of federal law, state legislation, executive guidance, and institutional policy rather than a unified regulatory framework.

Federal policy and the absence of comprehensive AI law

Federal AI governance has largely emerged through executive action and research coordination rather than binding statutory regulation. The *National Artificial Intelligence Initiative Act* of 2020 established national coordination for AI research and development but did not create enforceable rules governing how AI systems may be deployed in schools (U.S. Congress, 2020). Similarly, the 2023 *Executive Order on Safe, Secure, and Trustworthy Artificial Intelligence* directed federal agencies to develop standards addressing safety, civil rights, and algorithmic accountability (Federal Register, 2023). However, executive orders can be modified or rescinded by subsequent administrations and therefore do not provide durable regulatory architecture. As a result, the most stable legal protections affecting AI in education arise not from AI-specific legislation but from longstanding statutes governing data privacy and children's rights.

Sectoral privacy laws governing educational data

Several federal laws shape how AI systems may operate within educational environments by regulating the treatment of student information. The *Family Educational Rights and Privacy Act (FERPA)* governs access to and disclosure of student education records. It grants parents and students rights to inspect records and control the release of personally identifiable information. In AI contexts, FERPA becomes relevant when predictive analytics tools access transcripts, behavioural dashboards process disciplinary data, or tutoring platforms integrate with student record systems. If third-party vendors process this data, institutions must ensure contractual safeguards prevent redisclosure.

The *Children's Online Privacy Protection Act (COPPA)* regulates the collection of personal data from children under thirteen by online services (United States Congress, 1998). Schools may provide consent for educational tools used in classrooms, but this delegated consent creates institutional responsibility. AI systems collecting behavioural interaction data from younger students must therefore comply with strict requirements regarding transparency and data minimisation.

In addition, the *Health Insurance Portability and Accountability Act (HIPAA)* may apply when schools collaborate with external health providers or deploy AI-enabled wellbeing tools that process protected health information. While most school-held health records fall under FERPA, AI systems analysing mental health indicators or behavioural health data can intersect with both regulatory regimes depending on how information flows through institutional systems.

These statutes do not directly regulate algorithmic fairness or decision-making logic. Instead, they govern how data about students may be collected, stored, and shared. Nevertheless, they establish an important ethical baseline for AI: student data must remain within a framework of institutional trust.

State-level regulation and the Colorado example

Because federal AI legislation remains limited, states have begun developing their own governance frameworks. Privacy laws such as *California's Consumer Privacy Act (CCPA)* and its amendment, the *California Privacy Rights Act (CPRA)* provide residents with expanded rights to access and delete personal data held by organisations, including educational technology vendors.

One of the most significant developments is the *Colorado Artificial Intelligence Act*, adopted in 2024 and scheduled to take effect in 2026. The law regulates both developers and deployers of high-risk AI systems and requires documented risk management procedures and mitigation of algorithmic discrimination (Colorado General Assembly, 2024). Notably, the law places responsibility on deployers, including institutions that use AI systems, to exercise reasonable care in preventing discriminatory outcomes. For schools, this means that adopting AI tools affecting consequential educational decisions may trigger governance obligations such as documented risk assessments, monitoring procedures, and mitigation strategies.

Fragmentation and unequal protection

The decentralised nature of American regulation produces an important consequence: protections may vary significantly between states. A student moving from California to Florida, for example, may encounter different legal standards governing data rights and algorithmic transparency. Educational records and digital learning platforms travel across state lines, but the regulatory protections surrounding them do not always move in parallel.

This raises a broader ethical question. *Should children's rights in digitally mediated educational environments depend on jurisdictional geography?*

Federalism allows variation in law. Yet from an educational equity perspective, fragmented governance risks producing uneven safeguards for students exposed to the same technologies. For schools and universities, this complexity reinforces the importance of institutional governance beyond statutory minimums. Where law is uneven, ethical responsibility must fill the gap.

While the United States illustrates how federalism can produce regulatory fragmentation within a technologically advanced system, other regions confront a different governance challenge: building AI oversight structures in environments where regulatory capacity, infrastructure, and educational resources remain unevenly distributed.

AI governance in African contexts

The African continent does not operate under a single regulatory framework. AI governance varies widely across jurisdictions. However, regional guidance is emerging. The African Union adopted the Malabo Convention on Cyber Security and Personal Data Protection (African Union, 2014), though ratification remains uneven. Several countries, including Kenya, Nigeria, and South Africa, have enacted national data protection laws.

In 2023, the African Union published a Continental Artificial Intelligence Strategy, emphasising human rights, inclusion, and capacity building (African Union, 2024). While not binding, it signals an intent to shape AI governance around developmental priorities.

In many African educational systems, the governance challenge is not only fairness and oversight, but capacity. Limited technical infrastructure and regulatory enforcement mechanisms can make comprehensive AI oversight difficult. At the same time, AI adoption in education is often framed as a tool for expanding access and addressing teacher shortages. This creates a governance tension: innovation is positioned as necessary for development, yet oversight structures may lag behind deployment.

In such contexts, multi-level governance must account for resource constraints. Oversight committees may operate at ministry level rather than individual schools. Vendor accountability may depend on international contractual standards. Governance models must be adaptive to capacity realities without abandoning core principles of transparency and human oversight.

WHY THIS COMPARATIVE VIEW MATTERS

What emerges from these examples is not uniformity but pattern. They illustrate that AI governance in education is not emerging along a single institutional model. Across jurisdictions, the balance between decentralised institutional governance, market regulation, and centralised state oversight differs significantly.

Across global jurisdictions:

- Data protection is increasingly codified.
- Human oversight is emphasised.
- Deployer responsibility is expanding.
- Algorithmic discrimination is becoming a regulatory concern.

What differs is enforcement architecture, centralisation, and institutional capacity. For schools operating internationally or serving transnational communities, governance cannot rely on a single national template. It must meet the strictest applicable standard while remaining sensitive to local law.

The lesson is clear. AI governance in schools is a jurisdictionally embedded responsibility shaped by legal obligation, institutional culture, and state capacity. A multi-level governance framework must therefore be legally literate, culturally aware, and operationally precise. The next section translates that comparative awareness into concrete structural design.

PART IV: BEST PRACTICE—FROM LEGAL COMPLIANCE TO ETHICAL STEWARDSHIP

The most common mistake schools make is to treat regulation as the beginning and end of responsible AI use. It is neither. Law sets minimum obligations. Best practice begins one step earlier and goes one step further. It begins by asking whether a proposed use of artificial intelligence belongs in the institution at all. That is not a technical question. It is an ethical one.

Before a school asks whether a system complies with data protection law, it should ask whether the system aligns with its mission, vision, values, and curriculum. A school organised around human rights will approach AI differently from a school that defines itself through faith formation, democratic participation, sustainability, or commercial efficiency. A school committed to restorative discipline may reject behavioural risk scoring that a more compliance-oriented institution would accept. A school that claims to cultivate creativity should ask whether an AI tool expands intellectual agency or narrows it into optimisation (Sandel, 2012).

This is where ethical frameworks become useful. A rights based lens asks whether a system respects dignity, privacy, non-discrimination, and due process. A consequentialist lens asks whether the educational benefits outweigh foreseeable harms. A justice lens asks who bears the burden of error. A care ethics lens asks whether the system strengthens or weakens relationships of trust, attentiveness, and responsibility (Mittelstadt et al., 2016). None of these frameworks is sufficient alone. Together, they force schools to move beyond the seductive but shallow question of whether a tool is efficient. UNESCO's Recommendation on the Ethics of Artificial Intelligence is valuable precisely because it situates AI governance within a wider moral architecture of human rights, proportionality, and do no harm rather than within a narrow frame of technical performance (UNESCO, 2021). Floridi et al. (2018) make a similar point in the AI4People framework, arguing that beneficence, non-maleficence, autonomy, justice, and explicability must be treated as design and governance requirements rather than abstract aspirations.

For schools, the practical sequence should therefore be this: first, mission alignment; second, ethical analysis; third, legal compliance; fourth, implementation design; fifth, continuous review.

A useful example clarifies the difference. Consider a school that is offered an AI attendance prediction tool. The vendor claims it can identify students at risk of disengagement two months earlier than pastoral staff. A purely instrumental response asks whether the system is accurate enough to justify the purchase. A better response asks five prior questions. Does the system fit the school's educational philosophy? Does it support care or intensify surveillance? What variables generate the risk score? Are disadvantaged students more likely to be flagged because historical absenteeism correlates with poverty, disability, or family instability? What happens when the score conflicts with a teacher's knowledge of the student? Can the family challenge the result? It is only after those questions are answered that compliance analysis should begin.

Best practice in this area rests on three linked pillars: robust data governance, algorithmic impact assessment, and trust building.

Robust data governance policies

Data governance in education must begin with restraint. Schools should not collect data merely because a system can process it. They should collect only what is necessary for a clearly articulated educational purpose. That principle is already embedded in GDPR through data minimisation and purpose limitation, but its ethical force is broader than European law. Children's data is not institutional raw material. It is information entrusted to schools within a relationship of asymmetrical power.

A robust data governance policy should therefore define, in plain language, what data is collected, for what purpose, on what legal basis, for how long, with what access controls, and under what deletion schedule. It should also state clearly whether data may be used for model training, safety tuning, or product improvement. Schools should assume that deidentification is not the same as anonymisation, particularly in small communities where reidentification through context is possible. This matters in practice. A teacher who uploads "anonymised" essays to a generative AI system may still be processing personal data if writing style, subject matter, or embedded details allow identification.

Best practice also requires that governance policies distinguish between institutional data and vendor data. If a school uses an external platform, the contract should specify processor obligations, retention limits, breach notification timelines, subcontractor use, and deletion rights. The school remains accountable even when the infrastructure is outsourced. That is a legal point under GDPR and related regimes, but it is also an ethical one. Outsourcing labour does not outsource duty.

Algorithmic impact assessments

If data governance asks what information enters the system, algorithmic impact assessment asks what the system does to people.

Impact assessments should occur before deployment, not after controversy. Their function is not to predict every harm in advance but to force structured institutional reflection. The AI Now Institute's framework for algorithmic impact assessments remains useful because it treats assessment as a public accountability mechanism rather than a purely technical checklist (Reisman et al., 2018). The Canadian Directive on Automated Decision Making operationalised this logic in public administration by requiring risk assessment before deployment of automated systems affecting individuals (Government of Canada, 2019). The lesson for education is straightforward: if a system influences admission, grading, progression, support allocation, discipline, or wellbeing, assessment is not optional.

A strong educational impact assessment asks at least four levels of question.

First, educational purposes. What exactly is the system meant to improve, and what evidence supports that claim? If the answer is vague, efficiency, engagement, optimisation, then the school should pause. Schools are not obliged to adopt technology merely because it is novel.

Second, distributive impact. Which students are most likely to benefit, and which are most likely to be misread? The literature on algorithmic bias is clear that systems trained on historical data can reproduce inequality through proxy variables and sociotechnical abstraction (Barocas and Selbst, 2016; Selbst et al., 2019). A school serving multilingual learners, neurodivergent students, or highly mobile communities should assume that risk modelling and behavioural inference may perform unevenly across groups unless evidence shows otherwise.

Third, procedural fairness. Can the output be explained, challenged, and overridden? If the answer is no, the system has no place in consequential educational decision-making. This is where teachers can understand the matter clearly. If a student asks, "Why did the system say that about me?" the school must be able to answer.

Fourth, mission alignment. Even if a system is lawful and statistically effective, does it belong in this institution? A school committed to democratic participation may reasonably reject opaque predictive discipline tools on normative grounds. A sustainability-focused school may question the procurement of energy intensive AI tools whose educational benefit is marginal. A profit driven institution may emphasise efficiency, but even then it cannot ethically bypass children's rights and legal duties. The assessment must make these value choices visible rather than pretending they do not exist.

Fostering Trust

Trust is not produced by a privacy notice. It is produced by credible conduct over time.

In educational settings, trust requires transparency, participation, and restraint. Students and families should know when AI systems materially influence learning pathways or decisions. Teachers should know what systems are in use, how they work at a functional level, and where concerns should be reported. Governance committees should include, where appropriate, parent and student voice. Incident reporting mechanisms should exist not only for breaches but for patterns of unfairness, opacity, or inappropriate reliance.

Trust also depends on humility. Schools should be willing to say that they do not yet know enough to deploy a system safely. That is not institutional weakness. It is ethical maturity. Mittelstadt (2019) is right that principles alone cannot guarantee ethical AI. But the reverse is also true: technical sophistication alone cannot produce legitimacy. Legitimacy comes from a disciplined willingness to align technology with institutional purpose, to explain decisions, to correct errors, and to stop when harm is plausible.

This is why best practice is best understood not as a static checklist but as a mode of ethical stewardship. A school that asks only whether it may use AI is already behind. The better question is whether this use of AI is educationally justified, ethically coherent, legally defensible, and socially trustworthy.

Only when all four answers are yes should deployment proceed.

CONCLUSION: REGULATION AS FLOOR, NOT CEILING

The regulatory landscape surrounding artificial intelligence in education will continue to expand, differentiate, and harden as new technologies enter schools, as harms become more visible, and as public institutions confront the consequences of earlier regulatory delay. Generative systems, biometric tools, predictive analytics, emotional inference, and automated decision support will not all be governed in the same way, nor will they remain fixed in legal meaning over time. The lesson for schools is therefore not simply that they must comply with current law. It is that they must build governance structures capable of adapting as law evolves.

This is the deeper institutional challenge. Compliance cannot be treated as a static achievement. A policy written once and filed away is already obsolete. Data governance policies, procurement rules, safeguarding protocols, and impact assessments must function as living documents. They require review, revision, and reauthorisation as technologies shift, vendor practices change, and regulatory interpretation matures. What counts as low risk today may be treated as high impact tomorrow once deployed at scale or linked to other systems. Schools and universities must therefore govern for change, not only for the present.

At the same time, regulation has limits. Law can prohibit, constrain, require disclosure, impose duties, and create routes for redress. It can set floors beneath which institutions must not fall. But law does not, by itself, answer every moral question that education must confront. A system may be lawful and still pedagogically corrosive. It may satisfy technical compliance while undermining dignity, trust, or relational care. It may fit within a statutory framework yet remain misaligned with the educational purposes the institution claims to serve.

This is why regulation must be understood as the floor, not the ceiling, of responsible AI governance. The strongest institutions will be those that learn to hold three questions together at once. I*s this lawful? Is this ethically justified? Is this educationally worthy?* When those questions are separated, governance weakens. When they are asked together, schools regain agency.

That agency matters because the next phase of this debate is not merely legal. It is moral. Beneath privacy law, AI Acts, children's consent rules, and automated decision safeguards lies a more fundamental question: *what is a child owed in an educational environment increasingly mediated by intelligent systems?*

The next chapter turns to that question directly. It moves beneath regulatory architecture to the deeper normative foundation on which any legitimate educational use of artificial intelligence must rest: human rights. If regulation establishes procedural boundaries, human rights articulate the moral claims that make those boundaries necessary in the first place. Privacy, dignity, inclusion, participation, and equitable access are not supplementary concerns. They are the foundation. That is where the argument must now go.

REFERENCES

African Union (2014). *African Union Convention on Cyber Security and Personal Data Protection*. Available at: https://au.int/sites/default/files/treaties/29560-treaty-0048_-_african_union_convention_on_cyber_security_and_personal_data_protection_e.pdf

African Union (2024). *Continental Artificial Intelligence Strategy*. Available at: https://au.int/sites/default/files/documents/44004-doc-EN-_Continental_AI_Strategy_July_2024.pdf

ANPD (2024) *Tratamento de dados pessoais de crianças e adolescentes*. Brasília: Autoridade Nacional de Proteção de Dados. Available at: www.gov.br/anpd/pt-br/acesso-a-informacao/participacao-social/outras-acoes/documentos/ts_04_24_corrigido.pdf

ANPD (2025) *Regulatory Agenda for the 2025–2026 biennium*. Brasília: Autoridade Nacional de Proteção de Dados. Available at: www.gov.br/anpd/pt-br/acesso-a-informacao/institucional/atos-normativos/regulamentacoes_anpd/agenda_regulatoria_25_26___ingles___revisada_final_fev25.pdf

Barocas, S. and Selbst, A.D. (2016) 'Big data's disparate impact', *California Law Review*, 104(3), 671–732. Available at: https://doi.org/10.15779/Z38BG31

Benjamin, R. (2019) *Race after Technology: Abolitionist Tools for the New Jim Code*. Cambridge: Polity Press.

Brazil (2018) *Lei No. 13.709, de 14 de agosto de 2018: Lei Geral de Proteção de Dados Pessoais (LGPD)*. Brasília: Presidência da República. Available at: www.planalto.gov.br/ccivil_03/_ato2015-2018/2018/lei/l13709.htm

Chamber of Deputies (2025a) *Projeto de Lei No. 2338/2023: Dispõe sobre o desenvolvimento, o fomento e o uso ético e responsável da inteligência artificial com base na centralidade da pessoa humana*. Brasília: Câmara dos Deputados. Available at: www.camara.leg.br/proposicoesWeb/prop_mostrarintegra?codteor=2881712&filename=Avulso+PL+2338%2F2023

Citron, D.K. (2008) 'Technological due process', *Washington University Law Review*, 85(6), 1249–1313. Available at: https://openscholarship.wustl.edu/law_lawreview/vol85/iss6/2

Colorado General Assembly (2024). Senate Bill: SB24-205. *Consumer Protections for Artificial Intelligence*. Available at: https://leg.colorado.gov/bills/sb24-205

Department of Health, Education, and Welfare Advisory Committee (1973) *Records, Computers and the Rights of Citizens*. Published via the US Department of Justice. Available at: www.justice.gov/opcl/docs/rec-com-rights.pdf

Dubai Digital Authority (2026). *UAE Artificial Intelligence Act: Regulatory Framework and Compliance Guidance*. Available at: www.digitaldubai.ai/dubai-updates/dubai-ai-act-2026-comprehensive-guide

Eubanks, V. (2018) *Automating Inequality: How High-Tech Tools Profile, Police, and Punish the Poor*. New York: St Martin's Press.

European Union (2016) 'Regulation (EU) 2016/679 of the European Parliament and of the Council of 27 April 2016 on the protection of natural persons with regard to the processing of personal data and on the free movement of such data (General Data Protection Regulation)', *Official Journal of the European Union*, L119, 1–88. Available at: https://eur-lex.europa.eu/eli/reg/2016/679/oj

European Union (2024) 'Regulation (EU) 2024/1689 of the European Parliament and of the Council laying down harmonised rules on artificial intelligence (Artificial Intelligence Act)', *Official Journal of the European Union*. Available at: https://eur-lex.europa.eu/eli/reg/2024/1689/oj

Federal Register (2023) *Safe, Secure, and Trustworthy Development and Use of Artificial Intelligence. Executive order #14110*. Federal Register, 11/23. Available at: www.federalregister.gov/documents/2023/11/01/2023-24283/safe-secure-and-trustworthy-development-and-use-of-artificial-intelligence

Federal Senate (2024) *PL 2338/2023: Dispõe sobre o uso da inteligência artificial*. Brasília: Senado Federal. Available at: www25.senado.leg.br/web/atividade/materias/-/materia/157233

Floridi, L., Cowls, J., Beltrametti, M., Chatila, R., Chazerand, P., Dignum, V., Luetge, C., Madelin, R., Pagallo, U., Rossi, F., Schafer, B., Valcke, P. and Vayena, E. (2018) 'AI4People—An ethical framework for a good AI society', *Minds and Machines*, 28(4), 689–707. Available at: https://doi.org/10.1007/s11023-018-9482-5

Government of Canada (2019) *Directive on Automated Decision-Making*. Ottawa: Treasury Board of Canada Secretariat. Available at: www.tbs-sct.canada.ca/pol/doc-eng.aspx?id=32592

Human Rights Watch (2022) *"How Dare They Peep into My Private Life?" Children's Rights Violations by Governments that Endorsed Online Learning during the COVID-19 Pandemic*. New York: Human Rights Watch. Available at: www.hrw.org/report/2022/05/25/how-dare-they-peep-my-private-life/childrens-rights-violations-governments

Jobin, A., Ienca, M. and Vayena, E. (2019) 'The global landscape of AI ethics guidelines', *Nature Machine Intelligence*, 1(9), 389–399. https://doi.org/10.1038/s42256-019-0088-2

Mittelstadt, B.D. (2019) 'Principles alone cannot guarantee ethical AI', *Nature Machine Intelligence*, 1(11), November 2019, 501–507. https://doi.org/10.1038/s42256-019-0114-4

Mittelstadt, B.D., Allo, P., Taddeo, M., Wachter, S. and Floridi, L. (2016) 'The ethics of algorithms: Mapping the debate', *Big Data & Society*, 3(2), 1–21. https://doi.org/10.1177/2053951716679679

Noble, S.U. (2018) *Algorithms of Oppression: How Search Engines Reinforce Racism*. New York: New York University Press.

OECD (2019) *Recommendation of the Council on Artificial Intelligence (OECD/LEGAL/0449)*. Paris: OECD Publishing. Available at: https://legalinstruments.oecd.org/en/instruments/oecd-legal-0449

O'Neil, C. (2016) *Weapons of Math Destruction: How Big Data Increases Inequality and Threatens Democracy*. New York: Crown.

Parasuraman, R. and Riley, V. (1997) 'Humans and automation: Use, misuse, disuse, abuse', *Human Factors*, 39(2), 230–253. Available at: https://web.mit.edu/16.459/www/parasuraman.pdf

Personal Data Protection Act (PDPA) (2012) Singapore Statutes Online. Available at: https://sso.agc.gov.sg/Act/PDPA2012

Reisman, D., Schultz, J., Crawford, K. and Whittaker, M. (2018) *Algorithmic Impact Assessments: A Practical Framework for Public Agency Accountability*. New York: AI Now Institute. Available at: https://ainowinstitute.org/wp-content/uploads/2023/04/aiareport2018.pdf

Sandel, M.J. (2012) *What Money Can't Buy: The Moral Limits of Markets*. New York: Farrar, Straus and Giroux.

Selbst, A.D., Boyd, D., Friedler, S.A., Venkatasubramanian, S. and Vertesi, J. (2019) 'Fairness and abstraction in sociotechnical systems', *Proceedings of the Conference on Fairness, Accountability, and Transparency (FAT)**, pp. 59–68. Available at: https://doi.org/10.1145/3287560.3287598

UAE Government (2018) *UAE National Strategy for Artificial Intelligence 2031*. Available at: https://staticcdn.mbzuai.ac.ae/mbzuaiwpprd01/2022/07/UAE-National-Strategy-for-Artificial-Intelligence-2031.pdf

UNESCO (2021) *Recommendation on the Ethics of Artificial Intelligence*. Paris: UNESCO. Available at: https://unesdoc.unesco.org/ark:/48223/pf0000386693

United Arab Emirates (2021) *Federal Decree-Law No. 45 of 2021 on the Protection of Personal Data*. Available at: https://uaelegislation.gov.ae/en/legislations/1972/download

United Arab Emirates (2025) *Federal Decree-Law No. 26 of 2025 on Child Digital Safety*. Available at: https://uaelegislation.gov.ae/en/legislations/3912/download

United Arab Emirates (2026) *Artificial Intelligence Act*.

United States Congress (1998) Children's Online Privacy Protection Act (COPPA), 15 U.S.C. §§ 6501–6506. Available at: www.ftc.gov/legal-library/browse/statutes/childrens-online-privacy-protection-act

U.S. Congress (2020). H.R.6216—National Artificial Intelligence Initiative Act of 2020. Available at: www.congress.gov/bill/116th-congress/house-bill/6216

Westin, A.F. (1967) *Privacy and Freedom*. New York: Atheneum.

Winner, L. (1980) 'Do artifacts have politics?', *Daedalus*, 109(1), 121–136. Available at: https://faculty.cc.gatech.edu/~beki/cs4001/Winner.pdf

Human Rights as a Foundation 8

Equitable and Inclusive AI

At the conclusion of the previous chapter, we arrived at an important institutional insight: regulation is necessary, but it is not sufficient. Law establishes the minimum conditions under which artificial intelligence may be deployed responsibly in education. It defines procedural safeguards, allocates institutional duties, and creates mechanisms for accountability. Yet regulation alone cannot answer the deeper question that technological transformation inevitably raises.

What, fundamentally, is a child owed in an educational environment increasingly mediated by intelligent systems?

Legal frameworks such as data protection law and artificial intelligence regulation attempt to constrain risk. They define how systems should behave and where institutional responsibility lies. But beneath these procedural structures lies a deeper normative foundation. The justification for regulating AI in education does not ultimately arise from technical uncertainty or institutional caution. It arises from moral claims about human dignity, equality, and the protection of vulnerable persons.

Those claims are articulated most clearly within the language of human rights.

To understand the ethical boundaries of artificial intelligence in education, we must therefore move beneath regulatory architecture and examine the moral framework that precedes it. Human rights do not merely supplement AI governance. They provide the foundation upon which legitimate governance rests (UNESCO, 2021).

DOI: 10.1201/9781003662945-8

PART I: HUMAN RIGHTS, CHILDHOOD, AND THE MORAL ARCHITECTURE OF EDUCATION

A striking refrain often emerges when young people are asked about privacy in digital environments. Many respond with resignation rather than concern. They explain that the systems already know everything about them. Their search histories, their conversations, their locations, their preferences, their academic performance, even their emotional patterns are already recorded somewhere. Privacy, they conclude, belongs to an earlier generation.

This surrender should concern us deeply.

Privacy is not merely a technical preference about data handling. It plays a foundational role in the development of human freedom. The ability to think, experiment, err, and change without permanent surveillance is essential to intellectual growth and moral agency. A society in which young people believe that observation is constant and unavoidable risks producing citizens who internalise monitoring as the normal condition of life.

In educational settings, this risk becomes particularly acute. Schools are not simply service providers delivering knowledge. They are formative institutions in which individuals develop autonomy, identity, and civic capacity. If digital infrastructures within these institutions erode the conditions necessary for privacy, experimentation, and dissent, they alter not only educational practice but the architecture of democratic life itself. This is why the debate about artificial intelligence in education cannot remain confined to questions of efficiency or innovation. It must be located within the broader moral language that societies have developed to articulate the limits of institutional power. That language is the language of human rights.

The historical emergence of the human rights framework

The modern human rights framework emerged from the profound political and moral rupture of the twentieth century. The atrocities of the Second World War exposed the catastrophic consequences of state power unconstrained by universal moral principles. In response, the international community sought to articulate a shared normative foundation capable of protecting human dignity across political systems and cultural contexts. This effort culminated in the Universal Declaration of Human Rights (UDHR), adopted by the United Nations General Assembly in 1948 (United Nations, 1948).

The Declaration was not a treaty and therefore did not initially create binding legal obligations. Its significance lay elsewhere. It articulated a moral consensus that certain rights belong to every human being by virtue of their humanity. These rights were not granted by governments. They were recognised as inherent.

The UDHR established principles that would later become embedded in international law and national constitutions: the right to privacy, the right to education, freedom of expression, equality before the law, and protection against discrimination. Over time, these principles were translated into binding legal instruments such as the International Covenant on Civil and Political Rights (United Nations, 1966a), and the International Covenant on Economic, Social and Cultural Rights (United Nations, 1966b).

Through this process, human rights norms became progressively institutionalised. They entered constitutional law, judicial reasoning, administrative governance, and international diplomacy. Courts across the world increasingly interpret domestic legislation through a human rights lens. Public institutions, including schools and universities, now operate within legal environments shaped by these norms. Human rights therefore function simultaneously at three levels. They operate as moral principles, as legal obligations, and as interpretive frameworks guiding institutional decision-making. In the context of emerging technologies, they provide something that regulatory frameworks alone cannot offer: a stable normative compass.

Children as rights holders

For much of history, children were treated primarily as objects of protection rather than as holders of rights in their own capacity. Legal systems focused on parental authority and state guardianship, assuming that decisions about children should be made on their behalf rather than with their participation. This understanding began to shift in the late twentieth century.

The United Nations Convention on the Rights of the Child (CRC), adopted in 1989 and now ratified by nearly every country in the world, marked a profound conceptual transformation (United Nations, 1989). The Convention recognised children as individuals possessing inherent rights while also acknowledging their evolving capacities and particular vulnerabilities.

Several provisions of the Convention are especially relevant to the governance of artificial intelligence in education.

★ Article 3 establishes the principle that the best interests of the child must be a primary consideration in all actions concerning children.
★ Article 12 affirms the right of children to express their views in matters affecting them and to have those views taken seriously.
★ Article 16 recognises the child's right to privacy.
★ Article 28 affirms the right to education.
★ Article 29 emphasises that education should develop the child's personality, talents, and mental abilities to their fullest potential.

Taken together, these provisions articulate a vision of childhood that is deeply incompatible with purely technocratic governance. Children are not merely data subjects or future economic actors. They are rights-bearing individuals whose development requires protection, participation, and dignity. Artificial intelligence systems introduced into educational environments must therefore be evaluated not only in terms of performance metrics but also in terms of their compatibility with these rights.

Rights, ethics, and educational responsibility

Human rights frameworks do not operate in isolation from ethical reasoning. Rather, they translate moral commitments into institutional expectations. Philosophically, the protection of children's rights in educational contexts draws upon several ethical traditions. A rights-based approach emphasises dignity, autonomy, and protection from unjust interference. A justice-oriented perspective highlights fairness, equality of opportunity, and the prevention of structural disadvantage. A care-based framework emphasises relationships, attentiveness, and responsibility within educational communities. Together, these perspectives converge on a shared conclusion: educational institutions carry a special moral responsibility because they exercise authority over developing persons.

Artificial intelligence systems introduced into this environment inherit that responsibility.

When predictive models classify students, when behavioural analytics systems profile engagement, when generative tools reshape assessment practices, these technologies participate in the distribution of opportunity and recognition within the classroom.

The question therefore becomes not simply whether such systems function effectively, but whether they support the rights and flourishing of the children they affect.

Education, agency, and democratic participation

Human rights frameworks recognise education as more than the transmission of knowledge. Education is a foundational institution of democratic life. It prepares individuals to participate in collective decision making, to exercise freedom of expression, and to develop independent judgment.

The recognition of children as rights holders reinforces this democratic dimension. Young people are not merely future citizens. They are already participants in the moral community.

Artificial intelligence governance in education must therefore respect not only children's protection rights but also their participatory rights. Students should have opportunities to understand how algorithmic systems shape their learning environments. They should be able to question, challenge, and influence the technologies that affect them. If AI systems become opaque authorities whose outputs cannot be examined or contested, they risk undermining the very capacities that education is meant to cultivate. A rights-based approach to educational AI governance therefore insists on something deceptively simple: children must remain visible as subjects of education, not objects of optimisation.

Are human rights sufficient in the age of AI?

The modern human rights framework has demonstrated remarkable resilience. For more than 70 years, the principles articulated in the Universal Declaration of Human Rights have shaped constitutional law, international treaties, and judicial interpretation across much of the world. They have provided the moral vocabulary through which societies articulate claims of dignity, equality, and justice. Yet the durability of a framework does not guarantee its sufficiency.

The Universal Declaration of Human Rights was drafted in the aftermath of the Second World War, at a moment when the most immediate threats to human dignity were understood primarily in terms of state violence, discrimination, and political repression. The architecture of the Declaration reflects this historical context. Its articles address the protection of individuals from coercion, deprivation, and arbitrary authority within the structures of twentieth century political life. The technological environment in which those rights were formulated, however, bears little resemblance to the digital infrastructures shaping contemporary societies.

Artificial intelligence systems now mediate economic participation, social visibility, educational opportunity, and access to public services. They sort, rank, predict, and influence behaviour at a scale unimaginable in 1948. Decisions that once required human judgment increasingly occur through statistical inference embedded in computational systems. The power to shape individual trajectories no longer resides solely within state institutions or formal legal structures. It is distributed across complex technological ecosystems operated by governments, corporations, and transnational platforms. This shift raises an important question: *can a rights framework designed in the mid-twentieth century fully address the forms of power emerging in the twenty-first?*

Many scholars argue that existing rights can simply be interpreted expansively to cover new technological conditions. Privacy rights, for example, may be extended to address algorithmic surveillance. Anti-discrimination provisions may be applied to algorithmic bias. Procedural fairness doctrines may be adapted to automated decision making. In many cases, this interpretive strategy has proven effective. Courts and regulators have increasingly applied established legal principles to digital contexts. Data protection law, algorithmic accountability frameworks, and emerging AI regulations all draw heavily on existing human rights concepts. Yet, others suggest that the scale and character of technological transformation may expose structural gaps within the existing framework. One emerging line of scholarship therefore asks whether the human rights architecture itself may require expansion.

Proposals for a new human rights article

Within this debate, some scholars and policy thinkers have begun to explore the possibility of introducing an additional article to the Universal Declaration of Human Rights addressing the relationship between human dignity and advanced technological systems. Among these proposals is the argument for what has been described as a "31st Article" to the Universal Declaration (Hawking, 2026).

This proposal recognises that algorithmic systems increasingly shape the conditions under which individuals exercise many of the rights already recognised within the Declaration. Access to information, educational opportunity, employment prospects, and civic participation may all be influenced by automated classification systems whose logic remains opaque to those affected by them. If the exercise of fundamental rights increasingly occurs within algorithmically mediated environments, then the governance of those environments becomes a matter of human rights concern.

The proposal suggests that individuals should possess explicit rights in relation to automated decision-making systems that materially affect their lives. These rights may include meaningful transparency regarding algorithmic processes, the ability to challenge automated decisions, and protection from forms of computational manipulation or profiling that undermine autonomy. The objective of such proposals is not to replace the existing human rights framework but to extend it so that it remains responsive to new forms of power.

The argument introduced in Paris

This line of thinking has begun to appear in academic and policy discussions surrounding artificial intelligence governance. At an international conference at the International Association for Safe and Ethical Artificial Intelligence held at UNESCO House in Paris, Hawking (2026) introduced a proposal calling for renewed examination of whether the existing human rights framework is sufficient for the technological conditions emerging in the twenty first century.

In that analysis, Hawking argues that debates about artificial intelligence governance in education often begin with technological capability rather than institutional purpose. Yet, the more fundamental question should precede deployment: *why are AI systems being introduced into children's learning environments at all?*

Hawking proposes that institutions should evaluate AI adoption through a set of alignment questions: whether the technology supports the educational mission of the institution, whether it complies with regulatory obligations, whether it reinforces rather than distorts the curriculum, whether it respects the professional rights of staff, and most critically whether it upholds the dignity and rights of the child (Hawking, 2026).

While institutions frequently demonstrate competence in matters of compliance and efficiency, the final question often remains insufficiently addressed. According to Hawking, what is emerging across educational systems is not institutional collapse but a form of structural drift, in which technological infrastructures evolve more rapidly than the governance frameworks responsible for overseeing them. Children increasingly inhabit digital systems that observe, predict, and influence behaviour before they possess the developmental capacity to understand consent or the implications of data capture. Prompts, behavioural patterns, emotional signals, and performance indicators are recorded and analysed in ways that extend beyond the pedagogical intentions of educators or school leaders.

Generative systems may be introduced to improve efficiency in feedback and assessment. Yet, student data may be retained beyond what institutions originally anticipated. Behavioural analytics tools may influence perceptions of engagement or risk without families fully understanding the profiling practices involved. Writing assistance tools may begin to reshape norms of authorship and intellectual development before educational frameworks have had time to adapt.

In one documented case, an automated wellbeing system generated risk classifications using behavioural proxies that disproportionately flagged neurodivergent students as requiring intervention. The system was not designed with discriminatory intent. Yet, bias propagated through the structure of the model. For Hawking, such developments illustrate that artificial intelligence in education presents not merely a data governance challenge but a generational human rights question.

Why existing rights may not be enough

The argument for revisiting the human rights architecture rests on several observations. First, algorithmic systems introduce forms of influence that operate below the threshold of traditional legal categories. Behavioural nudging, predictive classification, and personalised information environments may shape human decision making without overt coercion. Second, many algorithmic systems operate through proprietary models whose internal logic is inaccessible even to those deploying them. This creates asymmetries of knowledge that challenge traditional notions of procedural fairness. Third, algorithmic infrastructures often operate across national borders, complicating the ability of individual states to guarantee rights protections through domestic law alone. Finally, children are particularly vulnerable within these environments. They encounter algorithmic systems during formative stages of cognitive and social development, often without the capacity to understand how their data is being used or how digital environments are shaping their behaviour. Taken together, these developments suggest that the traditional boundaries between technological governance and human rights protection may be dissolving.

If artificial intelligence increasingly structures the conditions under which individuals exercise their rights, then the governance of these systems becomes inseparable from the protection of human dignity itself. From this perspective, Hawking (2026) proposes that the human rights framework may eventually require explicit recognition of rights relating to algorithmic systems. Such an expansion could include protections from AI induced harm, rights to transparency in consequential automated decision-making, and equitable access to the benefits generated by advanced technologies.

Importantly, this proposal is framed not as a rejection of the human rights tradition but as its continuation. The history of human rights is itself a history of expansion. New conventions and legal instruments have repeatedly extended protections as social conditions evolved. The Convention on the Rights of the Child represented one such expansion. Artificial intelligence may represent another.

From general human rights to children's rights in the age of AI

These debates take on particular urgency in educational contexts. Children do not encounter artificial intelligence primarily as workers, consumers, or voters. They encounter it as learners. Schools are among the first institutional environments in which algorithmic systems influence daily experience, from digital learning platforms and behavioural analytics tools to generative educational assistants. This makes education a critical site for examining whether the existing human rights framework is sufficient. If the rights articulated in the Universal Declaration and the Convention on the Rights of the Child are to remain meaningful in an era of pervasive digital mediation, they must be interpreted and potentially expanded in ways that address the realities of algorithmic systems.

The next section therefore turns to another dimension of this challenge: how global technological development can reproduce historical patterns of inequality and cultural dominance if educational AI systems are designed without sensitivity to local pedagogical contexts and knowledge traditions. This issue is often described through the language of digital colonialism.

PART II: DIGITAL COLONIALISM, INDIGENOUS RIGHTS, AND THE ETHICS OF UNEQUAL AI FUTURES

If the previous section asked whether the existing human rights framework is sufficient for the age of artificial intelligence, the next question is more concrete and no less urgent: whose intelligence, whose values, and whose futures are being built into the systems now entering schools?

This is where the language of digital colonialism becomes useful. Couldry and Mejias argue that contemporary data extraction should not be understood merely as a new business model but as a social order in which human life is rendered available for continuous capture and appropriation. Their argument is not that digital systems replicate historical colonialism in identical form, but that they extend its extractive logic into the domain of data, prediction, and behavioural influence (Couldry and Mejias, 2019; Couldry and Mejias, 2021). In educational settings, that warning matters because schools can become sites where children's learning, behaviour, and identities are converted into data assets long before the children themselves can understand the terms of extraction.

Recent scholarship in educational technology has begun to make this concern explicit. Kohnke and Foung's review of predictive analytics studies in educational technology argues that data colonialism is not only a privacy problem but a broader culture of appropriation in which learner data is treated as a "free" resource for optimisation, prediction, and institutional value creation. Their central concern is that the language of innovation can normalise extractive practices while obscuring who benefits, who is rendered legible, and who bears the cost of being profiled (Kohnke and Foung, 2024). For a book on AI in education, this point is decisive. The ethical problem is not exhausted by asking whether data collection is lawful. It also requires asking whether educational relationships are being reorganised around extraction.

This issue is often framed as a Global South problem, and in one sense that is justified. Birhane's influential analysis of algorithmic colonisation in Africa shows how AI systems developed elsewhere can be imported into African contexts with minimal scrutiny, weak local accountability, and little alignment with local needs. Her argument is that such systems risk deepening dependency by displacing local innovation, imposing external categories, and embedding foreign assumptions into social infrastructures that are already shaped by unequal power relations (Birhane, 2020). That warning should be taken seriously in education, where imported AI tools may not fit local curricula, local languages, or local pedagogical aims.

At the same time, digital colonialism should not be treated as a phenomenon that exists only across continents. It can also be intensely local. The same ethical structure appears when one school has the resources to interrogate vendors, audit tools, and train staff, while another adopts the same systems under pressure, without technical expertise, legal support, or even reliable infrastructure. The divide is global, but it is also municipal, neighbourhood based, and institutional. Assefa and colleagues argue that digital inequality in developing educational contexts is not reducible to simple access. It also concerns the social, institutional, and pedagogical conditions under which technologies can be meaningfully used. Beckman and colleagues make a parallel argument in higher education, warning of a "GenAI divide" in which students do not benefit equally from AI systems because access, skills, policy clarity, and institutional support are distributed unevenly (Assefa et al., 2024; Beckman et al., 2025). The ethical conclusion is clear: unequal AI futures are produced not only by whether a system exists, but by who has the power to shape, question, and benefit from it.

A rights based response to this problem must therefore move beyond access alone. The question is not simply whether schools in the Global South or underfunded schools in the Global North can obtain AI tools. The deeper question is whether those tools reinforce local educational agency or erode it. Gallagher, Evans and Sarpong-Duah's work on digital educational governance in Ghana is especially useful here because it resists the assumption that innovation should always "scale up" from externally defined models. Instead, it argues for governance and policy instruments grounded in situated local needs and local decision-making (Gallagher, Evans and Sarpong-Duah, 2024). That insight should travel far beyond Ghana. It is a direct challenge to the idea that educational AI can be ethically deployed through one universal model designed elsewhere and exported everywhere.

This is also the point at which Indigenous rights become central. Recent scholarship is increasingly clear that AI governance cannot be treated as culturally neutral. Lewis and colleagues, in their Indigenous led "Abundant Intelligences" agenda, argue that Indigenous knowledge systems do not merely offer community consultation or post hoc ethical correction. They offer alternative epistemological foundations for thinking about intelligence, technology, and flourishing. Their work is important because it shifts the debate from inclusion within Western AI paradigms to the possibility of transforming those paradigms themselves (Lewis et al., 2025). Perera and colleagues' systematic review similarly finds that scholarship on Indigenous peoples and AI increasingly focuses on data sovereignty, language preservation, self-determination, and the need for direct engagement with Indigenous authorities rather than abstract ethical generalisation (Perera et al., 2025).

Here, Indigenous data sovereignty becomes a practical and moral bridge. Bowman and Bremner argue that Indigenous data sovereignty is not a symbolic add on to governance, but a framework concerned with rights, control, authority, and community determined use of data. In AI contexts, this matters profoundly. If data drawn from Indigenous communities are used to train systems without governance by those communities, then extraction is simply being modernised. If educational AI tools are introduced into Indigenous contexts without respect for local authority, language, protocol, and epistemology, then inclusion rhetoric may conceal a deeper dispossession (Bowman and Bremner, 2025).

The ethical space here is demanding. It requires schools and policy makers to resist two false moves at once. The first is technological universalism, the assumption that a system that performs well somewhere is therefore suitable everywhere. The second is romantic localism, the assumption that local context alone resolves all questions of rights, fairness, and accountability. A more defensible approach is plural and rights based. It asks whether AI systems support local pedagogical purposes, whether they preserve community authority over knowledge and data, whether they widen or narrow existing inequalities, and whether they allow children to remain subjects of education rather than objects of remote optimisation.

This means that "equitable and inclusive AI" cannot be defined as simply distribution of tools. It must include voice, governance, infrastructure, language, teacher capacity, and the right to refuse systems that distort educational purpose. In some contexts, the most ethical decision may be deployment with strong local adaptation. In others, it may be delay. In others still, it may be rejection.

The human rights question, then, is not whether everyone should receive the same AI. It is whether every child, every school, and every community has the right to educational technologies that respect dignity, support local flourishing, and do not reproduce old hierarchies in digital form. That is the threshold against which equitable and inclusive AI must now be judged.

PART III: TEACHER AGENCY, PROFESSIONAL JUDGMENT, AND THE LIMITS OF TECHNOLOGICAL SUBSTITUTION

Public discourse surrounding artificial intelligence in education has often been framed through a language of disruption. Headlines have repeatedly suggested that teachers may soon be replaced by intelligent tutoring systems, automated grading engines, or generative instructional assistants. In parallel, many education systems face genuine structural pressures: chronic understaffing, rising administrative burdens, and widening disparities in resources between schools. Within this environment, the claim that artificial intelligence could compensate for teacher shortages has gained considerable political and media attention.

Yet, the reality emerging in classrooms several years after the public release of large scale generative systems such as GPT-3 in 2022 and subsequent models has proven more complex. Rather than replacing educators, these technologies have largely revealed how deeply teaching remains a professional practice grounded in judgment, relational understanding, and pedagogical expertise.

Early encounters with generative AI in schools were often marked by uncertainty. Teachers were asked to adapt quickly to unfamiliar systems while navigating concerns about academic integrity, curriculum alignment, and their own professional futures. In many cases, the initial experience resembled a defensive response: rapid policy formation, emergency guidance documents, and urgent debates about plagiarism and assessment integrity.

Over time, however, a different pattern has begun to emerge. As educators experiment with AI tools, many are rediscovering the central fact that teaching is a skills driven profession. Effective teaching depends on a complex set of capacities developed through training and experience: the ability to interpret student misunderstanding, to adjust explanation in real time, to recognise emotional cues, to scaffold intellectual challenge, and to cultivate curiosity. These practices cannot be reduced to content delivery or information retrieval. They are forms of relational and contextual judgment developed over years of professional practice.

Research on the integration of artificial intelligence in education increasingly reflects this reality. Holmes, Bialik and Fadel (2019) emphasise that AI systems may augment certain instructional functions, but they do not replace the pedagogical role of educators. Instead, the presence of AI often amplifies the importance of human oversight and professional interpretation. Teachers remain responsible for determining when automated feedback is appropriate, when algorithmic recommendations require contextual correction, and when student wellbeing requires human attention rather than computational inference.

This insight has important implications for governance. If artificial intelligence is treated as a substitute for teachers, educational institutions risk undermining the professional expertise required to use these technologies responsibly. If, by contrast, AI is understood as a tool operating within a broader pedagogical framework, then teacher agency becomes a central component of ethical AI deployment.

Professional development therefore becomes critical. Educators require opportunities not only to learn how systems function technically, but also to examine how those systems interact with curriculum design, assessment philosophy, and classroom dynamics. The goal is not to transform teachers into engineers. It is to ensure that teachers possess sufficient conceptual literacy to question, adapt, and if necessary refuse technologies that conflict with educational goals.

Local capacity building is equally important. AI governance in education cannot be sustained solely through national policy or vendor documentation. Schools require internal expertise capable of evaluating tools, interpreting regulatory requirements, and supporting colleagues in responsible use. In practice, this often takes the form of interdisciplinary teams combining educators, school leaders, technical specialists, and safeguarding professionals.

Without such capacity, institutions risk falling into a pattern that has characterised earlier waves of educational technology: the gradual overshadowing of pedagogy by tools. When technological capabilities begin to dictate instructional practice rather than support it, educational purpose becomes secondary to platform design.

A rights based approach to artificial intelligence in education therefore implies a simple but powerful principle: pedagogy must remain sovereign. Technology may assist teachers, extend access to resources, and support administrative efficiency. It must not redefine the fundamental purpose of education or diminish the professional authority of those responsible for it.

CONCLUSION: HUMAN RIGHTS AS THE COMPASS FOR EDUCATIONAL AI

Artificial intelligence is entering education not as a single tool but as an infrastructure. Learning platforms, predictive analytics, generative assistants, behavioural monitoring systems, and automated assessment tools are beginning to shape how knowledge is produced, evaluated, and distributed within schools. Their presence will almost certainly expand. The question is not whether artificial intelligence will influence education. The question is under what conditions it will do so.

Throughout this chapter, one argument has remained constant. Artificial intelligence governance in education cannot be grounded solely in efficiency, innovation, or institutional convenience. It must be grounded in the protection of human dignity.

The human rights tradition offers precisely that foundation. From the Universal Declaration of Human Rights to the Convention on the Rights of the Child, the international community has repeatedly affirmed that education exists not merely to transmit knowledge but to cultivate the full development of the human person (United Nations, 1948; 1989).

Schools are entrusted with the intellectual and moral development of children—we would do well not to see them as sites of technological experimentation. Artificial intelligence systems introduced into these environments inevitably participate in that responsibility. They shape how students are evaluated, how attention is directed, how opportunity is distributed, and how authority is exercised within the classroom. When deployed carelessly, they risk amplifying inequality, narrowing intellectual autonomy, or normalising forms of surveillance incompatible with the conditions necessary for democratic life. When deployed responsibly, they may expand access to knowledge, support teachers in their work, and provide new tools for learning and creativity.

The difference between these outcomes will not be determined by technological capability alone. It will be determined by governance. Human rights frameworks provide the compass for that governance. They remind institutions that children are not merely future workers or data subjects within digital systems. They are rights holders whose dignity, privacy, agency, and participation must remain central to educational life.

This perspective also clarifies the role of educators. Teachers are not obstacles to technological progress. They are the professional stewards responsible for interpreting how new tools interact with curriculum, pedagogy, and student development. Artificial intelligence may assist them. It cannot replace the ethical judgment that teaching requires.

Seen in this light, the introduction of artificial intelligence into schools represents not simply a technological transition but a normative test. It asks whether societies are willing to preserve the moral commitments embedded in the human rights tradition even as new technological infrastructures emerge.

This question cannot remain abstract. The pace of technological development is accelerating. New forms of artificial intelligence are already emerging beyond the generative systems that first captured public attention. Agentic AI capable of autonomous task coordination, advanced learning analytics, robotics integrated into educational environments, immersive augmented and virtual reality systems, and even early quantum computing simulations are beginning to reshape how complex problems are explored in scientific and technical education. These developments will not remain confined to research laboratories for long.

As these technologies converge, the scale of both opportunity and risk will increase. Systems capable of adapting instruction in real time may transform personalised learning. Autonomous agents may assist in curriculum development or student support. Advanced analytics may help identify learning gaps earlier than traditional assessment. At the same time, the ethical questions examined in this chapter will intensify rather than diminish. Issues of surveillance, bias, autonomy, access, and institutional accountability will become more complex as technologies grow more powerful.

For this reason, the most important decisions about educational AI will not occur at the moment when these frontier systems arrive in classrooms. They will occur now, as institutions build the governance structures, ethical frameworks, and professional cultures that determine how such systems will eventually be used. Schools that develop strong foundations in human rights based governance, teacher capacity, and ethical reflection will be better prepared to integrate emerging technologies responsibly. Those that treat artificial intelligence as a purely technical procurement decision may find themselves reacting to systems that have already reshaped educational practice.

The future of educational AI must not be decided solely by engineers, policymakers, or technology companies. It must be shaped within classrooms, within school communities, and within the ethical commitments that societies choose to uphold. Human rights provide more than legal safeguards. They offer a moral orientation. They remind institutions that technological capability alone does not determine legitimacy.

Human rights were never intended to be static declarations. They are living commitments that must evolve alongside the societies they guide. In an age of increasingly intelligent systems, the task is not to resist technological change but to ensure that the moral architecture of education remains visible within it. If human rights remain the compass guiding those decisions, artificial intelligence may yet become a tool that expands educational possibility without sacrificing the dignity and agency of the next generation. The legitimacy of AI in education depends on whether it supports the flourishing of the children it affects, respects the professional judgment of educators, and strengthens rather than weakens the democratic purposes of schooling.

The next chapter turns to that future directly. It examines the technological horizon that may shape classrooms by the end of this decade and asks how educational institutions can prepare for a world in which artificial intelligence is no longer peripheral to learning but deeply integrated into it. The challenge will not simply be technological readiness. It will be ethical readiness.

And that work must begin long before 2030 arrives.

REFERENCES

Assefa, Y., Gebremeskel, M.M., Moges, B.T. and Tilwani, S.A. (2024) 'Rethinking the digital divide and associated educational in(equity) in higher education in the context of developing countries: The social justice perspective', *International Journal of Information and Learning Technology*, 42(1), 15–32. doi:10.1108/IJILT-03-2024-0058.

Beckman, K., Apps, T., Howard, S.K., Rogerson, C., Rogerson, A. and Tondeur, J. (2025) 'The GenAI divide among university students: A call for action', *The Internet and Higher Education*, 67, 101036. doi:10.1016/j.iheduc.2025.101036. Available at: www.sciencedirect.com/science/article/pii/S1096751625000454

Birhane, A. (2020) 'Algorithmic colonization of Africa', *SCRIPTed*, 17(2), 389–409. doi:10.2966/scrip.170220.389.

Bowman, D.N. and Bremner, L. (2025) 'Indigenous data sovereignty: Applying it by, with, for, and where it matters', *Canadian Journal of Program Evaluation*, 39(2), 265–287. doi:10.3138/cjpe-2024-0039. Available at: https://ces.journals.uvic.ca/index.php/cjpe/article/view/50

Couldry, N. and Mejias, U.A. (2019) *The Costs of Connection: How Data Is Colonizing Human Life and Appropriating It for Capitalism*. Stanford, CA: Stanford University Press.

Couldry, N. and Mejias, U.A. (2021) 'The decolonial turn in data and technology research: What is at stake and where is it heading?', *Information, Communication & Society*, 26(4), 786–802. doi:10.1080/1369118X.2021.1986102.

Gallagher, M., Evans, P. and Sarpong-Duah, J. (2024) 'Radiating out rather than scaling up: Horizontalism and digital educational governance in Ghana', *International Journal of Educational Development*, 111, 103168. doi:10.1016/j.ijedudev.2024.103168. Available at: www.sciencedirect.com/science/article/pii/S0738059324001950

Hawking, C. (2026) *'Why Are We Using AI in Schools?', Presentation at the International Association for Safe and Ethical AI*. Paris: UNESCO House, 24 February.

Holmes, W., Bialik, M. and Fadel, C. (2019) *Artificial Intelligence in Education: Promises and Implications for Teaching and Learning*. Boston: Center for Curriculum Redesign.

Kohnke, L. and Foung, D. (2024) 'Deconstructing the normalization of data colonialism in educational technology', *Education Sciences*, 14(1), 57. doi:10.3390/educsci14010057. Available at: www.mdpi.com/2227-7102/14/1/57

Lewis, J.E., Duarte, M.E., Kite, S., Pechawis, A., Tutuha, N., Brown, N., Curley, A., Gross, M., Hormel, K., Mika, C., Nabi-Bardhan, S., O'Neil, M., Poelina, A., Whyte, K. and Wylie, S. (2025) 'Abundant intelligences: Placing AI within Indigenous knowledge frameworks', *AI & Society*, 40, 2141–2157. doi:10.1007/s00146-024-02099-4. Available at: https://link.springer.com/article/10.1007/s00146-024-02099-4

Perera, M., Smith, L.T., Wihongi, H., Hudson, M., Kukutai, T., Rainie, S.C. and Lewis, J.E. (2025) 'Indigenous peoples and artificial intelligence: A systematic literature review', *Big Data & Society*, 12(2). doi:10.1177/20539517251349170. Available at: https://journals.sagepub.com/doi/10.1177/20539517251349170

UNESCO (2021) *Recommendation on the Ethics of Artificial Intelligence*. Paris: UNESCO. Available at: https://unesdoc.unesco.org/ark:/48223/pf0000380455.

United Nations (1948) *Universal Declaration of Human Rights.* New York: United Nations General Assembly. Available at: www.un.org/en/about-us/universal-declaration-of-human-rights

United Nations (1966a) *International Covenant on Civil and Political Rights.* New York: United Nations General Assembly. Available at: www.ohchr.org/en/instruments-mechanisms/instruments/international-covenant-civil-and-political-rights

United Nations (1966b) *International Covenant on Economic, Social and Cultural Rights.* New York: United Nations General Assembly. Available at: www.ohchr.org/en/instruments-mechanisms/instruments/international-covenant-economic-social-and-cultural-rights

United Nations (1989) *Convention on the Rights of the Child.* New York: United Nations General Assembly. Available at: www.ohchr.org/en/instruments-mechanisms/instruments/convention-rights-child

9 Vision for 2030

Preparing for the Classrooms of the Future

The release of ChatGPT in late 2022 did not merely introduce a new tool. It detonated a public mood.

Almost overnight, artificial intelligence moved from research labs and enterprise systems into kitchen table conversations, staff meetings, ministerial briefings, and school corridors. It triggered fascination, fear, career anxiety, academic integrity panic, and a familiar apocalyptic undertone about machines replacing humans. In education, the reaction was especially intense because schools were asked to respond publicly to a technology that appeared to arrive without warning and with enormous symbolic force (Dwivedi et al., 2023; Kasneci et al., 2023).

But it did not arrive without warning.

What caught much of the public by surprise was not the existence of artificial intelligence, but the speed with which one form of it became visible and socially usable. The underlying trajectory had been building for decades through machine learning, predictive analytics, recommendation systems, automation, and the long digitalisation of schooling (Selwyn, 2016; Holmes, Bialik and Fadel, 2019). By the time generative AI captured the headlines, classrooms had already spent more than twenty years absorbing data platforms, learning management systems, early warning tools, automated writing supports, and forms of algorithmic mediation that altered educational practice (Selwyn, 2016). ChatGPT was *the* spectacle. The infrastructure was already there. That distinction matters because it changes how the future should be read.

If the world treated generative AI as an unforeseen rupture, it was partly because it mistook public visibility for technological emergence. The more difficult truth is that

DOI: 10.1201/9781003662945-9

the broad direction of travel is already legible. The next phase of educational technology will not be defined by one chatbot or one platform. It will be shaped by *convergence*: advanced analytics, agentic systems, robotics, immersive and spatial computing, wearables and smart glasses, simulation environments, edge and cloud infrastructure, and, further out, quantum technologies and new forms of scientific modelling are all developing in parallel. Major technology outlooks in 2025 describe this wider movement clearly, pointing to simultaneous advances in immersive reality, cloud and edge computing, advanced connectivity, and quantum technologies rather than a single dominant innovation (McKinsey Global Institute, 2025).

This matters for ethics because risk exposure is compounding. Systems will become more embedded, more ambient, and more capable of acting across institutional workflows rather than sitting at the edge of them. Gartner has warned that through 2026, organisations will abandon 60 per cent of AI projects unsupported by AI ready data, and in 2025 it further projected that more than 40 per cent of agentic AI projects would be cancelled by the end of 2027 because of escalating costs, unclear business value, or inadequate risk controls (Gartner, 2025a; 2025b). These are not signs that institutions are struggling to build the governance, data foundations, and professional capacity required to carry it.

That struggle has an ethical dimension. When innovation advances faster than institutional readiness, the result is both technical and moral debt. Schools inherit systems they did not design, risks they are not prepared to govern, and behavioural shifts they have not had time to examine. It is less about educational institutions resisting the future, and more that they are being asked to absorb it before they have built the foundations required to do so with integrity (Pasquale, 2015).

This chapter argues that the period to 2030 should not be treated as a race to adopt the newest tools. It should be understood as a decisive window for institutional preparation. The central question is not which technologies will enter education. Many of them are already on the horizon. The real question is whether schools will develop the ethical, pedagogical, and organisational capacity to integrate them without surrendering professional judgment, widening inequality, or deepening digital debt (UNESCO, 2021).

To address that question, this chapter looks ahead to the technologies most likely to shape the next phase of K-12 education: agentic AI, advanced analytics, robotics, immersive and spatial computing, wearables, smart glasses, and increasingly sophisticated simulation environments, with quantum technologies appearing at the edge of the educational imagination. It considers not only their potential educational value, but also the compounding risks they bring. Most importantly, it argues that the work of preparing for 2030 does not begin in 2030. It begins now, in the slower and less glamorous labour of governance, professional development, pilot design, cultural change, and ethical discipline (UNESCO, 2021).

The future may be arriving quickly. But it is not arriving blindly. The outlines are already visible. The task now is to look at them with enough honesty to prepare.

PART I: FRONTIER TECHNOLOGIES AND THE CONVERGENCE OF EDUCATIONAL AI

If the release of generative AI exposed how quickly a single technology can reshape public debate, the next phase of artificial intelligence in education will likely be defined by something different. Not a single breakthrough, but convergence.

The systems most likely to shape classrooms over the coming decade are emerging simultaneously across several technological domains: advanced artificial intelligence, immersive computing environments, robotics, simulation technologies, and increasingly powerful computational infrastructures. None of these technologies alone will define the future of schooling. Their interaction will (Luckin et al., 2016; McKinsey Global Institute, 2025). Understanding that convergence matters because it clarifies why preparation must begin now rather than when a particular device or platform becomes widely adopted. By the time technologies become visible in classrooms, the underlying infrastructures are usually already in place (Selwyn, 2016).

Agentic AI

The first development shaping the next generation of educational technologies is the evolution from generative AI to agentic AI.

Generative systems respond to prompts by producing text, images, or other outputs. Agentic systems go further. They can plan, coordinate multiple tasks, retrieve information from multiple sources, and operate across software environments to accomplish goals with limited human intervention (Park et al., 2023).

Technology analysts increasingly describe this shift as the emergence of autonomous digital agents capable of executing complex workflows (IBM Institute for Business Value, 2025). These systems may analyse a learning objective, retrieve relevant resources, generate instructional material, adapt tasks based on student progress, and report learning outcomes back to institutional systems. For education, this could translate into AI systems capable of coordinating aspects of curriculum preparation, formative assessment, or student support. In principle, such systems could assist teachers by automating routine administrative tasks and synthesising educational resources (Holmes, Bialik and Fadel, 2019).

Yet the same capability also introduces new governance questions. When AI systems begin coordinating multiple actions across institutional infrastructure, they move from tools used by educators to systems operating within educational decision environments. The distinction matters because responsibility becomes more difficult to trace (Floridi et al., 2018).

Advanced learning analytics

A second development shaping the future of schooling is the expansion of advanced learning analytics.

For more than a decade, educational institutions have experimented with data driven systems designed to identify patterns in student engagement and performance. Early warning systems, predictive analytics dashboards, and adaptive learning platforms are already familiar within many universities and some school systems (Siemens and Baker, 2012; Ferguson, 2012).

The next generation of analytics systems extends these capabilities by integrating larger data streams, behavioural signals, and machine learning models capable of continuously updating predictions. Such systems may attempt to identify learning difficulties earlier, recommend targeted interventions, or dynamically adjust learning pathways (Siemens, 2013). Advocates argue that these tools may improve educational support by identifying students who might otherwise remain invisible within traditional assessment structures. Critics warn that predictive systems risk embedding historical bias, particularly when models are trained on datasets shaped by longstanding inequalities in educational access and achievement (Barocas and Selbst, 2016).

In both cases, the central point remains the same. These systems increasingly influence how educational attention and opportunity are distributed. Their governance therefore raises questions not only about accuracy, but about fairness, transparency, and institutional accountability.

Spatial computing and immersive learning environments

Another major technological trajectory is the development of spatial computing.

Spatial computing refers to technologies that merge digital and physical environments through augmented reality, virtual reality, and wearable interfaces such as smart glasses. Rather than interacting with information through traditional screens, learners interact with digital objects embedded within physical space (Billinghurst, Clark and Lee, 2015).

Immersive learning environments built through spatial computing could allow students to explore historical reconstructions, conduct virtual laboratory experiments, or manipulate complex scientific models in three dimensional environments (Radianti et al., 2020). Early forms of these technologies are already present in specialised training contexts such as medicine, engineering, and architecture. As hardware becomes lighter, more affordable, and more widely integrated into consumer ecosystems, similar capabilities may begin appearing in educational settings.

From an educational perspective, spatial computing offers new forms of experiential learning. From a governance perspective, it introduces new categories of data capture. Wearable devices and immersive systems may collect spatial movement data, gaze tracking, biometric indicators, and other behavioural signals that extend far beyond traditional educational records (Slater and Sanchez-Vives, 2016).

Robotics and embodied AI

The integration of robotics into educational environments represents another frontier.

Educational robotics has existed for many years as a tool for teaching programming and engineering concepts. However, recent advances in embodied artificial intelligence suggest that robots may increasingly participate in collaborative learning environments (Mubin et al., 2013).

Robotic systems capable of interacting with students, assisting in laboratory work, or supporting specialised educational needs are already under development in research contexts (Belpaeme, Kennedy and Ramachandran, 2018). In certain cases, such systems may assist students with disabilities by providing adaptive physical interfaces for learning activities.

The presence of embodied AI introduces a different set of ethical considerations from purely digital systems. Physical systems interact directly with human bodies and environments, raising questions about safety, supervision, and the social dynamics of human machine interaction in classrooms (Sharkey and Sharkey, 2012).

Simulation environments and scientific modelling

Simulation technologies also represent a growing area of educational innovation.

Advances in computational modelling now allow complex systems to be explored through interactive simulations that would previously have required expensive physical laboratories (de Jong and van Joolingen, 1998). Students can model climate systems, biological processes, chemical reactions, or engineering structures through digital environments capable of representing highly complex phenomena.

Simulation based learning offers significant pedagogical potential because it allows students to experiment with systems that are otherwise inaccessible (Rutten, van Joolingen and van der Veen, 2012). It can also support interdisciplinary problem solving, enabling learners to explore the interconnected dynamics of environmental, economic, and technological systems. These capabilities may become particularly important as education responds to global challenges such as climate change, public health, and sustainable development, which require systems thinking rather than isolated disciplinary knowledge (UNESCO, 2021).

Emerging computational infrastructures

Finally, the broader computational landscape is evolving.

Advances in cloud infrastructure, edge computing, and high performance computing are expanding the scale at which data intensive systems can operate (Armbrust et al., 2010).

At the frontier of this development lies quantum computing, which promises new forms of computational modelling capable of addressing complex optimisation and simulation problems beyond the reach of classical computing (Preskill, 2018). While quantum technologies are unlikely to enter everyday classrooms in the immediate future, their influence may shape advanced research environments and specialised educational programs. More importantly, they illustrate a wider point: the technological horizon facing education extends far beyond the generative AI systems that first captured public attention.

Convergence rather than replacement

Taken together, these developments suggest that the future of educational technology will not be defined by a single breakthrough. Instead, classrooms are likely to encounter a convergence of systems operating across different layers of infrastructure: intelligent software agents, immersive interfaces, physical robotics, data analytics, and advanced simulation environments (Luckin et al., 2016).

This convergence has two implications. First, it increases the potential for innovation in how students learn, explore complex problems, and access knowledge. Second, it increases the scale and complexity of the ethical questions surrounding educational technology. When systems observe behaviour, predict outcomes, adapt instruction, and operate across institutional infrastructures simultaneously, the governance challenges become qualitatively different from those posed by earlier educational technologies (Floridi et al., 2018).

It is precisely this expanding technological capability that reinforces the argument introduced in the previous chapter. As artificial intelligence becomes embedded within the environments through which individuals exercise fundamental rights such as education, privacy, and participation, the governance of these systems increasingly becomes a matter of human rights rather than merely technical regulation (UNESCO, 2021).

For that reason, the emergence of these technologies strengthens the case for revisiting the human rights architecture itself. If algorithmic systems shape how educational opportunity is distributed, how personal data is captured, and how institutional authority is exercised, then the protections surrounding those systems must evolve accordingly.

By 2030, the future classroom is unlikely to be organised around a single visible AI tool. It is more likely to involve a layered environment in which multiple systems operate at once: a teacher wearing lightweight translation enabled smart glasses; a learning platform dynamically adjusting tasks on the basis of prior interaction data; an analytics dashboard flagging patterns of disengagement; a simulation environment allowing students to model ecological or biomedical systems; and administrative agents generating reports, timetables, or parent communications in the background. None of these systems, taken individually, would appear to constitute a transformation of schooling. Together, however, they would alter the informational environment within which teaching, judgment, and institutional authority are exercised.

The next section therefore turns to the risks associated with this convergence. If the capabilities of educational technologies are expanding, so too are the ethical stakes of how they are deployed.

PART II: COMPOUNDING RISK AND THE ETHICAL GOVERNANCE OF CONVERGING TECHNOLOGIES

The technological developments outlined in the previous section promise significant educational opportunity. They also introduce a more complex risk landscape than earlier waves of educational technology.

In earlier phases of digitalisation, most educational technologies functioned as discrete tools. Learning management systems organised course material. Digital gradebooks stored assessment records. Video platforms extended access to lectures and learning resources. These systems altered educational practice, but their influence remained relatively contained within defined administrative functions.

The emerging generation of technologies operates differently. Artificial intelligence systems increasingly observe behaviour, generate content, predict outcomes, and interact across multiple layers of institutional infrastructure simultaneously. When these capabilities converge with immersive environments, wearable devices, advanced analytics, and autonomous agents, the result is not simply more technology in classrooms. It is a transformation of how educational environments function. Risk exposure therefore scales alongside capability.

The compounding nature of algorithmic risk

One of the defining characteristics of contemporary AI systems is that they accumulate influence over time.

Data gathered through learning platforms may feed predictive models. Predictive models may influence intervention strategies. Intervention strategies may alter how students are evaluated, supported, or categorised within institutional systems. Each layer appears manageable when viewed in isolation. Yet, when these layers interact, their cumulative effects become more difficult to anticipate or govern.

Research on algorithmic systems has repeatedly shown that errors or biases embedded within training data can propagate through decision systems at scale (Barocas and Selbst, 2016). In educational contexts, such dynamics can influence how students are identified as struggling learners, how behavioural risk is assessed, or how academic potential is interpreted.

This is not necessarily the result of malicious design. It often emerges from structural conditions. Models trained on historical educational data inevitably reflect patterns shaped by socioeconomic inequality, linguistic diversity, and institutional bias. When such models are integrated into decision processes, they risk reinforcing the very patterns institutions may be attempting to overcome. The ethical question therefore shifts from whether a particular system functions technically to whether its deployment reshapes opportunity structures within education.

Continuous profiling and the transformation of educational observation

A second emerging concern is the expansion of continuous profiling.

Earlier educational technologies captured discrete data points: exam scores, attendance records, assignment submissions. The new generation of systems increasingly captures behavioural signals as well. Engagement patterns, keystroke rhythms, eye tracking data, interaction timing, and platform navigation behaviour may all be incorporated into analytic systems attempting to model learning processes.

Some educational researchers argue that these signals can help educators identify students who need support earlier than traditional assessment allows. Others warn that behavioural inference systems may misinterpret neurodiversity, cultural communication styles, or non-linear learning pathways. From an ethical perspective, the issue is not simply whether such data improves predictive accuracy. It concerns the conditions under which children develop intellectual autonomy. When educational environments continuously analyse behaviour in order to generate predictions about performance or engagement, the distinction between observation and surveillance becomes difficult to maintain. For children and adolescents still developing their sense of identity and agency, the psychological implications of constant evaluation deserve careful consideration (United Nations, 1989).

Opacity and institutional responsibility

Another risk arises from the opacity of many contemporary AI systems.

Educational institutions increasingly procure technologies developed by external vendors whose models are proprietary and whose internal logic cannot easily be examined. Even when schools receive documentation describing system functionality, the underlying computational processes often remain inaccessible to educators and administrators.

This creates a governance paradox. Schools remain legally and ethically responsible for decisions affecting students, yet the tools influencing those decisions may operate through mechanisms that institutional actors cannot fully interpret.

Scholars have described this problem as a form of "black box" governance in which institutions rely on systems whose internal processes are difficult to audit (Pasquale, 2015). In education, where decisions influence life trajectories and developmental opportunities, such opacity raises serious questions about accountability. Human oversight becomes meaningful only when institutions possess the capacity to understand and evaluate the systems they deploy.

Global infrastructure and jurisdictional gaps

The global nature of digital infrastructure adds another layer of complexity.

Educational AI systems are often developed by multinational technology firms, hosted in distributed cloud environments, and deployed simultaneously across multiple jurisdictions. Data may move across national borders while regulatory frameworks remain territorially bounded. As discussed in earlier chapters, different jurisdictions approach AI governance through different regulatory models. Some rely on comprehensive frameworks such as the European Union's risk based regulatory structure. Others operate through sector specific rules or evolving national strategies.

For schools operating within global educational ecosystems, this creates overlapping governance obligations. Yet it also raises deeper ethical questions. When educational technologies are developed within one legal and cultural environment but deployed in another, whose values shape the system? The earlier discussion of digital colonialism illustrates how such dynamics can reproduce existing inequalities in knowledge production and technological control.

From technical risk to human rights

Taken together, these developments reveal why the governance of educational AI cannot be treated as a purely technical matter.

As algorithmic systems become embedded within the infrastructures through which children learn, communicate, and develop, they increasingly shape the practical conditions under which fundamental rights are exercised. Privacy, participation, equality of opportunity, and freedom of thought all become mediated by technological systems operating within educational institutions (United Nations, 1948).

This is precisely the concern raised in the previous chapter when considering whether existing human rights frameworks remain sufficient for the technological environment emerging in the twenty-first century. If artificial intelligence systems influence how educational opportunities are distributed, how personal data is interpreted, and how behavioural patterns are evaluated, then the governance of these systems becomes inseparable from the protection of human dignity. From this perspective, the argument for expanding the human rights architecture, including the proposal for an additional article addressing the rights of individuals within algorithmically mediated environments, becomes easier to understand. The aim is not to replace existing protections, but to ensure that they remain effective as new forms of institutional power emerge.

Ethical frameworks for educational AI governance

In practice, if educational institutions are to meet the demands of 2030, they will require structured governance frameworks capable of managing not only discrete risks, but the cumulative and evolving effects of artificial intelligence across educational systems. This need is increasingly reflected in regulatory and policy developments, where emerging approaches emphasise risk-based classification, proportional oversight, and the ongoing responsibility of institutions deploying AI systems.

Several approaches are already emerging within policy and research communities. The UNESCO Recommendation on the Ethics of Artificial Intelligence emphasises principles of proportionality, fairness, transparency, and human oversight (UNESCO, 2021). Algorithmic impact assessments, increasingly used in public sector governance, provide structured methods for evaluating potential harms before systems are deployed (Reisman et al., 2018). More recent regulatory models similarly reflect a shift towards risk-based governance, in which obligations are calibrated according to the potential impact of systems on individuals and institutions.

Within educational contexts, these frameworks can be translated into practical questions: what problem is the system intended to solve, and what evidence supports its effectiveness; whose data is being collected, and how it is protected; what biases may be embedded in training data or model design; who retains authority to override automated outputs; and whether students and families are able to understand and challenge decisions influenced by the system.

These questions are not merely procedural safeguards. They are expressions of the ethical commitments articulated within the human rights tradition. The purpose of governance is not to eliminate technological innovation, but to ensure that innovation unfolds within boundaries consistent with the dignity and development of the children whom educational institutions are entrusted to serve.

At the same time, the adequacy of existing frameworks cannot be assumed under conditions of rapid technological change. As artificial intelligence becomes more deeply embedded in educational environments, the object of governance shifts. Institutions are no longer evaluating discrete tools operating in isolation, but increasingly interconnected systems that evolve over time, interact with one another, and influence decision-making across multiple domains simultaneously.

Under these conditions, the application of ethical frameworks becomes more complex. A system may be evaluated at the point of adoption, yet its behaviour may change as models are updated or retrained. A single application may appear low risk in isolation, while its interaction with other systems produces cumulative effects that are difficult to anticipate. Decision-making processes that were once visible and attributable may become distributed across layers of infrastructure, making responsibility more difficult to trace.

The risk is therefore not limited to isolated instances of bias or error. It is the gradual erosion of visibility over how decisions are being shaped. In such contexts, governance challenges are compounded. Risks do not remain contained within individual systems, but emerge through their interaction, accumulation, and evolution over time. Regulatory approaches that emphasise risk classification and proportionality are, in part, a response to this shift. Yet their effectiveness depends on the capacity of institutions to recognise and manage risk not only at the point of adoption, but throughout the lifecycle of AI systems.

This is particularly evident in the phenomenon often described as *digital debt*. As new technologies are layered onto existing infrastructures without sufficient integration, governance, or professional capacity, institutions accumulate complexity that becomes increasingly difficult to manage. In the context of artificial intelligence, this complexity carries ethical implications. Systems introduced to improve efficiency or insight may, over time, create environments in which data flows, decision pathways, and accountability structures are no longer fully understood by those responsible for them. What begins as innovation can result in forms of institutional opacity that undermine both accountability and trust.

From this perspective, ethical frameworks must be understood not as static instruments, but as requiring sustained institutional capacity. Governance cannot be reduced to one-time evaluation or compliance processes. It must be maintained through continuous monitoring, periodic reassessment, and the ability to intervene when systems behave in ways that diverge from their intended purpose. In this sense, ethics becomes inseparable from risk management, organisational design, and professional practice.

From risk awareness to institutional preparation

Recognising these risks does not imply that educational institutions should reject emerging technologies. It does, however, require a shift in how adoption is understood. The introduction of artificial intelligence cannot be separated from the development of institutional capacity to govern it effectively and responsibly.

Preparing for the classrooms of 2030 will therefore require more than technological infrastructure. It will require professional knowledge, organisational coordination, and governance systems capable of operating under conditions of ongoing change. As technologies become more powerful and more embedded, the responsibility placed on educators and institutions becomes correspondingly greater. The central question is not whether schools will adopt artificial intelligence, but whether they will do so in ways that preserve their ability to understand, evaluate, and ultimately control how these systems shape educational practice.

PART III: INSTITUTIONAL READINESS AND THE GOVERNANCE OF EDUCATIONAL AI

If the previous sections examined the technological horizon and the ethical risks that accompany it, the final question is institutional. Are schools prepared to govern the systems they are beginning to adopt?

Technological change rarely fails because of a lack of innovation. It fails because institutions struggle to integrate new capabilities into existing structures of responsibility, professional practice, and cultural norms. Education is no exception. Over the past two decades, schools have absorbed successive waves of digital infrastructure, from learning management systems and cloud platforms to analytics dashboards and increasingly complex educational applications. Each cycle has introduced new capabilities, but also new dependencies and new forms of organisational complexity.

Artificial intelligence is likely to intensify this pattern rather than replace it. The challenge facing schools is therefore not only technological adoption, but institutional readiness.

From technological procurement to governance

One of the most persistent misconceptions surrounding educational technology is the belief that innovation begins with procurement. A school identifies a tool, signs a contract, and integrates the platform into its existing infrastructure.

Artificial intelligence does not fit comfortably within this model. AI systems influence decision-making processes, interact with data infrastructures, and often evolve through ongoing training and model updates. Their behaviour may change over time as new data enters the system. As a result, adoption cannot be treated as a single administrative event. It must be understood as an ongoing governance process.

Institutional readiness therefore begins with a shift in perspective. Schools must move from asking whether a technology works to asking how it will be governed over time. This includes establishing clear internal accountability structures, documenting system use cases, and ensuring that staff responsible for oversight possess sufficient technical and ethical literacy to interpret the behaviour of the systems they supervise. Without such capacity, institutions risk becoming dependent on systems they cannot fully evaluate.

Professional development and teacher capacity

The central actors in this process remain educators.

Public narratives about artificial intelligence often portray teachers as potential casualties of technological progress. Headlines regularly speculate about automated tutors, algorithmic curriculum design, or classrooms managed through intelligent systems. Such narratives overlook the fundamentally relational and interpretive nature of teaching.

Educational research has consistently shown that effective teaching depends on professional judgment developed through experience: the ability to recognise subtle learning difficulties, to adapt explanations dynamically, to respond to emotional cues, and to cultivate intellectual curiosity within diverse groups of students. Artificial intelligence may assist with certain instructional tasks, but it does not replicate the interpretive dimension of pedagogy.

For this reason, institutional readiness must include sustained professional development. Educators require not only familiarity with AI systems, but also an understanding of their limitations, assumptions, and potential effects on curriculum design, assessment practices, and student wellbeing. The objective is not to transform teachers into technologists, but to ensure that they remain the primary interpreters of how technology is used within the learning environment. Without this professional capacity, technological systems risk shaping educational practice by default rather than through deliberate pedagogical choice.

Leadership, change management, and organisational capacity for 2030

The question of institutional readiness cannot be reduced to teacher capacity alone. If schools are to govern increasingly complex technological environments by 2030, leadership itself will need to change. Artificial intelligence does not simply introduce new tools into educational settings. It alters the conditions under which decisions are made, risks are assessed, responsibilities are distributed, and trust is maintained. For that reason, institutional readiness is also a leadership challenge.

Educational leaders will require a broader repertoire of skills than has traditionally been expected in digital strategy. Technical procurement and basic platform oversight will no longer be sufficient. School leaders will increasingly need to understand risk classification, data governance, vendor accountability, organisational change, and the cultural conditions under which staff can adopt new technologies without being overwhelmed by them. They will need to distinguish between innovation that strengthens educational practice and innovation that merely accelerates complexity. They will also need the judgment to recognise when institutional enthusiasm for technological change is outpacing the organisation's capacity to absorb it responsibly.

This implies a significant programme of upskilling at leadership level. By 2030, the most effective school leaders are unlikely to be those who simply endorse innovation most enthusiastically, but those who can integrate technological decision making into wider frameworks of safeguarding, compliance, professional learning, and institutional risk management. Artificial intelligence governance will increasingly require leadership teams to interpret regulatory developments, understand lifecycle oversight, and assess not only whether a system is useful, but whether its deployment is proportionate, explainable, and sustainable over time.

There is also a change management dimension that educational institutions often underestimate. New technologies do not enter empty environments. They enter schools already shaped by workload pressures, uneven digital confidence, competing priorities, and varying levels of trust in leadership. If AI is introduced primarily through top down rhetoric about efficiency, disruption, or inevitable transformation, resistance should not be understood simply as conservatism. It may reflect legitimate concerns about safety, professional erosion, or institutional haste. Responsible implementation therefore depends not only on what systems are introduced, but on how the process of introduction is governed.

This is one reason why AI readiness should be understood in part as a safety and organisational health issue. In the same way that schools have developed cultures around safeguarding, health and safety, and child protection, they will increasingly need cultures capable of identifying, escalating, and managing technological risk. This includes clear reporting routes for concerns, leadership willingness to pause or withdraw problematic systems, and a shared understanding that ethical deployment is not a peripheral matter, but part of the institution's duty of care.

A culture of safe technological use is not created by policy language alone. It is built through repetition, leadership example, professional trust, and the normalisation of critical questioning.

From this perspective, compliance should not be understood narrowly as legal obligation. In the educational context, it is better understood as part of a wider institutional culture in which responsibility, documentation, review, and challenge are taken seriously before failure occurs rather than afterwards. Risk management, similarly, cannot remain confined to technical staff or procurement teams. It must become part of how leadership teams think about educational integrity, student protection, staff workload, and organisational resilience.

The schools best prepared for 2030 are therefore unlikely to be those that have adopted the greatest number of AI enabled systems. They are more likely to be those that have developed leadership structures capable of absorbing technological change without losing sight of educational purpose. In this respect, readiness is not a measure of how advanced an institution appears, but of how well it can govern complexity while maintaining trust.

Avoiding the expansion of digital debt

Institutional readiness also intersects with a broader organisational challenge increasingly discussed in technology governance: digital debt.

Digital debt refers to the accumulation of complexity that arises when new technologies are layered onto existing systems without sufficient integration, governance, or professional capacity (Protiviti, 2024). Over time, institutions may find themselves operating infrastructures that are difficult to maintain, poorly understood, and increasingly resistant to oversight.

In the context of artificial intelligence, this accumulation has distinct implications. Systems may draw on shared data sources, feed into one another, or influence overlapping decision processes. As layers of technology increase, the ability to trace how particular outcomes are produced may diminish. This is not simply an operational concern. It is an ethical one. When institutions cannot clearly understand how decisions are shaped, their ability to ensure fairness, accountability, and transparency is weakened. For schools, this emphasises the importance of integration planning and governance from the outset. Artificial intelligence cannot simply be added to existing digital infrastructures without careful consideration of how systems interact, how data flows across them, and how responsibility is maintained.

Pilot cultures and responsible experimentation

Another dimension of institutional readiness concerns the culture through which innovation is introduced. Educational institutions often face pressure to adopt new technologies rapidly. However, the complexity and evolving nature of AI systems make unstructured deployment particularly risky. A more sustainable approach involves structured experimentation.

Pilot programmes allow schools to test technologies within defined parameters, evaluate educational outcomes, and identify unintended effects before wider implementation. Crucially, such experimentation should include ethical as well as technical evaluation. Feedback from students, educators, and families can provide insight into how technologies are experienced in practice, while governance structures can assess alignment with principles of fairness, transparency, and student wellbeing.

In this sense, experimentation is not a preliminary stage prior to adoption, but a core component of governance. It provides a controlled environment in which risks can be identified before they become embedded within institutional systems.

Building institutional culture

Ultimately, institutional readiness is shaped as much by culture as by policy or infrastructure.

The ways in which educators interpret technological change, the extent to which leaders encourage critical engagement, and the degree to which institutions prioritise responsibility alongside innovation all influence how artificial intelligence is integrated into educational environments.

If AI is introduced primarily as a tool for efficiency or performance, it is likely to be adopted in ways that prioritise those outcomes. If it is approached through the lens of educational purpose, student development, and institutional responsibility, different choices follow.

A rights-based framework provides a useful point of reference. When institutions evaluate technological adoption in relation to human dignity, student development, and the broader aims of education, governance becomes anchored in purpose rather than driven by external pressures. Such alignment is essential if schools are to build cultures capable of sustaining compliance, managing risk, and ensuring that the deployment of artificial intelligence remains both safe and ethically defensible over time.

Preparing for 2030

The period leading to 2030 represents a critical window for educational institutions.

The technologies discussed earlier in this chapter will continue to evolve. Artificial intelligence systems will become more capable, immersive technologies more accessible, and data infrastructures more integrated into everyday educational practice. Yet the fundamental question facing schools will remain unchanged.

Will institutions shape these technologies according to educational values, or will technologies reshape educational institutions by default?

The answer depends less on technological progress than on institutional preparation. Schools that invest in teacher capacity, governance structures, ethical reflection, and responsible experimentation will be better positioned to integrate emerging technologies without sacrificing their core mission. Those that treat artificial intelligence as simply another procurement decision may find themselves adapting to systems whose implications were never fully examined. The future of educational AI will therefore not be decided solely by engineers or technology companies. It will be shaped within classrooms, within school leadership teams, and within the professional cultures of education systems around the world. Preparing for that future requires more than technical readiness. It requires moral clarity about the purpose of education itself. And it requires beginning that work now.

CONCLUSION: PREPARING THE ETHICAL FOUNDATIONS OF THE FUTURE CLASSROOM

The argument of this chapter has been forward looking, but its central claim is about preparation, not technology.

Artificial intelligence will continue to evolve rapidly in the coming years. Agentic systems, immersive environments, advanced analytics, robotics, and simulation technologies will expand the ways in which knowledge can be explored, modelled, and shared. These developments hold genuine promise for education. They may allow students to investigate complex systems, collaborate across distances, and access forms of learning that were previously limited by physical or institutional constraints.

Yet the trajectory described in this chapter also reveals a deeper truth. The challenge facing schools is less about technological adoption, and more about the ethical governance of increasingly powerful infrastructures that shape how students learn, how educators teach, and how opportunity is distributed within educational systems. The future classroom will be defined by the choices institutions make about how technology is integrated into the moral architecture of education. The platforms and tools chosen are of secondary importance.

Earlier chapters in this book traced how digitalisation has already transformed educational environments over the past two decades. They examined the governance challenges created by artificial intelligence, the regulatory frameworks emerging across jurisdictions, and the human rights principles that provide a foundation for evaluating technological change. This chapter has extended that discussion by looking ahead to the technological horizon that may shape the next phase of educational development.

Across these discussions, a consistent theme emerges. Artificial intelligence does not determine the future of education. Institutions do. Technological systems reflect the priorities, assumptions, and governance structures of the societies that deploy them. When those systems are introduced into schools, they interact with an environment that carries particular responsibilities. Education is not merely an administrative function or an economic pipeline. It is a formative institution responsible for cultivating intellectual agency, social participation, and the capacity for independent judgment.

This is why the ethical questions surrounding artificial intelligence in education cannot be postponed until technologies mature. The foundations that determine how these systems will be used are being established now. Decisions about data governance, institutional oversight, teacher capacity, and ethical frameworks will shape the conditions under which future technologies enter classrooms. If those foundations are weak, technological capability will outpace institutional control. If they are strong, innovation can unfold within boundaries that protect students, support educators, and sustain the democratic purposes of education.

The task ahead therefore requires both imagination and restraint. Educational institutions must remain open to new forms of learning made possible by emerging technologies, while maintaining the ethical clarity necessary to question systems that threaten to distort educational purpose.

Artificial intelligence may become an important component of future classrooms. It should never become their defining authority.

***

The chapters of this book have examined artificial intelligence in education from multiple perspectives: technological development, regulatory frameworks, ethical governance, human rights, global inequality, and institutional readiness. Together, they suggest that the debate about educational AI is not simply about tools. It is about how societies choose to organise the relationship between technology, knowledge, and human development.

The final chapter—the conclusion—draws these threads together. It returns to the central question that has run beneath every discussion in this book: *what kind of educational future are we willing to build in an age of intelligent systems*? Answering that question requires more than policy guidance or technical expertise. It requires moral judgment about the role education should play in shaping human flourishing in a technologically mediated world.

The conclusion therefore turns from analysis to reflection. It considers the lessons emerging from this moment of technological transformation and asks what responsibilities educators, policymakers, and societies must accept if artificial intelligence is to serve education rather than redefine it. The future of learning is being constructed now. The final chapter asks what principles should guide its design.

REFERENCES

Armbrust, M., Fox, A., Griffith, R., Joseph, A.D., Katz, R., Konwinski, A., Lee, G., Patterson, D., Rabkin, A., Stoica, I., and Zaharia, M. (2010). 'A view of cloud computing', *Communications of the ACM*, 53(4), 50–58. Available at: https://doi.org/10.1145/1721654.1721672.

Barocas, S. and Selbst, A. (2016) 'Big data's disparate impact', *California Law Review*, 104(3), 671–732. Available at: https://papers.ssrn.com/sol3/papers.cfm?abstract_id=2477899

Belpaeme, T., Kennedy, J. and Ramachandran, A. (2018) 'Social robots for education: A review', *Science Robotics*, 3(21). Available at: www.science.org/doi/10.1126/scirobotics.aat5954

Billinghurst, M., Clark, A. and Lee, G. (2015) 'A survey of augmented reality', *Foundations and Trends in Human–Computer Interaction*, 8(2–3), 73–272. Available at: www.researchgate.net/publication/277637661_A_Survey_of_Augmented_Reality

de Jong, T. and van Joolingen, W. (1998) 'Scientific discovery learning with computer simulations', *Review of Educational Research*, 68(2), 179–201. Available at: www.jstor.org/stable/1170753

Dwivedi, Y.K. et al. (2023) 'So what if ChatGPT wrote it? Multidisciplinary perspectives on opportunities, challenges and implications of generative conversational AI', *International Journal of Information Management*, 71. https://doi.org/10.1016/j.ijinfomgt.2023.102642

Ferguson, R. (2012) 'Learning analytics: Drivers, developments and challenges', *International Journal of Technology Enhanced Learning*, 4(5–6), 304–317. Available at: https://dl.acm.org/doi/10.1504/IJTEL.2012.051816

Floridi, L. et al. (2018) 'AI4People—An ethical framework for a good AI society', *Minds and Machines*, 28, 689–707. Available at: https://pubmed.ncbi.nlm.nih.gov/30930541/

Gartner (2025a) *Gartner Says Lack of AI-Ready Data Puts AI Projects at Risk.* Stamford, CT: Gartner. Available at: www.gartner.com/en/newsroom/press-releases/2025-02-26-lack-of-ai-ready-data-puts-ai-projects-at-risk

Gartner (2025b) *Top Strategic Technology Trends for 2025.* Stamford, CT: Gartner Research.

Holmes, W., Bialik, M. and Fadel, C. (2019) *Artificial Intelligence in Education: Promises and Implications for Teaching and Learning.* Boston: Center for Curriculum Redesign. Available at: www.researchgate.net/publication/332180327_Artificial_Intelligence_in_Education_Promise_and_Implications_for_Teaching_and_Learning

IBM Institute for Business Value (2025). *Agentic AI's Strategic Ascent.* Available at: www.ibm.com/thought-leadership/institute-business-value/en-us/report/agentic-ai-operating-model

Kasneci, E. et al. (2023) 'ChatGPT for good? On opportunities and challenges of large language models for education', *Learning and Individual Differences*, 103. https://doi.org/10.1016/j.lindif.2023.102274

Luckin, R. et al. (2016) *Intelligence Unleashed: An argument for AI in Education.* London: Pearson. Available at: www.researchgate.net/publication/299561597_Intelligence_Unleashed_An_argument_for_AI_in_Education

McKinsey Global Institute (2025) *Technology Trends Outlook 2025.* McKinsey & Company. Available at: www.mckinsey.com/capabilities/tech-and-ai/our-insights/the-top-trends-in-tech

Mubin, O., Stevens, C.J., Shahid, S., Al Mahmud, A., and Dong, J.J. (2013) 'A review of the applicability of robots in education', *Journal of Technology in Education and Learning.* Available at: https://roila.org/wp-content/uploads/2013/07/209-0015.pdf

Park, J. et al. (2023) 'Generative agents: Interactive simulacra of human behavior', *Proceedings of the ACM Conference on Human Factors in Computing Systems.* Available at: https://dl.acm.org/doi/10.1145/3586183.3606763

Pasquale, F. (2015) *The Black Box Society: The Secret Algorithms that Control Money and Information.* Cambridge, MA: Harvard University Press. Available at: https://raley.english.ucsb.edu/wp-content/Engl800/Pasquale-blackbox.pdf

Preskill, J. (2018) 'Quantum computing in the NISQ era and beyond', *Quantum*, 2, 79. Available at: https://quantum-journal.org/papers/q-2018-08-06-79/

Protiviti (2024) *Global Technology Executive Survey: Digital Debt and the Future of Enterprise Technology.* Menlo Park, CA: Protiviti. Available at: www.protiviti.com/gl-en/global-technology-executive-survey

Radianti, J., Majchrzak, T.A., Fromm, J., and Wohlgenannt, I. (2020) 'A systematic review of immersive virtual reality applications for higher education', *Computers & Education*, 147. Available at: www.sciencedirect.com/science/article/pii/S0360131519303276

Reisman, D., Schultz, J., Crawford, K. and Whittaker, M. (2018) *Algorithmic Impact Assessments: A Practical Framework for Public Agency Accountability.* New York: AI Now Institute. Available at: https://ainowinstitute.org/wp-content/uploads/2023/04/aiareport2018.pdf

Rutten, N., van Joolingen, W. and van der Veen, J. (2012) 'The learning effects of computer simulations in science education', *Computers & Education*, 58(1), 136–153. Available at: https://dl.acm.org/doi/abs/10.1016/j.compedu.2011.07.017

Selwyn, N. (2016) *Education and Technology: Key Issues and Debates.* 2nd edn. London: Bloomsbury.

Sharkey, N. and Sharkey, A. (2012) 'Granny and the robots: Ethical issues in robot care for the elderly', *Ethics and Information Technology*, 14(1), 27–40. Available at: https://link.springer.com/article/10.1007/s10676-010-9234-6

Siemens, G. and Baker, R. (2012) 'Learning analytics and educational data mining', *Proceedings of the 2nd International Conference on Learning Analytics and Knowledge.* Available at: https://dl.acm.org/doi/10.1145/2330601.2330661

Siemens, G. (2013) 'Learning analytics: The emergence of a discipline', American Behavioral Scientist, 57(10), 1380–1400. Available at: https://journals.sagepub.com/doi/abs/10.1177/0002764213498851?journalCode=absb

Slater, M. and Sanchez-Vives, M. (2016). 'Enhancing our lives with immersive virtual reality', *Frontiers in Robotics and AI*, 3, 74. Available at: https://doi.org/10.3389/frobt.2016.00074. Available at: www.researchgate.net/publication/311778884_Enhancing_Our_Lives_with_Immersive_Virtual_Reality

UNESCO (2021) *Recommendation on the Ethics of Artificial Intelligence*. Paris: UNESCO. Available at: https://unesdoc.unesco.org/ark:/48223/pf0000380455

United Nations (1948) *Universal Declaration of Human Rights*. New York: United Nations General Assembly. Available at: www.un.org/en/about-us/universal-declaration-of-human-rights

United Nations (1989) *Convention on the Rights of the Child*. New York: United Nations General Assembly. Available at: www.ohchr.org/en/instruments-mechanisms/instruments/convention-rights-child

Conclusion *Keeping It Real—Moving Forward* 10

This book began with a practical concern and arrived at a deeper one. At first glance, the subject appeared to be solely concerned with artificial intelligence in schools: what it is, how it works, where it is already being used, and what risks it carries. But as has been explored in depth, the question is far more about thc institutional and moral impact of artificial intelligence. The technological aspects are of lesser importance as they are developing constantly and are therefore harder to quantify.

What happens when systems that sort, predict, generate, recommend, and increasingly act begin to shape the environments in which children learn, teachers teach, and schools make decisions? When educational institutions, already shaped by two decades of uneven and often ineffectual digitalisation, are asked to absorb a new wave of technologies without sufficient time, capacity, or ethical preparation? And most importantly, what happens to the purposes of education itself when intelligent systems begin to occupy roles once reserved for human judgement? These are questions that deserve to be wrestled with, and which this book has attempted to answer.

What has been offered through this book is more demanding than either utopia or apocalypse. Artificial intelligence in education is a test of whether schools, policymakers, and societies are willing to govern technological power with enough seriousness to protect the dignity, agency, and developmental needs of the children at the centre of education. The AI in education market is set to grow exponentially in the coming years, creating an opportunity to capture a user base desperate for improvement and change. This market has no intention of waiting for evidence to mature, governance to be built, or ethical questions to be resolved. There is money to be made, and education is an attractive sector in which to do so.

That is the thread running through every chapter. The ethics and governance of AI is the story—the technologies themselves simply how this story is told. And beneath governance lies a still deeper concern: whether education remains accountable to human purposes in an age increasingly shaped by machine systems.

DOI:10.1201/9781003662945-10

WHAT THIS BOOK HAS SHOWN

One of the book's first arguments was historical. Artificial intelligence entered a system already altered by earlier waves of digitisation. Chapter 2 traced this lineage from the calculator debates of the 1980s through interactive whiteboards, Building Schools for the Future, MOOCs, tablets, and virtual learning environments. The promises accompanying each wave were remarkably consistent: personalised learning, improved outcomes, reduced workload, and modernised classrooms. The evidence, examined honestly, told a different story. Meta-analyses of educational technology research consistently showed modest average effects on student learning, with significant variation depending on implementation and context (Hattie, 2009; Tamim et al., 2011). The gap between promise and evidence became one of the defining features of educational technology adoption. Yet the pattern repeated, almost word for word, each time a new technology arrived.

This history matters because it punctures the myth of sudden rupture. ChatGPT may have captured public attention dramatically, but the conditions that made its arrival feel plausible had been developing for years. Digital infrastructures, data habits, weak oversight, and the gradual normalisation of platform dependence all prepared the ground. The interactive whiteboard experience alone should have provided an enduring warning: the United Kingdom invested heavily in a technology that produced, at best, modest and often short-lived gains in attainment, yet the investment continued and the technology became embedded before the evidence base was established (Higgins, Beauchamp and Miller, 2007). Education systems have demonstrated a limited institutional memory regarding technology adoption, and that institutional amnesia is now repeating itself with AI.

The pandemic years intensified these patterns. Emergency remote learning exposed the fragility of educational systems, the depth of digital inequality, and the extent to which rapidly adopted platforms carried hidden costs in data extraction, surveillance, and opacity. Chapter 3 documented how the crisis did not create all the problems discussed in this book but made them visible. The Sutton Trust found that 54 per cent of private schools had devices ready for online learning, compared to just 5 per cent of state schools (Sutton Trust, 2021). A Human Rights Watch investigation later found that 89 per cent of educational technology products recommended by governments during the pandemic had the capacity to surveil children in ways unrelated to education (Human Rights Watch, 2022). Those platforms became the default infrastructure, a legacy schools the world over now wrestle with. The crisis revealed how quickly educational institutions can become dependent on technical systems they neither fully govern nor fully understand.

As AI Ed Tech moved into the mainstream, public discourse often fixated on novelty. Adaptive tutors, automated grading, behavioural prediction, and now generative and agentic systems were framed either as revolutionary breakthroughs or as existential threats. But as Chapter 4 demonstrated, the ethical questions that mattered most were more grounded. Who benefits? Who is misread? Who is excluded? Who remains accountable when the system fails? The history of Ed Tech is littered with cautionary tales. Knewton, once valued at over $180 million and hailed as the future of personalised learning, ended in a fire sale to Wiley: a reminder that venture capital enthusiasm is a poor substitute for demonstrated educational impact. The Ofqual A-level algorithm disaster of 2020, the racial bias documented in proctoring software, and the Anne Frank Holocaust denial chatbot all stood as case studies in what happens when technology is deployed without adequate oversight. What appears as personalised support in one context may become intensified surveillance in another. What is sold as innovation may in practice shift power away from teachers, families, and students toward opaque technical infrastructures.

THE ETHICAL CORE

Running through every chapter of this book are five recurring ethical tensions. They are worth naming explicitly now, because they define the terrain on which the future of AI in education will be contested.

The first is *power without visibility*. Artificial intelligence systems increasingly shape educational life through classification, prediction, recommendation, and behavioural analysis. Yet these forms of power often remain difficult to see. The greater danger lies less in overt misuse than in ordinary adoption without sufficient understanding. As Chapter 5 argued, much of the ethical problem lies in normalisation: Google's education suite became the default in thousands of schools, yet adoption occurred with limited public debate about corporate power, data extraction, or democratic accountability. By 2018, 80 million teachers and students relied on it globally. Plagiarism detection tools shifted pedagogy from trust to surveillance. Learning analytics systems began labelling students as "at risk" using algorithms whose assumptions teachers were not trained to interrogate.

The second is *efficiency without reflection*. Again and again, this book has shown that educational institutions are vulnerable to the language of efficiency. Tools that promise to save time, personalise learning, detect risk early, and scale support. These are seductive promises, particularly in systems already under strain and teachers without enough hours in the day. But efficiency remains a managerial principle, and education has obligations it alone cannot satisfy. The EEF-funded trial that found a 31 per cent reduction in planning time for Key Stage 3 science was real and welcome, but it amounted to roughly an hour per week (AICERTS, 2025). The promise of efficiency is only as good as the governance that surrounds it.

The third is *data without dignity*. Student data deserves better than to be endlessly captured, repurposed, or modelled as though it were raw material. Chapter 8 argued that privacy plays a foundational role in the development of human freedom—far beyond a technical preference about data handling. The ability to think, experiment, err, and change without permanent surveillance is essential to intellectual growth and moral agency. Once educational environments become sites of continuous extraction, the conditions of freedom, experimentation, and intellectual development begin to narrow. The Convention on the Rights of the Child remains a living articulation of the moral principles that should govern how technology is deployed in the lives of vulnerable people.

The fourth is *innovation without accountability*. Innovation detached from governance creates institutional drift. New systems are introduced before rules are clear, before staff are trained, before families understand the stakes, and before children can meaningfully participate in decisions affecting them. The result amounts to a transfer of power without adequate democratic control. Chapter 6 argued that AI governance must operate at multiple levels simultaneously: classroom, school leadership, local authority oversight, vendor accountability, and participatory engagement with parents and students.

The fifth is *access without justice*. Asking whether schools have AI tools misses the point. The harder question is whether institutions have the capacity to govern them, adapt them to local educational purposes, and ensure they do not deepen old inequalities under new digital forms. The Sutton Trust's 2025 report revealed that teachers in private schools were more than twice as likely to have received formal AI training as their state school counterparts, and private schools were three times more likely to have a school-wide AI strategy (Sutton Trust, 2025). Technology benefits those already advantaged, unless governance explicitly addresses this tendency. The same logic that produces digital colonialism across countries can reproduce itself between neighbouring schools divided by funding, expertise, and institutional power.

FROM CRITIQUE TO CONSTRUCTION

These five tensions are dimensions of a single structural challenge, and they compound one another: how to govern powerful technologies within institutions whose core purpose is the development of young human beings. Each tension, left unaddressed, compounds the others. Power without visibility makes accountability impossible. Efficiency without reflection erodes the purposes that governance is supposed to protect. Data without dignity undermines the trust on which educational relationships depend. Innovation without accountability produces institutional drift. And access without justice ensures that the benefits of technology flow to those who need them least. Alongside its diagnosis, this book has articulated responses.

The first response, developed across Chapters 5 and 6, is that AI must be treated as a safeguarded educational practice rather than a procurement event. Ethics must shape classroom use, institutional policy, and oversight from the start, rather than being bolted on after deployment. Schools need governance architectures that clarify who is responsible, how systems are reviewed, how risks are escalated, and how students and families can challenge decisions. Accountability needs concrete expression: documented impact assessments before deployment, safeguarding leads involved in procurement decisions, override authority retained by trained educators in every high-stakes decision, and students treated as rights-bearing participants rather than passive data subjects: these are the structural components of responsible adoption.

The second response, drawn from Chapter 7, is regulatory seriousness. The GDPR, the EU AI Act with its risk-tier model for classifying AI systems, COPPA in the United States, Brazil's LGPD, and emerging frameworks internationally all set vital floors beneath which institutions must not fall. Education is explicitly identified as a high-risk domain under the EU AI Act, with specific obligations imposed on both providers and deployers. Schools need legal literacy as a means of protecting educational trust, well beyond a compliance exercise. Yet regulation, important as it is, sets only a floor. Governance must build the ceiling.

The third response is deeper still. Chapter 8 argued that human rights must serve as the normative foundation for AI in education. The Universal Declaration of Human Rights and the Convention on the Rights of the Child articulate the moral principles that should govern how technology is deployed in the lives of vulnerable people. Privacy, dignity, participation, equality, and educational development remain the standards by which legitimacy must be judged. The chapter also examined digital colonialism and argued that movements such as Indigenous data sovereignty offer an important counter-narrative: governance must be grounded in local educational agency and community voice, not imposed from above.

The fourth response is the preservation of teacher judgement. This book has repeatedly argued that AI may support educators, but it must not displace the interpretive and relational work that defines teaching. No amount of clever wordplay by an AI tutor will replace the warm and encouraging words of a teacher a student trusts. The relational aspect of learning can only be gained over time and is often hard won. As the American Enterprise Institute has warned, the risk of professional deskilling in education is uniquely high because what is being eroded is not merely a job skill but a human connection (AEI, 2025). Professional development, mentoring, communities of practice, and local capacity building are therefore core conditions for responsible AI adoption, as essential as the governance frameworks themselves.

The fifth response, articulated in Chapter 9, concerns timing. The period before 2030 offers a window to build ethical readiness, pilot carefully, strengthen data governance, and establish cultures capable of absorbing technological change without surrendering educational purpose. The next phase of educational technology will be shaped by the simultaneous development of agentic AI systems, advanced learning analytics, spatial computing, robotics, and simulation environments. Risk exposure is compounding rather than stabilising. Schools that have built robust governance foundations will be positioned to sculpt rather than merely survive what Mustafa Suleyman has called "the coming wave" (Suleyman and Bhaskar, 2023). Those that have not may find themselves swept along by forces beyond their control.

CROSS-SECTOR COLLABORATION: WHAT MOVING FORWARD ACTUALLY REQUIRES

A persistent finding across this book is that no single sector can solve these challenges alone. The problems are too distributed, too interconnected, and too deeply embedded in institutional practice for any one actor to address them comprehensively. Educators understand pedagogy, developmental needs, classroom dynamics, and institutional realities. Policymakers shape the legal and funding conditions under which technologies are deployed. Technology developers design systems whose assumptions and affordances structure educational possibilities. Families and communities understand local context, values, and the lived consequences of policy choices. Students themselves, too often omitted from decision-making, possess crucial knowledge about how digital systems are experienced from within.

Responsible AI in education therefore requires genuine collaboration across sectors, including shared governance, reciprocal accountability, and sustained structures through which concerns can travel across institutional boundaries. Developers must be required to explain systems in terms educators can use. Policymakers must avoid imposing innovation agendas without supporting governance capacity. Schools must not accept vendor language as a substitute for independent judgement. Communities must be treated as participants in shaping educational technology, not merely as recipients of decisions already made.

As Stuart Russell has argued, the most important thing we can do is build systems and frameworks that are "provably safe and beneficial for humans" (Russell, 2019). Cross-sector partnership, at its best, exists to prevent any one actor from holding unchecked power over the technical and moral design of schooling.

SUSTAINING ETHICAL CULTURE: PROFESSIONAL LEARNING AND MENTORSHIP

An ethical framework survives only inside an institution that knows how to sustain it. Continual professional learning must therefore be treated as a structural necessity. AI literacy in schools needs to go far beyond a one-off workshop on prompt writing or a temporary policy response to plagiarism concerns, developing instead into an ongoing professional formation in how intelligent systems work, what they obscure, how they shape judgement, and where educators retain authority. There is much evidence in support: 76 per cent of teachers report receiving no training or substantial guidance from their school on how to use AI effectively (Twinkl, 2025). The DfE's own Technology in Schools survey found that while 61 per cent of leaders believed technology had reduced staff workload, only 43 per cent of classroom teachers agreed—a gap that hints at the distance between leadership perception and frontline reality (DfE, 2025).

Mentorship networks matter here. Much of the most meaningful knowledge about technology adoption does not emerge from formal guidance alone. It travels through trusted professional relationships: experienced teachers supporting newer colleagues, school leaders learning from peers across systems, safeguarding specialists advising curriculum teams, and interdisciplinary groups working through difficult cases together. These communities of practice can become the ethical immune system of a school. They create the conditions in which concerns are raised early, uncertainty is discussed openly, and professional confidence is preserved rather than eroded.

It is well known that teaching attracts a disproportionate number of professionals with a strong moral sense. The narrative around AI—that it is a tool for shortcuts—sits uncomfortably with many teachers who see the graft of lesson preparation and marking as core to their professional identity. The BETT 2025 survey found that 44 per cent of teachers felt they were "cheating" when they used AI (BETT, 2025). Teacher Tapp data revealed that while 58 per cent of teachers now use AI for their work, only a third of those using it for lesson preparation had admitted as much to their senior leadership team, illustrating the growth of shadow AI across education (Teacher Tapp, 2025). Tackling this mindset—not by dismissing the moral instinct behind it, but by channeling it toward responsible and transparent use—must be a core part of the school leader's role. An ethically aware school culture grows from confidence that difficult questions can be asked without institutional defensiveness—rather than from fear of getting AI wrong.

WHAT WE STILL NEED TO KNOW

This book has argued for ethical vigilance, but vigilance must be informed by evidence. That requires more research than currently exists. The rapid pace of technological adoption has outstripped the depth of the empirical record. Many tools are marketed with confidence long before their educational effects are well understood. The evidence base for AI in education remains, as UNESCO's 2023 Global Education Monitoring Report warned, deeply uneven, with 2.6 billion people still lacking internet access and only 40 per cent of primary schools globally having connectivity (UNESCO, 2023). Any governance framework that ignores these realities designs policies for a minority of well-resourced schools while leaving the majority behind.

Future research should move in several directions at once. We still need longitudinal evidence on how AI systems affect learning, attention, creativity, agency, and developmental trajectories over time. Emerging research into what UNESCO terms "AI-chatbot-induced cognitive atrophy" suggests that overreliance on large language models may reduce memory retention, motivation, and critical thinking, but these findings remain preliminary and require sustained investigation (UNESCO, 2023).

Much current research is system-centred or institution-centred; we need more work grounded in children's lived experiences, especially across age groups and vulnerabilities. There is an urgent need for comparative work across regions, particularly outside dominant Anglo-American and European contexts, including research on AI in low-resource systems and across diverse legal traditions. More research is needed on how AI changes teacher labour, emotional workload, professional judgement, and institutional authority. The field needs stronger ways of measuring whether AI systems in education actually uphold dignity, participation, equality, and developmental rights rather than simply meeting technical performance targets. And further research must continue on Indigenous data sovereignty, local pedagogical adaptation, and non-extractive models of educational AI design.

THE LIMITS OF THIS BOOK

This book also has limits, and they should be stated plainly.

Artificial intelligence in education is not only a technical and institutional challenge. It is also a material one. The systems now entering schools depend on energy intensive infrastructure, large-scale computations, and physical resources that carry environmental cost. That dimension has not been the central focus of this book. The argument developed here has concentrated on governance, ethics, and institutional responsibility within education systems.

Nevertheless, questions of sustainability cannot be entirely separated from those concerns. Decisions about when and how AI is used are not neutral. They reflect judgments about necessity, proportionality, and value. Not every task requires the use of a large-scale model. In many cases, simpler tools, existing resources, or professional reasoning are sufficient. The risk is not only misuse, but overuse. If AI becomes the default response to every problem, then efficiency begins to displace judgement. For that reason, the responsible integration of artificial intelligence must also include restraint. Knowing when not to use these systems is part of ethical practice, even where their use is technically possible.

Artificial intelligence in education is a moving target. Technologies, regulations, and institutional practices are changing quickly, often faster than scholarship can stabilise. Not every jurisdiction could be treated in equal depth. Not every technology discussed here will mature in the way current forecasts suggest. And because the evidence base remains uneven, especially in K–12 settings, some arguments in this book necessarily rely more on governance analysis, rights-based reasoning, and analogies from adjacent domains than on long-term educational outcome data that does not yet exist.

That limitation belongs to the field itself, and to the present historical moment. We are being asked to make decisions of lasting consequence in conditions of partial evidence. That is precisely why ethical reasoning and institutional restraint remain so important. Gartner's warning that more than 40 per cent of agentic AI projects may be cancelled by the end of 2027 due to escalating costs, unclear business value, or inadequate risk controls tells us something important about institutional readiness (Gartner, 2025).

Every sector—not only education—is struggling to build the governance, data foundations, and professional capacity required to carry it responsibly. If large corporations with dedicated AI teams and substantial budgets are finding this difficult, schools operating with far fewer resources and far greater safeguarding obligations should not be expected to move faster. They should be expected to move more carefully.

A FINAL WORD

Artificial intelligence will continue to enter education as deep infrastructure. That much is already clear. The harder question is whether education will continue to recognise itself as a moral enterprise while it does.

Schools have always prepared young people for a world they cannot yet fully see. That task now includes technologies capable of shaping how knowledge is encountered, how behaviour is interpreted, and how futures are distributed. It includes the transformation of classrooms into data-rich environments where algorithms mediate attention, structure feedback, and increasingly influence how educational opportunity is distributed. The temptation will be to treat this as a technical challenge and to hope that enough innovation, regulation, and policy will eventually settle the matter.

But the deeper task is older and more demanding. It is to decide, again and again, what education is for. Not what it can be optimised to deliver, but what it owes to the young people who pass through it.

If education is merely a delivery system for skills, then increasingly intelligent systems may seem sufficient. If education is a human project concerned with judgement, freedom, dignity, responsibility, and the formation of persons capable of living with others in a democratic world, then no technological advance removes the need for moral clarity. It sharpens it.

That is the truth this book has tried to keep in view. With the next decision, rather than the next platform. With the values education is asked to serve, rather than the technology asked to serve them.

The future of AI in education will be decided less by what machines can do than by what human beings refuse to forget.

And that, in the end, is where moving forward must begin.

REFERENCES

AEI (2025) *The Illusion of Learning: The Danger of Artificial Intelligence to Education.* American Enterprise Institute. Available at: www.aei.org/op-eds/the-illusion-of-learning-the-danger-of-artificial-intelligence-to-education/

AICERTS (2025) *Education Readiness: UK Teachers Face AI Skills Gap.* AICERTS. Available at: www.aicerts.ai/news/education-readiness-uk-teachers-face-ai-skills-gap/

BETT (2025) AI in Education. Available at: https://uk.bettshow.com/ai-in-education

DfE (2025) *Technology in Schools Survey 2024 to 2025: Research Report.* London: Department for Education.

Gartner (2025) *Gartner Predicts More Than 40% of Agentic AI Projects Will Be Scrapped by End of 2027.* Gartner. Available at: www.gartner.com/en/newsroom/press-releases/

Hattie, J. (2009) *Visible Learning: A Synthesis of Over 800 Meta-Analyses Relating to Achievement.* London: Routledge.

Higgins, S., Beauchamp, G. and Miller, D. (2007) 'Reviewing the literature on interactive whiteboards', *Learning, Media and Technology*, 32(3), 213–225.

Human Rights Watch (2022) *How Dare They Peep into My Private Life?' Children's Rights Violations by Governments that Endorsed Online Learning during the Covid-19 Pandemic.* New York: Human Rights Watch.

Russell, S. (2019) *Human Compatible: Artificial Intelligence and the Problem of Control.* New York: Viking.

Suleyman, M. and Bhaskar, M. (2023) *The Coming Wave: Technology, Power, and the Twenty-First Century's Greatest Dilemma.* London: Bodley Head.

Sutton Trust (2021) *Remote Learning: The Digital Divide*. London: Sutton Trust.
Sutton Trust (2025) *Artificial Advantage? AI Use in Schools*. London: Sutton Trust.
Tamim, R.M., Bernard, R.M., Borokhovski, E., Abrami, P.C., and Schmid, R.F. (2011) 'What forty years of research says about the impact of technology on learning: A second-order meta-analysis and validation study', *Review of Educational Research*, 81(1), 4–28. 10.3102/0034654310393361. Available at: www.researchgate.net/publication/258182794_What_Forty_Years_of_Research_Says_About_the_Impact_of_Technology_on_Learning_A_Second-Order_Meta-Analysis_and_Validation_Study
Teacher Tapp (2025) *The Rise of AI-Enabled Teachers, Stressed Teachers, and Our Tapp Behaviour Tracker*. Teacher Tapp. Available at: https://teachertapp.com/articles/the-rise-of-ai-enabled-teachers-stressed-teachers-and-our-tapp-behaviour-tracker/
Twinkl (2025) *Majority of UK Teachers Rely on AI Despite Training Gap*. IT Brief. Available at: https://itbrief.co.uk/story/majority-of-uk-teachers-rely-on-ai-despite-training-gap
UNESCO (2023) *Global Education Monitoring Report 2023: Technology in Education — A Tool on Whose Terms?* Paris: UNESCO.

Appendices

OVERVIEW

Appendix A

Model Policy Language for AI Governance and Ethical Use

SHORT FORM INSERT FOR SCHOOL POLICY FRAMEWORKS

Purpose of this model text

The following wording is offered as a model for schools developing or revising policy language relating to artificial intelligence (AI). It is designed to support institutional alignment between AI use, educational purpose, and ethical governance. It should be adapted to local context and incorporated into wider policy frameworks, including safeguarding, assessment, data protection, staff conduct, and acceptable use policies.

Important note

This model language focuses specifically on governance, ethics, academic integrity, and institutional responsibility. It is not intended to function as a complete standalone AI policy, nor does it replace legal review. All schools should ensure that final policy wording is reviewed and approved in accordance with the legal and regulatory requirements of the relevant jurisdiction.

Model wording

This policy is designed to align with the school's mission, vision, values, and curriculum. The school recognises that AI may be used in ways that support teaching, learning, administration, accessibility, and institutional effectiveness. At the same time, the school affirms that the use of AI must remain consistent with its educational purpose, safeguarding responsibilities, and commitment to professional and academic integrity.

AI is understood by the school as a tool that may assist human work, but not replace human responsibility. Teachers and school leaders retain responsibility for decisions affecting students, including decisions relating to learning, assessment, well-being, behaviour, progression, and support. The use of AI does not remove or reduce professional accountability.

The school expects all uses of AI to be transparent, proportionate, and educationally justified. Students, staff, and families should be able to understand when AI is being used in meaningful ways, for what purpose it is being used, and what limits apply to that use. No AI system should be used in a manner that obscures responsibility, prevents challenge, or undermines trust.

AI may be used to support low-stakes educational and administrative tasks where appropriate professional oversight is maintained. Any use of AI that materially influences assessment, student evaluation, access to opportunity, safeguarding processes, or significant educational decisions must be subject to explicit institutional review and approval. Fully automated decision-making in matters affecting students is not permitted without meaningful human review and clear accountability.

The school will not rely solely on vendor assurances when adopting AI-enabled products or services. External systems must be subject to appropriate institutional scrutiny, including consideration of privacy, fairness, explainability, safeguarding implications, and alignment with the school's educational values. The school remains accountable for the use of systems deployed within its own environment, including those provided by third parties.

Academic integrity remains a core expectation of the school. The use of AI by students or staff must not misrepresent authorship, distort assessment evidence, or undermine the validity of educational work. Where AI use is permitted in learning or assessment contexts, expectations for disclosure and appropriate use must be made clear. Staff should rely on professional judgement, supported by institutional processes, rather than assume that automated detection tools provide definitive evidence of misconduct.

The school will establish appropriate mechanisms for reporting concerns relating to AI use, including concerns raised by staff, students, and families. AI-related risks, ambiguities, or unintended effects should be reviewed through existing governance structures and may result in revision, restriction, or withdrawal of tools or practices where necessary.

This policy language should be read alongside the school's wider framework of safeguarding, academic, behavioural, and data governance policies. It is intended to support coherent institutional practice and should be reviewed regularly in light of technological, legal, and educational developments.

Author note

This model language is intentionally written as policy wording schools can adapt rather than as a complete standalone policy. In practice, AI governance should be integrated into existing institutional frameworks rather than treated as a separate technical issue. Schools should therefore revise related documents in parallel, particularly those concerning safeguarding, academic integrity, assessment, consent, procurement, and data protection.

Appendix B

AI Governance Blueprint and Implementation Framework

MODEL INSTITUTIONAL DESIGN TOOLKIT FOR SCHOOLS

Purpose of this model framework

This blueprint provides a structured approach for schools to design, implement, and sustain AI governance as part of institutional practice. It translates the governance architecture developed in Chapter 6 into an operational model that schools can adapt to their own context.

This framework is intended to support:

- Clear allocation of responsibility
- Consistent decision-making across the institution
- Alignment with safeguarding, assessment, and legal obligations
- Ongoing review and correction of AI use in practice

Important note

This blueprint is not a fixed organisational model. Schools should adapt roles, structures, and processes according to their size, governance context, and regulatory environment. AI governance should be embedded within existing institutional systems rather than implemented as a standalone structure.

FOUNDATIONAL PRINCIPLE: GOVERNANCE AS INSTITUTIONAL COORDINATION

AI governance should be treated as a coordination function across the school, not as a technical responsibility located within a single department.

AI intersects multiple domains simultaneously, including:

- Safeguarding
- Curriculum and pedagogy
- Assessment and academic integrity
- Data protection and privacy
- Procurement and vendor management
- Professional development

Without deliberate coordination, responsibility becomes fragmented and accountability weakens. The purpose of this blueprint is to prevent that fragmentation by making authority explicit and visible.

STEP ONE: INSTITUTIONAL ROLE DELINEATION

Before any AI system is adopted or used at scale, the school should define where decision-making authority resides.

Schools should establish clarity across four core functions:

Operational supervision
Who oversees day-to-day use of AI in classrooms and administrative processes?

Institutional approval
Who authorises the adoption of AI systems and ensures alignment with safeguarding, assessment, and policy?

Structural oversight
Who monitors system level risks, including bias, vendor compliance, and equity impact?

Participatory accountability
How are student and parent perspectives incorporated into review and governance?

These roles may sit with existing leadership structures, but they must be explicitly assigned and documented. Responsibility should never remain implied.

STEP TWO: CLASSIFYING AI USE BY DECISION IMPACT

Not all AI use carries the same level of risk. Schools should classify AI systems according to the level of influence they have on students and institutional outcomes.

A simple three tier model can be used:

Low impact use

Administrative support, lesson planning, resource generation, accessibility tools

Requires: professional oversight, no formal approval beyond local use

Moderate impact use

Feedback tools, learning support systems, formative assessment assistance

Requires: departmental or leadership awareness and review

High impact use

Assessment, grading, progression decisions, behavioural or predictive analytics

Requires: formal institutional approval, documented oversight, and ongoing review

Classification should be revisited as systems evolve or uses change.

STEP THREE: ESTABLISHING A GOVERNANCE BODY OR FUNCTION

Schools should designate a clear governance function responsible for AI oversight.

This does not necessarily require a new committee. It may be:

- An extension of an existing safeguarding or digital governance group
- A cross functional leadership group
- A designated senior leader with defined authority

The governance function should be responsible for:

- Reviewing and approving AI systems
- Monitoring risk and impact
- Coordinating across departments
- Ensuring alignment with institutional policies
- Maintaining documentation and institutional memory

Authority and remit must be clearly defined.

STEP FOUR: EMBEDDING HUMAN OVERSIGHT

Human oversight must be treated as a professional obligation, not an optional safeguard.

Schools should ensure that:

- AI outputs are reviewed before being acted upon in meaningful contexts
- Educators understand the limitations and uncertainty of AI systems
- Responsibility for decisions remains clearly assigned to individuals, not systems

Oversight should be proportionate to the level of impact. High impact uses require more rigorous review and accountability structures.

STEP FIVE: ALIGNING WITH SAFEGUARDING AND EXISTING FRAMEWORKS

AI governance should be integrated into existing institutional frameworks rather than developed in isolation.

This includes alignment with:

- Safeguarding and child protection structures
- Data protection and privacy governance
- Curriculum and assessment policies
- Behaviour and conduct expectations

AI should be treated as part of the school's duty of care, not as a separate technical domain.

STEP SIX: VENDOR GOVERNANCE AND PROCUREMENT

Schools should establish clear expectations for external providers.

Before adopting AI enabled systems, schools should:

- Conduct due diligence on functionality, data use, and limitations
- Require transparency about how systems generate outputs
- Assess risks related to bias, privacy, and safeguarding
- Ensure contractual clarity regarding responsibilities and liabilities

A system that cannot be adequately explained or scrutinised should not be adopted.

STEP SEVEN: BUILDING FEEDBACK, REPORTING, AND REVIEW LOOPS

Governance must include mechanisms for continuous learning and correction.

Schools should establish:

- Clear reporting channels for staff, students, and families
- Processes for documenting incidents, concerns, and unintended effects
- Regular review cycles for AI systems and practices
- Criteria for revising, restricting, or withdrawing systems

Governance becomes credible when it can respond to real world use, not just planned use.

STEP EIGHT: PROFESSIONAL CAPACITY AND CULTURE

AI governance depends on professional capability.

Schools should:

- Provide structured training in critical evaluation of AI systems
- Support staff in understanding both capabilities and limitations
- Reinforce that professional judgement remains central
- Build shared norms around responsible and transparent use

Governance is sustained through culture as much as through structure.

IMPLEMENTATION SEQUENCE (PRACTICAL GUIDE)

Schools may use the following sequence as a starting point:

1. Map existing AI use across the institution
2. Define and document roles and responsibilities
3. Classify current and proposed AI systems by impact
4. Assign or establish a governance function
5. Review high impact uses and pause where necessary
6. Align governance with safeguarding and data protection frameworks

7. Introduce reporting and review mechanisms
8. Provide staff guidance and training
9. Document decisions and create institutional records
10. Schedule regular review and update cycles

GOVERNANCE BLUEPRINT IN TABLE FORMAT

Operational Overview for Leadership Teams

TABLE B.1 Institutional Roles and Responsibilities

GOVERNANCE FUNCTION	*CORE QUESTION*	*TYPICAL RESPONSIBILITY (ADAPT TO CONTEXT)*	*KEY OUTPUTS/ EVIDENCE*
Operational supervision	Who oversees day-to-day AI use?	Teachers, department heads, operational leaders	Classroom practices, usage norms, reporting
Institutional approval	Who authorises AI adoption?	Senior leadership, academic leadership	Approved tools list, documented decisions
Structural oversight	Who monitors risk and system-level impact?	Safeguarding lead, data protection, governance group	Risk logs, review reports, compliance records
Participatory accountability	How are student and parent voices included?	Parent councils, student representatives, leadership	Feedback records, consultation outcomes

TABLE B.2 AI Use Classification by Decision Impact

IMPACT LEVEL	*DESCRIPTION OF USE*	*EXAMPLES*	*GOVERNANCE REQUIREMENT*
Low impact	Supports tasks without affecting outcomes	Lesson planning, admin tasks, resource generation	Professional oversight at point of use
Moderate impact	Influences learning processes but not final decisions	Feedback tools, formative assessment support	Departmental review and visibility
High impact	Affects outcomes, evaluation, or opportunity	Grading, progression decisions, predictive analytics	Formal approval, documented oversight, ongoing review

TABLE B.3 Governance Structure and Oversight Function

ELEMENT	*KEY QUESTION*	*MINIMUM EXPECTATION*	*INDICATORS OF STRONG PRACTICE*
Governance ownership	Who is responsible for AI governance?	Named individual or group	Clear mandate, cross-functional representation
Decision authority	Who can approve or reject systems?	Defined approval pathway	Documented criteria and escalation routes
Cross-institution coordination	How are departments aligned?	Regular coordination between key functions	Integrated governance across safeguarding, curriculum, and data
Documentation	How are decisions recorded?	Basic record of approvals and reviews	Structured logs, institutional memory

TABLE B.4 Human Oversight and Professional Responsibility

AREA	*EXPECTATION*	*PRACTICAL APPLICATION*
Decision accountability	Humans remain responsible for outcomes	Staff validate AI outputs before use
Oversight by impact level	Higher impact requires stronger oversight	Formal review for high-impact decisions
Professional judgement	AI supports but does not replace expertise	Teachers interpret, not defer to, outputs
Transparency in practice	AI use is visible and explainable	Students informed when AI contributes meaningfully

TABLE B.5 Safeguarding and Policy Alignment

DOMAIN	*GOVERNANCE REQUIREMENT*	*ALIGNMENT ACTION*
Safeguarding	AI use must not introduce harm or risk	Integrate AI into safeguarding reviews
Data protection	Compliance with legal data handling standards	Align with existing privacy frameworks
Assessment integrity	AI must not undermine validity of evaluation	Update academic integrity policies
Behaviour and conduct	Expectations for responsible AI use	Embed in student and staff codes of conduct

TABLE B.6 Vendor Governance and Procurement

STAGE	*KEY QUESTIONS*	*EXPECTED PRACTICE*
Pre-adoption	Do we understand how the system works?	Due diligence on functionality and data use
Risk assessment	What risks does this system introduce?	Review bias, privacy, safeguarding implications
Contractual clarity	Who is responsible for what?	Defined obligations and accountability
Ongoing monitoring	Is the system performing as expected?	Regular review and vendor engagement

TABLE B.7 Feedback, Reporting, and Review

MECHANISM	*KEY QUESTION*	*MINIMUM PRACTICE*	*STRONG PRACTICE*
Reporting channels	Can concerns be raised easily?	Defined reporting pathway	Multiple access points, clear communication
Incident documentation	Are issues recorded and tracked?	Basic incident log	Structured tracking and pattern analysis
Review cycles	Are systems reviewed regularly?	Periodic review	Scheduled, criteria-based evaluation
Escalation	What happens when risks are identified?	Defined escalation route	Clear authority to suspend or withdraw systems

TABLE B.8 Implementation Sequence (Quick Start Guide)

STEP	*ACTION*	*OUTCOME*
1	Map current AI use	Institutional visibility
2	Define roles and responsibilities	Clear accountability
3	Classify AI systems by impact	Risk-based governance
4	Establish governance function	Coordinated oversight
5	Review high-impact uses	Immediate risk control
6	Align with safeguarding and data frameworks	Integrated governance
7	Introduce reporting and review mechanisms	Continuous monitoring
8	Build staff capacity	Informed professional practice
9	Document decisions	Institutional memory
10	Schedule review cycles	Adaptive governance

Author note

These tables are designed as working tools rather than descriptive summaries. Schools are encouraged to adapt them into internal planning documents, governance charters, or leadership meeting materials. The purpose is not to create additional bureaucracy, but to make responsibility, decision-making, and accountability visible and actionable.

Appendix C

Practical Tools and Templates for AI Governance

OPERATIONAL INSTRUMENTS FOR SCHOOLS

Purpose of this section

This appendix provides practical tools that schools can use to implement and sustain AI governance in day-to-day practice. These instruments are designed to support consistent decision-making, documentation, and accountability, aligned with the governance framework outlined in Chapter 6.

These tools are not exhaustive. Schools should adapt them to their institutional context and integrate them into existing systems wherever possible.

Tool 1. AI System Registration and Inventory Template

Purpose:
To ensure that the school maintains a clear and up-to-date record of AI systems in use across the institution.

Model template fields:

- Name of system/tool
- Vendor/provider
- Description of functionality
- Area of use (teaching, assessment, administration, safeguarding, other)
- Type of AI capability (generative, predictive, analytical, embedded feature)
- Users (staff, students, both)
- Data processed (personal data, student data, sensitive data, none)
- Decision impact level (low, moderate, high)
- Date introduced

- Approval status (approved, under review, not approved)
- Responsible owner (named role or individual)
- Notes on risks or limitations

Guidance:
This should function as a living institutional register, not a one-time audit document.

Tool 2. AI Use Risk and Impact Assessment Template

Purpose:
To support structured evaluation of AI systems before and during use.

Model assessment questions:

Educational purpose

- What is the intended educational benefit of this system?
- Is this use necessary, or could the same outcome be achieved without AI?

Impact on students

- Does this system influence learning, assessment, or opportunity?
- Could it affect different groups of students in unequal ways?

Human oversight

- Who reviews and validates outputs?
- What decisions are made based on this system?

Transparency

- Will students and families know this system is being used?
- Can its function be explained in clear terms?

Data and privacy

- What data is processed?
- Is this data necessary and proportionate?

Safeguarding

- Could this system expose students to harm, bias, or inappropriate content?

Vendor reliability

- Is the provider transparent about how the system works?
- Are there known limitations or risks?

Final determination

- Approved
- Approved with conditions
- Not approved

Tool 3. AI Decision and Approval Record

Purpose:
To document institutional decisions regarding AI adoption and use.

Model record fields:

- System name
- Date of review
- Reviewing body or individual
- Summary of intended use
- Risk-level classification
- Key risks identified
- Mitigation measures required
- Decision outcome
- Conditions for use (if applicable)
- Date for review

Guidance:
This record creates institutional memory, which is essential for accountability and continuity.

Tool 4. Incident Reporting and Review Template

Purpose:
To ensure that concerns, failures, or unintended consequences are captured and acted upon.

Model fields:

- Date of incident
- System involved
- Description of issue
- Who reported the issue
- Immediate action taken
- Impact on students or staff
- Severity level (low, moderate, high)
- Follow-up action required
- Responsible person

- Date of resolution
- Lessons learned

Guidance:

Governance becomes credible only when institutions respond to real-world use, not just planned use.

Tool 5. Staff Guidance Prompt (Operational Use Checklist)

Purpose:
To support educators in making informed decisions at the point of use.

Model prompt (for staff-facing guidance):
Before using AI in your practice, consider:

- Am I clear about why I am using this tool?
- Does this support, rather than replace, my professional judgement?
- Could this affect how a student is evaluated or treated?
- Would I be comfortable explaining this use to a student or parent?
- Do I understand the limitations of this system?

If the answer to any of these is unclear, pause and seek guidance.

Tool 6. Student Disclosure Guidance (Model Language)

Purpose:
To support transparency and academic integrity in student use of AI.

Model language:

Students may use AI tools where permitted by the school or teacher. Where AI is used, students may be required to disclose:

- The tool used
- The purpose of use
- The extent to which AI contributed to the final work

Failure to disclose AI use where required may be treated as a breach of academic integrity.

Tool 7. Governance Review Cycle Template

Purpose:
To ensure ongoing evaluation of AI systems and practices.

Model structure:
Frequency:
At least annually, with additional reviews for high-impact systems
Review questions:

- Is the system performing as expected?
- Have any risks or unintended consequences emerged?
- Are there disparities in impact across student groups?
- Does the system remain aligned with institutional values and policies?

Outcomes:

- Continue use
- Modify use
- Restrict use
- Withdraw system

Closing note

These tools are designed to make governance visible, repeatable, and accountable.

AI does not introduce entirely new responsibilities into schools. It exposes where responsibility was previously assumed but not defined.

The purpose of these instruments is to ensure that responsibility is made explicit, decisions are documented, and institutional practice remains aligned with educational purpose.

Appendix D

Pre-Audit and Institutional Readiness Questions

SELF-ASSESSMENT FRAMEWORK FOR SCHOOLS

Purpose of this section

This framework is designed to support schools in assessing their current level of preparedness for governing AI. It can be used prior to formal audit, inspection, or internal review, and as a working tool for leadership teams.

The questions are intentionally direct. Inability to answer them clearly is itself a governance signal.

Visibility and Awareness

- Do we know which AI systems are currently being used across the institution?
- Do we know which staff are using AI, and for what purposes?
- Do we know whether students are using AI in their learning, and how?
- Do we maintain a current inventory of AI systems and tools?

Indicator of readiness:
AI use is visible, documented, and understood at institutional level.

Purpose and Educational Justification

- Can we clearly explain why each AI system is being used?
- Is each use aligned with our mission, curriculum, and educational priorities?
- Have we identified where AI adds value, and where it does not?
- Are any systems in use because they are available rather than necessary?

Indicator of readiness:
AI use is intentional, not incidental.

Roles and Accountability

- Do we know who is responsible for approving AI systems?
- Do we know who is responsible for monitoring their use and impact?
- Are responsibilities formally assigned, or informally assumed?
- If something goes wrong, is it clear who is accountable?

Indicator of readiness:
Responsibility is explicit and traceable.

Risk Classification and Oversight

- Have we classified AI uses by their level of impact on students?
- Do we distinguish between low-, moderate-, and high-impact uses?
- Are high-impact uses subject to formal approval and review?
- Do we revisit classifications as systems evolve?

Indicator of readiness:
Oversight is proportionate to impact.

Human Oversight and Professional Judgement

- Are AI outputs reviewed before influencing decisions about students?
- Do staff understand the limitations and uncertainty of AI systems?
- Is there any area where decisions are effectively automated?
- Do educators feel able to question or override AI outputs?

Indicator of readiness:
Human judgement remains central and active.

Safeguarding and Student Protection

- Have we assessed whether AI systems introduce safeguarding risks?
- Could any system expose students to harmful, biased, or inappropriate content?
- Are AI tools used in ways that could influence student well-being or behaviour?
- Are safeguarding teams aware of and involved in AI governance?

Indicator of readiness:
AI is treated as part of safeguarding, not separate from it.

Data Protection and Privacy

- Do we know what data each AI system processes?
- Is the use of data necessary, proportionate, and lawful?
- Are staff aware of data risks when using AI tools informally?
- Are external providers compliant with relevant data protection requirements?

Indicator of readiness:
Data use is understood, justified, and controlled.

Vendor and Procurement Governance

- Do we evaluate AI systems before adopting them?
- Do we understand how systems generate outputs, at least at a functional level?
- Are vendor claims independently assessed or simply accepted?
- Are contractual responsibilities and liabilities clear?

Indicator of readiness:
The institution, not the vendor, holds control.

Academic Integrity

- Do we have clear expectations for student use of AI?
- Do staff understand how AI affects assessment design?
- Are we relying on detection tools without understanding their limitations?
- Are we able to distinguish between support and substitution in student work?

Indicator of readiness:
Integrity is upheld through design and judgement, not assumption.

Transparency and Communication

- Do students know when AI is used in meaningful ways?
- Are parents informed about how AI may affect their child's learning or data?
- Can we explain our use of AI in clear, non-technical terms?
- Do we provide channels for questions or concerns?

Indicator of readiness:
Trust is built through clarity, not opacity.

Monitoring, Reporting, and Learning

- Do we have a way to report concerns or incidents related to AI?
- Are issues documented and reviewed systematically?
- Do we learn from mistakes or unintended outcomes?
- Do we review AI use regularly, or only at adoption?

Indicator of readiness:
Governance is continuous, not static.

Closing note

These questions are not a compliance checklist. They are a test of institutional awareness.

Schools that can answer them clearly are not necessarily risk-free.

But schools that cannot answer them are operating without visibility, and therefore without control.

Appendix E

Consent and Communication Models for AI Use

REFRAMING CONSENT IN THE AGE OF ARTIFICIAL INTELLIGENCE

Purpose of this section

This appendix provides model approaches to consent and communication relating to AI use in schools. It reflects a shift from one-time, static consent toward ongoing, informed, and context-sensitive engagement with students and families.

Foundational Principle: Consent as Ongoing Process
In the context of AI, consent cannot be reduced to a single checkbox or annual form.

AI systems:

- Evolve over time
- Are embedded across multiple tools and contexts
- May be used in ways that are not visible to students or parents

Consent must therefore be:

- Ongoing rather than one-time
- Informed rather than implied
- Contextual rather than generic

When Consent Is Required
Schools should consider consent, or explicit communication, where AI use involves:

- Processing of personal or sensitive student data
- Systems that influence learning, assessment, or opportunity

- Use of generative AI involving student interaction or content creation
- Third-party tools that extend beyond core educational provision

Consent requirements will vary by jurisdiction, but ethical expectations remain consistent.

Model Parent Communication Language

Example: General AI Use Notice

The school uses AI systems in certain areas of teaching, learning, and administration. These systems are used to support educational processes and improve efficiency, while maintaining appropriate human oversight.

Where AI systems involve the processing of student data or contribute to educational decisions, the school ensures that their use is aligned with safeguarding, data protection, and educational standards.

Parents and guardians may contact the school for further information about how AI is used in relation to their child's education.

Model Context-Specific Consent Language

Example: Use of AI-Enabled Learning Tool

The school intends to use an AI-enabled learning tool to support specific purpose, e.g., personalised feedback or language development.

This tool may process student inputs in order to generate responses or feedback. All use is subject to teacher oversight, and no significant educational decisions are made solely by the system.

Parents are invited to review this use and may raise questions or request further information before consenting to their child's participation.

Age-Appropriate Student Communication

Consent is not only a legal matter. It is also an educational one.

Schools should ensure that students are informed in ways appropriate to their age and understanding.

Example (younger students):

"We sometimes use computer tools that help teachers and students with learning. These tools are designed to support your work, but your teacher is always in charge of what happens in class."

Example (older students):

"Some tools used in your learning use artificial intelligence to generate feedback or suggestions. These systems are not always correct, and your teacher remains responsible for evaluating your work. You are expected to use these tools responsibly and transparently."

Frequency and Review of Consent
Schools should:

- Review consent practices regularly
- Update communication when systems or uses change
- Avoid relying on outdated or overly broad consent agreements

Consent should reflect actual practice, not assumed practice.
Right to Question and Challenge

Students and parents should have:

- The ability to ask how AI is used
- The ability to request clarification or raise concerns
- Clear channels for communication with the school

Consent without the possibility of challenge is not meaningful.

Appendix F

Red Lines and Non-Negotiables for AI Use in Schools

MINIMUM STANDARDS FOR ETHICAL AND INSTITUTIONAL INTEGRITY

Purpose of this section

This appendix sets out minimum conditions for the use of AI in schools. These are not aspirational principles. They are boundary conditions. They define practices that should not occur, regardless of perceived efficiency or innovation benefits, because they are incompatible with the purpose of education and the duty of care owed to students. These red lines are designed to support leadership teams, educators, and governing bodies in making clear, defensible decisions.

Guidance for Use

These red lines should be:

- Integrated into policy frameworks
- Used in procurement and approval processes
- Referenced in governance decisions
- Communicated clearly to staff and stakeholders

They are not designed to prevent the use of AI. They are designed to ensure that its use remains aligned with the purpose of education.

TABLE F.1 Institutional Red Lines

AREA	*RED LINE (NON-NEGOTIABLE)*	*RATIONALE*
Decision-making	No fully automated decisions affecting student outcomes	Educational decisions require human judgement and accountability
Transparency	No use of systems that cannot be meaningfully explained	Institutions must be able to justify how decisions are influenced
Accountability	No delegation of responsibility to AI systems or vendors	Responsibility remains with the school
Safeguarding	No deployment of systems that bypass or weaken safeguarding processes	Student protection overrides technological convenience
Data Use	No use of student data beyond clearly defined and justified educational purposes	Data minimisation and purpose limitation are essential
Academic integrity	No reliance on AI detection tools as sole evidence of misconduct	Such tools are unreliable and cannot replace professional judgement
Equity and fairness	No use of systems where bias risk is known but unexamined	Schools must not introduce or amplify inequality
Vendor dependency	No adoption of systems that cannot be independently scrutinised	Black box dependency undermines institutional control

TABLE F.2 Conditional Red Lines (Require Explicit Justification and Oversight)

AREA	*CONDITION*	*REQUIREMENT FOR USE*
Assessment	AI involvement in grading or evaluation	Must include human review and documented oversight
Student interaction	Generative AI tools used directly by students	Must include clear guidance, supervision, and age-appropriate boundaries
Behavioural analytics	Systems predicting behaviour or risk	Must be critically assessed for bias and safeguarding implications
Personalisation systems	AI shaping learning pathways or recommendations	Must be transparent and open to challenge
Third-party tools	External platforms processing student data	Must meet institutional and legal standards for privacy and accountability

Appendix G

First 90 Days Implementation Plan

PRACTICAL STARTING FRAMEWORK FOR SCHOOLS

Purpose of this section

This appendix provides a structured implementation pathway for schools beginning to establish AI governance. It translates the broader framework into a time-bound sequence of actions.

This is not a complete transformation plan. It is a starting point designed to establish visibility, control, and accountability within the first 90 days.

TABLE G.1 90-Day Implementation Overview

PHASE	*TIMEFRAME*	*FOCUS AREA*	*OUTCOME*
Phase 1	Days 1–30	Visibility and control	Understanding current AI use
Phase 2	Days 31–60	Structure and governance	Defined roles and processes
Phase 3	Days 61–90	Integration and communication	Operational and cultural alignment

TABLE G.2 Phase 1 (Days 1–30): Visibility and Immediate Risk Control

ACTION	*DESCRIPTION*	*OUTPUT*
Map AI use	Identify all AI tools used by staff and students	Initial system inventory
Identify high-risk unknowns	Flag tools affecting assessment, data, or safeguarding	Immediate risk awareness
Pause unreviewed high-impact uses	Temporarily suspend unclear or high-risk applications	Risk containment
Assign interim responsibility	Designate a lead or small group for AI oversight	Named accountability
Communicate initial position	Inform staff that AI use is under review	Institutional clarity

TABLE G.3 Phase 2 (Days 31–60): Structure and Governance

ACTION	*DESCRIPTION*	*OUTPUT*
Classify AI systems	Apply low-, moderate-, high-impact framework	Risk-based categorisation
Establish approval process	Define how new tools are reviewed and approved	Governance pathway
Formalise governance function	Confirm oversight group or responsible leader	Structural accountability
Begin risk assessments	Review high-impact systems using structured criteria	Documented evaluations
Develop staff guidance	Provide initial expectations for responsible AI use	Operational clarity

TABLE G.4 Phase 3 (Days 61–90): Integration and Communication

ACTION	*DESCRIPTION*	*OUTPUT*
Implement reporting mechanisms	Introduce channels for concerns and incident reporting	Feedback infrastructure
Review high-impact systems	Confirm, modify, or withdraw based on assessment	Risk-controlled usage
Align with existing policies	Integrate AI governance into safeguarding and data frameworks	Coherent institutional approach
Communicate with parents and students	Provide clear information about AI use	Transparency and trust
Plan ongoing training and review cycles	Establish next phase of governance development	Sustained implementation

Key principles for the first 90 days

Start with visibility, not perfection. Prioritise high-impact risks. Make responsibility explicit early. Use existing structures where possible. Communicate clearly and consistently. The first 90 days are not about solving AI governance in full but about moving from uncertainty to control. From informal use to structured oversight. From assumption to accountability.

Appendix H

A Letter to Educators *On Teaching, Trust, and Artificial Intelligence*

You may have heard the message. That AI will transform education, save you time, reduce workload, maybe even replace parts of what you do. In many schools, this conversation is already underway. New systems are being introduced. Expectations are beginning to shift. Decisions are being made, sometimes quickly, about how these technologies will be used. But your daily practice tells you something different.

What you have probably encountered is ambiguity. A growing number of tools, each claiming value, often not aligned with how classrooms actually work. A pressure to engage with systems that no one around you fully understands, including those responsible for implementing them. And underneath it all, something harder to name. A sense that your professional judgement, honed over years of experience, is being asked to defer to technologies that have not yet earned that authority.

The discomfort this generates is worth taking seriously. Because the starting point was never about learning a new tool. It is instead a deeper question that most of the policy and vendor narrative often avoid. What happens to the foundations of education when decision-making is no longer a solely human responsibility?

AI does not just introduce new capabilities. It reorganises how decisions are made, how authority is distributed, and how accountability must be understood within schools. This cannot be managed through tools alone. It requires institutions to take responsibility for how these systems are introduced, governed, and used. It also requires that educators remain at the centre of that process.

Teaching is the exercise of judgement: the ability to interpret context, to respond to uncertainty, and to recognise when a student is struggling for reasons that will never surface in a data dashboard. This is what builds trust. And trust remains the foundation of effective education.

AI *can* assist in aspects of your work. It can help generate resources, organise information, and surface patterns you might not otherwise see. But it does not understand your students in the way that you can. It does not carry responsibility nor care for their outcomes. It does not carry the ethical and legal obligations that define your role. The introduction of AI into schools is therefore a question of safety, trust, and institutional responsibility before it is a question of capability.

As institutions, schools must change. They must move away from informal and unstructured AI use toward clear, structured, and transparent practice. Systems must be reviewed before use. Risks must be understood and mitigated before they are encountered. Responsibility must be defined in advance, not assigned after the fact.

Schools also have a responsibility to support you. This includes setting clear expectations, defined boundaries, providing relevant training, and building governance structures that allow these systems to be used responsibly. It includes creating space to question, to challenge, and where necessary, to refuse use when evidence or context does not support it. It also requires open communication with students and families about what is being used and why. This is not an aspiration. It is a minimum standard.

There is a risk that this narrative becomes one of inevitability. That systems will advance regardless, and that educators must simply adapt or be left behind. We do not accept this narrative. Education is a public institution with a defined responsibility to those it serves. Technology that does not meet that responsibility has no place in schools. Your judgement remains central because it is the only mechanism through which the interests of the children you serve are consistently protected. Governance frameworks support this, but only when they are enacted by professionals with knowledge, responsibility, and accountability. That responsibility remains with you.

AI will become more capable, more embedded, and more present in our lives. The question this book has tried to hold open across every chapter is whether it will be governed in a way that protects the purpose of education itself. That work belongs to institutions. And it belongs to the educators within them. It begins with clarity about what should be adopted, what should be questioned, and what should not be accepted at all.

Author note

This text is written both as a reflection on the role of educators in the age of AI and as a model communication that school leaders may adapt for their own institutions. Schools are encouraged to use and modify this text to support clear, transparent, and respectful dialogue with staff as they develop their approach to AI governance.

Index

For Product Safety Concerns and Information please contact our EU representative GPSR@taylorandfrancis.com Taylor & Francis Verlag GmbH, Kaufingerstraße 24, 80331 München, Germany

Batch number: 10837650

Printed by Printforce, the Netherlands